PRAISE FOR

TEN STEPS TO NANETTE

"For fans of Gadsby, her delivery on the page will delight just as it does on screen. She remains honest, with stories that draw laughter over situations that are always based in truth—harsh or otherwise." —*Time*

"A joyful read . . . Gadsby's voice is intimate and close, and spending time with it is a lot like listening to a good friend relay a fascinating life story over a couple of pints at the bar." —*Oprah Daily*

"Enthralling . . . Gadsby embeds her memories with wit, reflection, and self-deprecation; she eschews convention by meticulously framing her life through her defining work." —*The Washington Post*

"The sweetest, warmest, and most delightfully and casually funny comedian memoir in a decade. Yes, Gadsby addresses traumas and frightening moments in her years as an unabashedly sensitive child and young person, but the book is, by and large, the answer to the question that most memoirs never really address because the author remains too guarded: Who *is* this person, really, and why do they do the work that they do?" —*Vulture*

"If you want to see what led to Gadsby's emergence as a whip-smart social critic, *Ten Steps to Nanette: A Memoir Situation* covers it all." —*Esquire*

TEN STEPS TO NANETTE

HANNAH GADSBY

TEN STEPS TO NANETTE

A MEMOIR SITUATION

BALLANTINE BOOKS ✛ NEW YORK

2023 Ballantine Books Trade Paperback Edition

Copyright © 2022 by Hannah Gadsby

All rights reserved.

Published in the United States by Ballantine Books, an imprint of
Random House, a division of Penguin Random House LLC, New York.

BALLANTINE is a registered trademark and the colophon
is a trademark of Penguin Random House LLC.

Originally published in hardcover in the United States by
Ballantine Books, an imprint of Random House, a division of
Penguin Random House LLC, in 2022.

ISBN 978-1-9848-1980-2
Ebook ISBN 978-1-9848-1979-6
International edition ISBN 9780593159224

Printed in the United States of America on acid-free paper

randomhousebooks.com

2 4 6 8 9 7 5 3 1

Book design by Jo Anne Metsch

FOR MUM AND DAD

"Art is restoration: the idea is to repair the damages that are inflicted in life, to make something that is fragmented—which is what fear and anxiety do to a person—into something whole."

—LOUISE BOURGEOIS

TEN STEPS TO NANETTE

Introduction

Technically, this is my second book. But I wouldn't bother trying to find a copy of my first effort as it was only published in an edition of one, and I've misplaced it. This is no great loss to literature because my first book was a very bad book. Although, I shouldn't be too hard on myself, the story does have a bit of charm considering I was only seven years old when I penned it. But as a stand-alone piece of writing, it is terrible. Even the title is bad:

How Siffin Soffon became friendly with a Dragon. Part One

I put a spoiler in the title. What a fool. Why would you bother reading a book when you already know that no matter how dramatic the narrative twists and turns might be, Siffin Soffon and the Dragon will eventually end up on pretty good terms.

Clearly, I had an epic series in mind when I added "Part One" to the title, but sadly I never got round to writing the second installment. Even so, one would assume I'd have left the reader with a cliffhanger so as to whet their appetite for Part Two, but no, Part One ends with Siffin Soffon and his new dragon pal waving a happy goodbye from the pleasant shores of "Holiday Island." No wonder I never got round to writing the sequel, I couldn't even think of a name for an island beyond the singular purpose I'd invented the island for. I was clearly all out of ideas.

I suppose you might want to read the book just to find out who this Siffin Soffon character is, but here, again, you'll find my writing falls short because, apparently, I didn't think it was necessary to offer a description of the central character of my novella. My accompanying drawings could have been enlightening, but again, ambiguity reigns; Siffin Soffon begins his epic journey as a carefully executed, albeit childishly rendered, little red goat, but by the time he becomes friendly with the Dragon he is just a lazy tangle of orange squiggles because I'd grown bored of drawing and had also, presumably, lost the red pencil. Fortunately, I do have some insider knowledge on this matter, and I can report that Siffin Soffon was neither a red goat nor an orange squiggle, he was the imaginary friend of my older brother, Hamish, and according to him, Siffin Soffon was a tiny footballer who lived in the toilet with his best friend Kinnowin.

When the one copy of my very bad book found its way back to me recently, I was inundated with a cluster of memories that I didn't even know I had. I'm not talking about repressed memories, they didn't return with a shocking jolt, they just quietly worked their way to the front of my thought queue as if they'd never left.

The cover, two pieces of red cardboard bound by masking tape, had faded and softened over time, but my poorly planned title still looked as if it had only been poorly executed just yesterday. As I held it in my hands, I recalled how angry seven-year-old me had become the moment I realised that I didn't have enough space for the last six words of the title, and I felt the heat of my self-admonishment rise as sharp as if thirty-five years had not passed. Flipping through to the back page, I saw the note of praise written by the vice principal next to a reward sticker of the Pink Panther curving himself around a giant pen with the words "Well Done!" spilling from its point. I remembered how lovingly I'd traced around the sticker with my finger, almost bursting with pride. I also recalled that I had felt a little bit annoyed that it was only the vice principal, and how I'd wondered what the hell I had to do to get the principal's attention. I could also remember how my teacher had insisted she write my story out for me because I was too young to have my pen licence and how she had then insisted that I read my story to the whole class, and how everyone in my whole class had HATED both me and my book. I don't blame them. It was, after all, a very bad book.

The return of my literary debut stirred up memories that went well beyond the object itself, and included the emotional roller coaster that had precipitated my urge to put pen to paper. It had all begun with my obsession with Hamish's imaginary friends and the mounting distress I felt because they didn't want to be my friends too. I hadn't known what "imaginary" meant and had just assumed that Hamish had cool friends who refused to talk to me, which made for many toilet-time tears. I also remembered how, after it was explained to me that Hamish's friends lived inside his head, I had asked if I was allowed to imagine Siffin Soffon too, and when Hamish said no, I'd burst into tears again and this prompted Hamish to offer me the thoroughly unacceptable compromise of the imagined friendship of Kinnowin. I did not accept, because I only really wanted Siffin Soffon, who I'd imagined was a little red goat and had managed to convince myself that I could sometimes hear him *clip-clopping* on the plumbing. I did not care for Kinnowin, I hardly knew her, I didn't even know what she looked like.

I also remembered how, at one point, I'd attempted to conjure my own imaginary friends and began galloping about on my horse, Sergeant, while chatting to my good friend Mr. Dog, who was a dog I'd obviously named in the tradition of Holiday Island. It was not a winning moment, as I could only recall how profoundly foolish I had felt because I knew my friends were not real, and, to make matters worse, I had imagined them to be incredibly large chaps, which meant I still didn't have any friends to talk to in the toilet. I don't know what to call my next move, as I don't think it is possible to kill beings that do not exist, so let's just say that I ghosted Sergeant and Mr. Dog, violently. It felt humane at the time, but really, I just wanted them out of the way so I could try my luck with Siffin Soffon again.

After my needless imaginary horse-and-dog ritual sacrifice,

Hamish told me I was too late. His friends were gone. When I pressed him for their whereabouts, he very sombrely reported that they were in Heaven helping God. Throughout my childhood and well into adulthood I worshipped Hamish and it often felt, painfully so, that he deliberately abused the power that he had over me. But when I remember episodes like this, I know that simply couldn't be true of a small boy who not only assumed that God would need the help of tiny football players but who also felt such levels of loneliness that he had to invent friends he could talk to, and poo on. He clearly had issues of his own.

Despite all these memories returning with such wonderful clarity, the story itself failed to ring a single bell in my brain. It was so unfamiliar, in fact, that the ending would have come as a complete surprise had I not spoilt it with the title. Another striking element of the very bad book that I don't recall authoring was the high level of violence, bloodthirst and death it contained, not to mention how matter-of-factly seven-year-old me described the guts and gore of it all. I should have been given counselling, not a Pink Panther sticker.

Yet, despite the foreign story line with all its beheadings, torture and other blood-filled whatnot, there was still a familiarity to the story, because Part One essentially reads like a thinly veiled auto-biography. Siffin Soffon hated dresses, had dreams about being a dog and was a big fan of food. But the most astonishing thing about my very bad book is that it reads like a blueprint for my future, a map, if you will, for the way that adult Hannah emerged from that strange and childish little author. Much like my own life, Siffin Soffon's journey was defined by accidents, isolation and exile and his survival, as much as his perils, were, like mine, brought about by an abundance of misplaced trust and a passive acceptance of circumstance, no matter how grim.

Ten Steps to Nanette, which I guess could be dubbed a very delayed Part Two, is more of a traditional memoir. It begins with my birth and ends with a publishing deadline. It has two stories to tell—one is about my rather odd start to life, and the other is about my rather odd decision to end my life in comedy. I have tried to approach this book with as much honesty as possible; however, what follows is also a thinly veiled fantasy. I've chosen a bit of fantasy over fact in a few places because some of my stories are not entirely mine. I've changed some names, and even merged people, times and places, because I don't believe I have the right to publicly open anybody else's can of worms. But, please! I implore you not to fall into the trap of playing "truth detective," because most of my life has been lived inside my own head and, unless you are Mr. Dog and/or Sergeant, you have never ever been there, so you will just have to take me at my word.

And although I am inclined toward extracting a laugh when I tell a story, you should be forewarned that some horrible things have happened to me, and some of my stories might very well upset you. They certainly upset me.[⊗] But I don't want you to fret, so let me just spoil your journey now, before you even get your foot on the first step, by giving away the ending, which is to say, as I'm writing this, I am on pretty good terms with the Dragon and there is plenty of food.

⊗ Seriously, though. I am triggering all of the warnings. If you are distressed by things like assault, molestation, rape, injury, isolation, suicidal ideation, body image or other mental health difficulties, please read on with caution, if you decide to read on at all. I see you, I support you. Breathe easy, my friends.

EPILOGUE

I had to know if the lawn was real. It looked too perfect to be made of organic matter, the vast green square around the picture-perfect pool had a uniformity that bordered on unsettling, every single blade of grass was as tall and as straight as its neighbour. Surely, I thought, it had to be plastic. But then again, that didn't make any sense. Fake grass is for people who are house-proud but water and/or time-poor.⊗ Fake grass is not for the stupidly rich who have a household staff with a gardening division. I broke free of the mingling and quietly made my way to the edge of the path, dropped my serviette and, as I bent down to pick it up, I brushed my hand over the mysterious lawn. Fuck me. It was real. I made my way back to the party, with a new mystery to solve: Why would you manicure real grass to make it look fake?✐

I knew I was behaving abnormally. And by "abnormal," I don't mean my failure to blend in with all the celebrities and Hollywood power players who had gathered in Eva Longoria's unnervingly perfected garden. Personally, I think that it's normal to be abnormal in

⊗ All plastic plants are an ecological hate crime.
✐ Answer: Garden variety anxiety.

the midst of that strange a milieu. I didn't feel at all bad that I'd rocked up in jeans and a T-shirt while everyone else was wrapped in fancy, because I don't think it's abnormal for a Hollywood outsider to not know that a dress code is an actual code that has to be cracked. The invitation had said *dress for brunch,* and because brunch is not a real meal, I took that to mean I didn't have to make a real effort. So, I felt perfectly normal about my inability to match the ethereal magnificence of Janelle Monáe. What is *not* normal, however, is abruptly walking away from a conversation *with* Janelle Monáe to satisfy a sudden urge to pat some strange-looking lawn.

It was not the first time I'd been distracted by underfoot landscaping decisions in the presence of celebrity. At the Netflix Emmys party a few months earlier, I couldn't think about anything other than the white carpet. What kind of monster would choose white carpet for an outdoor event?[*] The outdoors, no matter how fancy, is just not the natural habitat of carpet—white or otherwise. The issue plagued me so doggedly that I failed to notice I was in the middle of what could have easily been a genuine fever dream.

When John Stamos introduced himself to me and gushed glowingly about my work, I could only watch his mouth move and hope he didn't notice that my mind was elsewhere. The only thing I really wanted to talk about was under our feet: What do you reckon will happen to this carpet tomorrow? Will it have a life beyond this event, Sir Stamos? It was only much later—months in fact—that I was able to process the fact that I had been approached by Uncle Jesse because he knew who I was and wanted to let me know that he liked my work. There is nothing reasonable or logical about that set of facts.

When Jodie Foster asked to have her photo taken with me, I failed to be as flattered as I should have been because I was too worried about all the damage the carpet was doing to the turf underneath it. And when I was introduced to three of the *Queer Eye* boys,

---

[*] Ted Sarandos.

I was not curious about the absence of the other two, the only thing on my mind was how it was possible that the white carpet could still be so white hours into a crowded schmooze-and-booze fest.[⊛]

I couldn't accept that it was one single piece of carpet, the area was huge and it didn't have a straight-edged perimeter like an indoor room would, but I was having trouble finding any joins. Even I knew, however, that it would be inappropriate to get down on my knees and start sweeping around with my hands to feel it out, so I decided to make my way to the edge and see if I could find some answers there. That was when I bumped into Norman Lear. He turned around and apologised to me. What a nice man, I thought, and smiled back as he introduced himself, which was just as well, because I had no idea who he was. I made a note to google him later and then politely left to resume my quest, failing to seize my opportunity to pick the brains of the king of television sitcoms himself.

My obsession with the carpet situation was finally broken when I got a tap on the shoulder by a very small woman.

"Are you Hannah Gadsby?"

I nodded, praying that she would introduce herself, because I had no idea who she was, but she simply nodded back and then announced, "Jennifer Aniston would like to meet you." I expected that the introduction would take place where I stood, but the small woman instead told me to follow her before turning abruptly and disappearing into the crowd. *How curious,* I thought; this was not an invitation, it was a summons. Intrigued, I trotted after her, forgetting all about the white carpet.

Jennifer Aniston greeted me with great enthusiasm and incredible warmth, which is not at all what I expected from somebody who curates their own mingling experience without moving an inch. If that were me, I would surely be messing with people.[✐]

After Jennifer Aniston told me how excited she was to meet me, I

⊛ Witchcraft or white supremacy—only the algorithm can tell.
✐ (*tap, tap*) "Hannah Gadsby would like you to know that . . . YOU'RE IT." (*run away!*)

told her that I was also very excited to meet her. I was being polite, of course, I was not excited, I was terrified. I am autistic, I don't know how to navigate small talk with my best friend,[*] so the prospect of conversing with one of the most enduringly beloved famous people there is, was not at all relaxing. What level of admiration does she expect from riffraff? Would she require that I confirm her identity and status through the metaphor of flattery? Should I inform her that I had not seen *Friends*? I needn't have worried, because apparently Jennifer Aniston just wanted to let me know that she had not seen my show. Touché.

It had the rhythm of a compliment, but really, it was just a fact. As a fact, it might have been an insult but somehow, Jennifer Aniston managed to make it sound like enthusiastic approval. It was shocking nonetheless, and I forgot myself, and replied more bluntly than appropriate: "Why are you telling me this?" My question gave her pause, and as she did, I began to regret my whole existence. "I don't know," she laughed. I laughed too. It seemed like the polite thing to do. She continued, "It's just that I was on location and everyone kept telling me that I had to see *Nanette*, and I didn't have the chance and when I heard you were here, I just wanted . . ." She trailed off, almost embarrassed, but I was just relieved that I wasn't the only one who had no idea what the endgame was. She grabbed my hands as if to reassure us both. "I will watch it! And I know I will love it," she promised, offering me a clear path out of the awkwardness, which I did not take. "But what if you don't? What if you hate it?" She patted my hands and replied, "I won't tell you!" Classic L.A.

This was my first-ever[**] Emmys party and I have to say, I think I did a pretty good job at not making a buffoon of myself. Unlike with my brunch couture disaster, I came close to cracking the dress code, I'd had a shower, but I still managed to bring a raggedy incongruence to my presence. I put it down to the fact that my gown had

[*] In my defence, my best friend, Douglas, is a Dog.
[**] And only.

not been made for the occasion and I was wearing my own shoes. I was not wearing a gown, of course, I was wearing my only suit. But you know what I mean. My only regret is that I did not stay long enough to use the bathroom. I wanted to know what kind of strange flooring decisions had been made for the occasion of fancy people abluting.

The show that Jennifer Aniston had not yet seen was my stand-up comedy special, *Nanette*. When it had dropped on Netflix on June 19, 2018, it made such a big splash that within a few months I'd become the talk of the town, and by that I mean THE TOWN. I'd only ever been to L.A. on layovers before, and so it was a bit rude that on my first time in the city proper I had to pass my own giant face plastered on billboards and bus stops® as I was being dragged all over town, rubbing shoulders and having the kind of meetings that my peers would kill for.

The few months that followed the release of *Nanette* were amongst the strangest and most unsettling of my life. I went from relative obscurity to intense visibility in such a short period of time that I sustained spiritual whiplash. Ironically, all the chaos that followed my "overnight success" is actually a lot funnier than the show itself. Like way, way funnier. But that is hardly surprising, given that on paper, *Nanette* is arguably the most deliberately miserable, unfunny hour of comedy ever made.

For the record, as of yet, Jennifer Aniston has not found me to tell me that she loved *Nanette*. I suppose I could take that to mean she hated it—she wouldn't be alone. But I think it is more likely that she is quite busy and may not even remember having a conversation with me. But I do hold out hope that one day I will get a tap on my shoulder and a small woman will tell me that Jennifer Aniston wanted me to know that she didn't think *Nanette* lived up to all the hype. That would be Amazing.

I might have been living the showbiz dream, but, and I can't

® Which might have been triggering had it not been so supremely uncanny.

stress this enough, this so-called dream was never my dream. I know the more cynically minded will want to read that as faux humility, but I'm actually quite happy to own my ambitions where they exist⊗—but when it came to breaking into the ranks of the La La people, it was blunt pragmatism that steered me away from ever giving it a second thought. I just don't see the point of indulging any fantasy that, in practice, could only ever amount to being a monumental waste of time and energy, because that's what chasing Hollywood success could only ever be for someone like me, given that for most of my life I have been a financially insecure autistic Australian genderqueer vagina-wielding situation who does not have a bird-like skeletal system.⌀ I might have had a reasonable shot with only one or two of those "quirks," but not the whole set, and certainly not with Cate Blanchett already in town hogging all the moody lesbian roles. But, honestly, my biggest impediment is that I'm quite lazy.

It was only the coalescence of some extreme luck forged by an unforeseeable cluster of circumstances that pushed me into the peripheral vision of the movers and shakers of the so-called town of tinsel. It could have been a transformational experience save for one very big problem: I had nothing to pitch. Which, except for a strategically leaked sex tape, left me with absolutely no way of capitalising on my big moment. This isn't to say that I had nothing more to offer, it was more that I had put absolutely everything I had into the piece of work that had turned me into an "overnight success." *Nanette* sucked me dry and I was an empty shell, a veritable husk of a human, and it felt like I was just pissing this huge and rare opportunity right up the wall. I felt hopeless and helpless and it was all I could do to lurch from one incredible moment to the next and hope I didn't make mistakes I couldn't recover from. At least I managed to get a book deal.

Nanette's success might have taken me completely by surprise,

---

⊗ I am a total "girrrl" boss.

⌀ I am now financially secure—for the first time in my life. I am also white. Which remains a distinct advantage whether I acknowledge it or not.

but the backlash that followed it was entirely expected.⊗ I had, after all, written a show denouncing the two most overly sensitive demographics the world has ever known: straight white cis men and self-righteous comedians. I have only myself to blame.✒

"I'LL TELL YOU WHAT SHOULD BE THE TARGET OF OUR JOKES RIGHT NOW—OUR OBSESSION WITH REPUTATION. REPUTATION. THAT'S WHAT WE VALUE MOST. NOT HUMANITY—REPUTATION. YOU KNOW WHO TAKES THE MANTLE OF THIS MYOPIC ADULATION OF REPUTATION? CELEBRITIES. AND COMEDIANS ARE NOT IMMUNE." (NANETTE 56:42)

When Ellen DeGeneres was interviewed by *The New York Times* to promote the release of her own Netflix special, *Relatable,* she was asked what she thought about *Nanette* and responded by saying that she "loved" it, but then kind of undid that idea by making it clear that she didn't think it was stand-up. She called it "a solo show." I got stuck on the word "solo" when I read that. Stand-up comedians nearly always perform solo—Ellen certainly did—so how is that a distinction? I supposed that if by "solo" she meant that I didn't work with a team of writers, then yes, I suppose, by contrast, Ellen's special was not a solo show.⑥

Ellen was not the first comedian to make this kind of mild jab about *Nanette,* but I will only flag her because she is "my people," and that feels like a safe space in this moment in time.☼ I have been made well aware that a lot of comedians hate both me and my work, and while it is not an entirely pleasant scenario, I can't blame them for being so peeved. I kind of agree on one level, a comedy show that

---

⊗ Not to scale, however.
✒ This is a very clever subtext joke about victim blaming. Which is not funny.
⑥ What? I am being kind.
☼ I look forward to the time when there can be a public adult conversation about intersectionality.

is defiantly unfunny has no right being crowned the "next big thing in comedy." But I didn't do the crowning, so I don't know what the fuck they want me to do about it.

Ultimately, I don't feel compelled to defend *Nanette* as comedy, because that's a dull game, but I do want to take a moment to directly address any Americans who may be reading this: your comedy gods are not mine. I have heard all about your *Saturday Night Live* thing; and I acknowledge its place in your pantheon of yuk-yuks—but ultimately, it means nothing to me. *SNL* could be a freight company for all I care. All jokes aside, which is what got me into this mess to begin with, I should stress that the Australian comedy scene is very, very different to the American model, and that my work is not simply a reflection of who I am as an individual, but also very richly informed by the culture and circumstance of where I learnt my craft.⊗

I am what you could call a "festival comic," which means I am something of a long-form comic. I don't build sets by stacking jokes one on top of the other, I shape shows out of interconnecting material that is designed to pull an audience through a cohesive hour-long experience. To be clear, I don't think this approach to comedy is superior, it is simply different. Furthermore, I should stress that I am not the inventor of this approach, or even the best at it. The Australian and U.K. festival circuit is full of incredible comedians crafting utterly marvellous hours of comedy, year after year, and the quality and depth of the talent pool was such that I never had to pay much attention to what my American peers were saying or how they said it, because I had more than enough brilliance around me to occupy all of my creative curiosity. I was always aware of all the big hitters of American comedy, of course I was, because that's how aggressive cultural imperialism works, but I never felt inspired enough to think of it as any kind of relevant benchmark for myself.

⊗ G'day, mate.

Before *Nanette* made her big splash in 2018, I already had eight hour-long stand-up comedy shows sitting in my oeuvre, and four comedy-adjacent art history lectures, so I don't think not being able to snag a set at Caroline's on Broadway has held me back at all. And with all this experience and exposure to the art of the "comedy hour," it shouldn't be a surprise that I was able to take sixty minutes of abject misery and turn it into a very compelling and hugely successful piece of work. I have skills, people, I know what I am doing, even if you don't like it.

PEOPLE FEEL SAFER WHEN MEN DO THE ANGRY COMEDY. THEY'RE THE KINGS OF THE GENRE. WHEN I DO IT, I'M A MISERABLE LESBIAN, RUINING ALL THE FUN AND THE BANTER. (NANETTE 58:09)

I am still bewildered by the howling rage in which other comedians demanded that I be cancelled from comedy because I went too far with all my not-not-jokes. George Carlin once said that it is the job of a comedian to find the line and then cross it. That is what I have done. The line I found is the definition of comedy itself, and given the considerable nerve I struck, I would say that makes me an excellent comedian. Except I won't. Because I don't think of myself as a comedian, I am a stand-up performance artist, or, as Andy Kaufman would say, a song-and-dance man.

Make no mistake, though, comedy is in a real bind at the moment. None of the whingey whiners are wrong to be concerned, they're just wrong about where they're directing their panic and blame. I am not the problem. The witch they are looking for is context.[⊗] It is no longer the case that jokes only live in the room where they're told. Rightly or wrongly, everything you say on stage, or anywhere for that matter, has the potential to be taken out of context,

---

[⊗] Context would definitely float if you threw it in a river. As would I.

which makes satire next to impossible to execute without some snag or another. Comedy is not Vegas anymore. I don't imagine there's a comedian alive who doesn't have at least one really toxic joke lurking in their back catalogue waiting to come back to haunt them. I'm sure my turn will come. It would be impossible to think, for all the material I've pushed out into the world, that there isn't some bad-taste shit amongst it. I was, after all, born ignorant and steeped in the same bucket of prejudices as everybody else.⊗

I do think, however, I might have a little bit of an advantage over most comedians because the predominant demographic of my core audience has always been lesbians. If an audience of lesbians don't like your comedy, they will shut you down. And lesbians don't need to retreat to the safety of the internet, either, they'll hold you to account right there and then. And I'm not talking about quaint interventions like heckling or booing. It's so much worse than that. It's cold.

"WHAT KIND OF COMEDIAN CAN'T EVEN MAKE A LESBIAN LAUGH? EVERY COMEDIAN EVER! HA, HA, HA. GET IT? LESBIANS DON'T HAVE A SENSE OF HUMOUR!" (NANETTE 15:40)

Lesbians, you see, form their call-out subcommittees while you're still on stage, and as a team they will mute you with their clicking fingers. Lesbians are happy to cut your jokes off at the punch line, hack out the heart of your set and kill all the comedy before your material has even had a chance to live its best life. It is all you can do

---

⊗ So let me get ahead of the curve as best I can. In *Nanette*, I kept using the term: "straight white man." And what I should have said was "straight white *cis* man." I also flicked around a few "fellas" and "guys," which was not cool, and I was too cavalier about generalising the experience of "women." I regret not being more explicit about the intersections of race, gender, and sexuality (which is to say, my privilege), and for not being more consistent and careful about using language inclusive of non-binary and trans folk. I also used some dodgy language around mental illness, which I regret. I sincerely apologise for the harm I may have caused, and I hereby withdraw my availability to host the Oscars for the next ninety-nine years.

to watch your best work bleed out in front of you as your audience deconstructs a long list of triggers you've never even heard of, much less intended to pull. I would very much like to back this point up by making a joke about hazing but I know better than that now. As frustrating as it was to be policed by the lesbian feedback complex, I am terribly grateful for it now, as I think the worst of my ideas were nipped in the bud before they could do real harm to my career . . . and to other people, of course.

Well before I even began writing *Nanette*, I was bored by emotionally reactive comedians who have no problem defending bigotry in the name of laughter. And while it does sound very logical to insist that the singular purpose of comedy is making people laugh, I would argue that we have the internet nowadays, and that really has cornered the market of mindless laughs: it's free, forever and you don't have to leave the house. And why would you leave the house to go to a comedy club and risk a surprise set from Louis C.K. being all sad and talking about how he wanks like a teenage fascist?[⊛] Personally, I would say that if you care more about the effect of your words than you do about the meaning behind them, then you have a recklessly Machiavellian worldview. Laughter is rarely benign, but it is often malicious. So, I don't think it really matters much if you think your jokes are "pure," you're a chump if you think an audience cares about your intentions. They'll take your "harmless" jokes and laugh for their own harmful reasons, or, in the case of me, not laugh at all, because I won't rest until comedy is dead.

You could be forgiven for thinking that *Nanette* is first and foremost a deconstruction of comedy. You'd still be wrong, but I could forgive you, only because I *wanted* you to think that *Nanette* was a deconstruction of comedy. But really, all my chat about that was just a decoy. A McGuffin, if you will. I wanted to destroy the myth of the "genius" and draw attention to the long history of abuses of power that dominate the story of Western art. I wanted to deflate the egos of mythologised artists and I could think of no better medium than

---

[⊛] Which is to say, with great frequency and absolutely no humanity.

stand-up comedy to do this with . . . given that it is also an industry full of immature boys fighting in a vacuum to be the best at something fewer and fewer people actually care about.

If I were pushed to categorise *Nanette,* I would call her "stand-up catharsis," an experiment in the transmutation of trauma. You see, I was not simply telling my audience about my traumas; my goal was to simulate a feeling in the room that was akin *to* trauma, because I wanted to see if I could create an experience of communal empathy in a room full of strangers. Not just for me, but for all the people who have ever gone to comedy shows and been triggered by all the rape celebrations, violence, misogyny, homophobia and transphobia that gets spewed into microphones the whole world over.⊗

I understand, better than most, that *Nanette* is not "technically" a comedy show, but the twist is, she is not comedy in the same way that Frankenstein's monster is not a human. I did not write a speech and then call it comedy. I took everything I knew about comedy, then I pulled it all apart and built a monster out of its corpse. *Nanette* would not have worked if it were just a theatre show gate-crashing a comedy stage. People know the difference. My delivery was the same as I used for stand-up.⌀ The room was in play, there was no fourth wall, no heckle was ignored, walkouts were acknowledged. There was no director, no dramaturg, just me.

I should also point out that *Nanette* is not completely devoid of jokes. The first half is crammed full of very solid punch lines, and every time I performed the show, I filled the room with a lot of big laughter, without fail. That is important, not just as a bragging point, but because that's how I built the trust. And I needed my audience to trust me because I needed my audience to feel safe, and I needed my audience to feel safe so that I could take that safety away and not give it back. Why? Because that is the shape of trauma.

⊗ If you have been triggered at all by my anti-comedy, feel free to borrow my template to free yourself from your own prison of sads.
⌀ Except for the bits where I am ranting. That style is known as "angry archetypal man having a monologue." Which is what many would call "pure comedy."

"THAT IS MY JOB. I PUT TENSION IN A ROOM AND THEN I CURE IT WITH A LAUGH. AND YOU SAY—THANKS FOR THAT! I NEEDED A LAUGH. BUT I MADE YOU TENSE! THIS IS AN ABUSIVE RELATIONSHIP. WHY DO YOU STAY WITH ME? SEE THAT? I JUST MADE YOU LAUGH WITH A JOKE ABOUT DOMESTIC VIOLENCE. COMEDY IS NASTY WORK." (NANETTE 30:36)

Nanette was dropped into the stream smack-bang in the middle of the #metoo movement, which is the only time to release a comedy show which includes a story about a violent assault followed by a ten-minute screed calling bullshit on the patriarchy. But that's why I am such a great comedian, because comedy is, after all, all about timing. The show may not be funny, but you can't accuse me of not knowing how to read a room. But to be clear, I did not create *Nanette* with a Netflix special in mind. I didn't even have a deal in place when we filmed it, and the only reason *Nanette* became a Netflix phenomenon was because she had already inadvertently become a phenomenon on her own.

"ARTISTS DON'T INVENT THE ZEITGEIST. THEY RESPOND TO IT." (NANETTE 45:03)

The purpose of *Nanette* was never to catapult me into the top rung of the comedy conversation, quite the opposite, I was trying to *cull* my audience, I was trying to find my small pocket of genuine fans so I could be who I wanted to be on stage, without worrying about making a broad audience feel comfortable. But from the very first time I performed *Nanette* my audience refused to let me push them away, they made it clear that they understood my pain and that they cared. And so, what I had thought would effectively seal me off into an obscure corner of both my life and my art form instead became something far bigger than me, something of an international cultural phenomenon that not only shook the comedy world out of its tree but pushed my own existence into a shape I no longer recognise.

I DO THINK I HAVE TO QUIT COMEDY, THOUGH. AND SERIOUSLY. I KNOW IT'S PROBABLY NOT THE FORUM . . . TO MAKE SUCH AN ANNOUNCEMENT, IS IT? IN THE MIDDLE OF A COMEDY SHOW. (NANETTE 16:53)

One of the most talked-about points of *Nanette* was that early on in the show I declared that I was quitting comedy. I try not to get annoyed by all the people who took that statement so literally because, to be fair, there were times that I felt as if I really did want to quit, because performing the show was incredibly stressful and so overwhelming that it felt like the only sensible thing to do. But I was never really serious about quitting.

"MY CV IS PRETTY MUCH A COCK AND BALLS DRAWN UNDER A FAX NUMBER." (NANETTE 31:53)

I owe stand-up comedy my life: it gave me the platform and the purpose to playfully interrogate my own story and unravel the immature and sometimes toxic versions of events that my younger, traumatised brain had settled on. I have no doubt that without comedy I would not have had much of a chance in life, let alone been able to develop the kind of confidence and courage I needed to be able to "quit." I believe that stand-up—with or without the comedy— is one of the greatest art forms there is. To be able to wrap your own voice around your own mind, and to be able to craft it into something that has the capacity to make a room full of strangers think and feel differently, even if it's just for a moment in time, is an incredible and humbling thing to be able to do. Why would I want to quit that?

"WHAT I HAD DONE WITH MY SHOW ABOUT COMING OUT OF
THE CLOSET WAS FREEZE AN INCREDIBLY FORMATIVE EXPERIENCE
AT ITS TRAUMA POINT AND THEN SEAL IT OFF WITH JOKES.
MY STORY BECAME MATERIAL, A ROUTINE, AND THEN THROUGH
REPETITION THIS VERSION FUSED WITH MY ACTUAL MEMORY.
THE PROBLEM IS THAT MY JOKE VERSION WAS NOT NEARLY
SOPHISTICATED ENOUGH TO ACCOMMODATE FOR THE DAMAGE
DONE TO ME IN REALITY. YOU LEARN FROM THE PART OF THE
STORY YOU FOCUS ON. I NEED TO TELL MY STORY PROPERLY."
(NANETTE 40:26)

I performed *Nanette* for the very last time at the Montreal Comedy Festival and it was a truly unsettling experience. It was after the special had dropped on Netflix, and I knew as soon as I walked onto the stage that something dramatic had shifted. The fever pitch that hit me was quite unlike anything I'd experienced before, and it gave me the impression that I could have toured *Nanette* indefinitely. There was clearly an audience for it, no doubt, but once her reputation preceded her, *Nanette* was no longer a viable show. That's the tricky thing about *Nanette*, you see, because while she isn't comedy, she also can't exist without it. So, when people began applauding my setups and joining in with my punches, it was clear that a large chunk of the audience was too comfortable with their own thinking, and I knew it was over. As I walked off stage to rapturous applause, I understood I had to let her go.

Nanette belongs to the world now.

FOUNDATION MYTHOLOGY

IN THE BEGINNING

The first time I stepped up to a microphone to do the jokes, I wasn't at all anticipating that such a habit was to become my life. There wasn't much about me up until that point that would have suggested I was a natural performer. I'd had next to zero exposure to any creative industries when I was growing up, and on the rare occasion I spoke, I was barely heard and I barely cared. When I first tried stand-up, I was in my late twenties and too old to begin a career that demands all the best habits of young people, such as late-night loitering, talking about yourself all the time and masking low self-esteem with false confidence. But I am a late-blooming type, so I took to it all very well.

Although my parents were always incredibly supportive of all their children's ambitions, they, like most small-town folk of minimal means, were understandably biased toward more reliable career avenues, or at least ones that existed. So, it is unsurprising that Mum would sometimes stray into the badlands of active discouragement, like the time I declared, when I was about eight years old, that I wanted to be a dog when I grew up, and she counselled me to consider a more practical vocation, like not being so bloody stupid.

I tried to explain that I didn't want to be just any old dog and told her of my intention of becoming a paratrooping German shepherd in the S.A.S. To which Mum sensibly replied, "The army wouldn't let you join, sweetheart. You've got flat feet."

Even when she would knock a dream dead the very first time she met it, there was always an immutable truth to be found at the root of her "no can do" attitude. I think I was about twelve when she casually flicked my writing ambitions out of contention by observing, "But you don't have anything to say. You have to be interesting to be a writer, you know."

During the early stages of writing this memoir I began asking a lot of questions about what I was like when I was a little kid, but each time I broached the subject she would respond in a way that suggested she didn't think it was any of my business who I am. "Why do you need to know that?" she'd retort, as shocked and defensively as if I'd enquired about her post-menopausal habits of masturbation. The closest I ever got to an answer was a list of the defining traits of my siblings; Justin was the loving one, Jessica was the leader, Ben was the most intelligent, and Hamish was the funny one. This was likely just an attempt to encourage me to be more interested in other people, but I'm more inclined to believe she meant it as an inventory of qualities that do not apply to me.

Mum's determined efforts to raise her children to become humble humans paid off, as I think all of us tend to use the good manners and self-deprecation she drilled into us, more often than we don't. But I don't think her success was achieved entirely through encouraging good behaviour. Some credit does need to go to some of her more hard-line strategies, such as celebrating our successes through the metaphor of our failures. For example, when I won an award for creative writing in primary school, Mum made sure any pride I felt about awards was tempered with a sobering reminder that I still hadn't made any friends.

I made my final attempt to express artistic ambition when I was a sullen fifteen-year-old and told Mum I wanted to be an artist. She asked me why I would want to become an alcoholic before adding, "Because you'll wear a winter coat with holes in the pocket and your bottles of grog will keep falling out and smashing on the pavement."

To this day, the specificity of her cautionary scenario still stuns me.

So when, at age twenty-seven, I told her that I was going to pursue a career as a stand-up comedian, I was shocked when instead of total resistance she was simply confused, exclaiming "But I'm funnier than you!"

Such unbridled encouragement probably came from a sense of relief, because, although I had managed to avoid both alcoholism and artistry, I'd still carved out a fairly tragic existence for myself. At twenty-seven years of age, I was thoroughly unemployed, drifting, without a home and profoundly alone. I don't think any of my friends or family really knew that my existence was so utterly grim, because to be fair, nor did I. I've only recently been able to comprehend just how terrible a life I'd been leading. Sure, I was alive, but that was about it; I didn't have anything to look forward to, much less a dream to fall back on.

Perhaps if Mum had encouraged me like a "normal" parent, then I might have ended up in the army, wearing camouflage orthotics and barking my orders like a dog, but I very much doubt I would've ever become interesting enough to be a writer with so much to say. And besides, even if my mum had taken to pumping me full of positive affirmations and other guff, I have no doubt that I would have still had a painful and slow start to my adult life, courtesy of my brain and the big old quirk built into the very heart of its function. And that's why I can safely say I was only ever going to be a late bloomer in life.

ONCE UPON A TIME

I have a very clear memory from the day I was born, and I'm certain it is a complete fabrication. As a memory, it starts out believably enough with Mum relaxing on a hospital bed, propped up on a tri-pillow, drinking a cup of instant coffee, smoking a celebratory cigarette, and basking in the glow of me, her fifth child. After a moment, Mum stubs out her cigarette in an abalone shell and reaches for the phone on the bedside table and calls my dad with the wonderful news of me.

While it is feasible that I could have witnessed something like this as a newborn, it is harder to believe that I also saw my dad's beaming face as he marched into my older siblings' bedroom, gently waking them so they could all celebrate their new sister with a feast of green cordial and chips. If my memory is correct, which it clearly isn't, given that I appear in two places at once, there should be four children celebrating with Dad, not two, and they should look something like my brothers and sister, but they don't. They look like Dick and Fanny from *The Magic Faraway Tree*.

False memories aside, there is no doubting that I was born. Aside from my bodily existence, I also have a birth certificate that confirms the fact of my birth and that it happened in Burnie, Tasmania, in 1978. The only other primary resource I have is my mum, who, every time we'd drive past the Burnie Hospital, would point up to the window decorated with a giraffe and tell me that's where I was born. I like giraffes but that is hardly a fact-check.

Mum says that I was an uneventful pregnancy, aside from a prolonged bout of indigestion, and she also insists that I was a very easy birth. I was her fifth child, so I tend to believe her. I probably came out like a slippery fish.

According to Mum, as soon as I took my first lungful of air I shat on the nurse, copping her right on the chest. Apparently, the doctor had joked, "It's a good thing you're not a foot shorter!"—the implication being that I would have shat on the nurse's face. Mum loves this story. She applauds the doctor's wit every time she tells it, but his joke has always troubled me. Most people instinctively hold a baby to their bosom, so I really don't think a nurse would've held me to her face just because she was a foot shorter. All jokes aside, I still can't escape the apparent fact that I began my life with a rather aggressive ablution.

LONG, LONG AGO

I was most likely two years old in my first genuine memory of life, because Mum says that's how old I was when I got chickenpox. Mum's clearly not a reliable source when it comes to facts, but I do remember being very low to the ground, so I may very well have been two. My brother Hamish is the only other player in this memory, and if I was two then he would've been four, and we were both covered in the horribly itchy red pock of the chicken.

The dining room floor also features quite heavily in this memory, which is a testament to its ugliness. It was a swirl of multi-toned brown, very thick of the pile and capable of hiding an enormous amount of debris. It was covered in stains and bared its threads at every doorway it approached. I grew up to loathe that carpet, though at the time of this memory I was still of an age when learning about the world meant accepting it wholesale.

In my little memory, Hamish and I were sitting on this sea of hairy chocolate—well, Hamish was managing to sit, whereas I was flopping about like a guppy out of water. Relief came in the form of distraction, when two giant pieces of cardboard and some delicious-looking crayons were placed in front of us. With my urge to scratch muted, I set about rendering a picture of a horse by a fence. (I can only assume that's what I drew because it was a motif I revisited again and again throughout my childhood.)

I was pretty happy with my effort until I looked over at what Hamish had drawn. It was a masterpiece: a real human head with a smile, freckles, a pencil-thin neck and curly hair. I looked down, expecting my horse and fence to buoy my jealous spirits, but instead my gaze was met by a collection of indecipherable scribbles and I burst into tears, consumed by inferiority; and, to make it worse, my body was painfully itchy all over again. Eventually I was lifted off the carpet, scratching and bawling, and that is where my first coherent memory ends.

THERE ONCE WAS A CHILD

My family had established itself by the time I came onto the scene. Hamish was already the youngest, so I just got attached to him and we became known as "the little kids." Our older siblings—Justin, Jessica and Benjamin—were known as "the big kids." I should say at this point that all five of us were born within nine years of each other, so the big kids were quite small when they got their promotion, and despite Hamish and I now both being in our forties, we are still known as "the littles."

As the little kids, Hamish and I spent an enormous amount of time in each other's company. We were constantly playing games, most of which were the type that could produce a winner, and therefore a loser, and therefore I was always the latter. The two years between Hamish and I were the bane of my existence for most of my life. As a grown-up, this kind of age gap means absolutely nothing, but back then it was literally a lifetime. This is not to say I wasn't competitive—our games were usually very fiercely fought—I just never quite managed to take home the trophy, which was a block of wood that Hamish had glued to another block of wood.

If Hamish had had it his way, however, he would've been in constant competition with Ben, but the three-year age gap between them was crueler to Hamish than ours was to me. Still, if ever Ben felt compelled to play against his younger brother, I would be dropped immediately and left to my own devices. I never felt particularly rejected whenever this happened, because I have always been particularly talented at the art of self-occupation. In fact, spending time alone was the one thing I was supremely better at than Hamish.

Simply filling up a bucket, emptying it and then filling it back up again could keep me occupied for hours. When the weather would drive me inside, there was still plenty to do. I could easily spend an entire afternoon drawing a horse by a fence over and over again or rearranging my half of the bedroom. There was also a monstrous collection of Lego that always needed stacking and sorting. You might be surprised to know that for all the hours I spent playing with Lego, I only ever managed to build a wall. Sometimes I'd attempt a corner, but not often, and I never aspired to roofing any of my builds. You see, without a competition or a brother to drive my sense of purpose, I was never interested in the results of any given activity. As far as I was concerned, the only reason to do something was so that you could do it again. And again. And again.

THE INFAMOUS FIVE

There were times, and as far as I was concerned, they were the most wonderful times, when the big kids joined forces with Hamish and I, and we would play as a pack. It was usually for something like a game of cricket, but on rare occasions we would turn our backyard into a town and pretend we were all pillars of the community. Our future lives could've easily been predicted through the roles we all chose when we played Towns. Hamish would always be the shopkeeper and sell bric-a-brac for Monopoly money, and now he keeps an actual shop and sells fruit and vegetables for real money. My oldest brother, Justin, would always be the town bus driver, and he is now a bus driver and he's never considered any other job for himself. If ever there was a perfect opposite to myself, it is Justin. The only things we have in common are our parents. He is sunny, optimistic, welcoming, open, confident, boisterous, social, generous and kind; and as a kid, he had an unshakable commitment to imaginary play.

Justin once convinced Hamish and Ben to play a game called Bus Depot with him, which involved them re-riding their paper route on their bikes and pretending to deliver parcels. Justin had taken the game too seriously and hadn't noticed his recruits were not really listening to him describe the rules. They weren't listening because they were openly laughing at the way Justin was talking into his hand as if he were using a two-way radio, and how at the end of each sentence, he'd make the sound of static: "[*schhhhhhhtttt*] So, ah, you both have about five deliveries all up, over [*schhhhhhhtttt*]. It's very important you deliver every parcel, over [*schhhhhhhtttt*]."

After finishing his instructions, Justin made one last static noise before riding off to do his share of the deliveries, at which point Hamish and Ben remember looking at each other, dropping their bikes to the ground, and going inside to watch the cricket. About three hours later the phone rang; it was Justin. By the time Ben hung up he was laughing so hard he could barely relay the message, because Justin was still communicating through an imaginary bus radio despite having been just hit by a car. Apparently, he'd been clipped by a car reversing out of a driveway, but miraculously, he wasn't injured at all—probably because he'd been imagining so hard that his bike was a bus that the laws of physics had begun to believe it as well.

It's never not funny to us all to think about the poor bloke who'd knocked Justin off his bike/bus. How awful he must've felt at first, then how frightened of my parents' reaction he'd have been, but the thing that gets us the most is how bewildering it must have been for the bloke to see the kid he'd just run over call up an imaginary bus depot and interrupt his own accident report with radio static.

When we played Towns, my sister Jessica would always volunteer to be the schoolteacher. Although she didn't become a teacher, she did become a project manager, which is effectively the role she always took in our games. A natural leader, Jessica saw herself as the boss of the kids. I don't know how the others felt about her assumption of authority, but I was more than happy for her guidance because I had no desire to lead and I certainly didn't possess the skills I needed to survive on my own.

Each and every time we set about playing Towns, I always made the same job request: "I want to be a dog."

"No! Hannah, you can't be a dog!" Jessica would reply, already exhibiting her talent for project management. "How many times do I have to tell you? You have to be a doctor, or a nurse. Someone needs to run the hospital." And although I would always accept my reappointment without protest, like a good dog, it was never without disappointment.

You may well laugh at the absurdity of wanting to be a dog, but I have grown up to become an incredibly successful one. I am a very trusting adult with devastatingly simple needs, I like being told I am good, I'm distressed by loud noises, I always feel much better after a walk, and I am very easily bribed with the promise of food.

Out of all of us, it's Ben who's landed the furthest from his chosen career when we played Towns. Being a policeman was never really going to suit the quietest and gentlest member of our clan. After studying law, Ben eventually became a teacher and has recently discovered a talent for working with children with autism. In retrospect, this talent was clearly in evidence when we played Towns because every time my job application for "town dog" was denied, he would always make me feel better by quietly pulling me aside to tell me that I could be a dog if I really wanted to be—so long as I was a doctor dog.

CHALK AND CHEESE

My parents' marriage proves that as painful as the process is, something worthwhile can result when you persevere for long enough with the merging of chalk and cheese. When I was growing up it seemed as if I was destined to be 100 percent my father's daughter, as evidenced by my inheriting some of his more distinctive physical features, like good facial symmetry, flat feet, weak ankles and having the heart rate of an elite athlete housed in the body of an elite potato. But sadly, like most women, I am making a very convincing, late-in-life run at turning into my mother.

I once made the mistake of asking Mum who she thought I took after more, and she responded with the saddest little sound, I hardly needed to hear the answer: "You got all the useless bits of both of us!" Sadly, she's not wrong. Being an equal mix of the chalk and cheese of my parents didn't necessarily have to end so badly for me, I could have turned out to be a delicious snack that could also mark up an emergency hopscotch pitch on the pavement. But instead, I'm just someone who crumbles easily and yet still manages to block the exits. I have Dad's preference for non-participation and quiet, and yet I'm constantly shattering my own peace with the disruptive, shit-stirring genes I inherited from my mum.

Mum was a hairdresser by trade, but with five kids all born within a decade of each other she understandably didn't seek to simultaneously dress the hair professionally. So whenever there was a school form that asked for *Mother's Occupation,* Mum would simply write *convict labourer.* But that was not the whole truth, she also had a job cleaning the local golf club.

Mum was the boss of our family and as such she did all the yelling. I think one of the reasons my siblings and I remain so close is because when we were growing up, we shared a common enemy. Every fight we ever had would inevitably end with the plea: "Don't tell Mum!" Like the time Hamish stabbed me in the neck with a cricket wicket. It wasn't an official cricket wicket, just a sharpened stick Dad used as a garden stake. Hamish and I had been fighting over it for most of the day. He wanted to use it to practice bowling and I wanted it because he had it. For a long time, it was just a process of snatch-and-run, but when we both ended up with a grip on each end, it turned into a game of tug-of-war. The game ended when, at the height of my tug, Hamish decided not to tug back, and let go. He thought that I would just lose my balance, but instead the pointy end of the stick lodged itself into my throat. We stood there, stunned, the stick swinging ever so slightly from my neck. I was pretty sure I was going to die, but that wasn't the real issue. "I'll tell you what," Hamish offered in a careful voice, "you can have the wicket. If you don't tell Mum."

It was a win-win in my mind and I pulled the bounty out of my neck, making a satisfying popping sound. True to my word, I wore skivvies for a few weeks to cover up my scab. I hated skivvies, but anything was better than telling Mum.

At her most frustrated, Mum would threaten to run away from the family. I never really thought she was serious, but I remember once Jessica called a meeting and managed to convince us all that Mum and Dad were going to get divorced and that we should punish them both by going out on our own, just like the Famous Five. Although I was quite excited about the prospect of being Timmy the Dog, I was ultimately very anxious about the prospect of a disruption to my existence. But as usual I trusted Jessica unquestioningly and backed her 100 percent when she herded us into our parents' bedroom to tell them of our plans. Apparently, it was the first Mum and Dad had heard of their impending breakup, but after hearing Jessica's plan for total independence, Dad said he thought divorce sounded really great.

Dad was a high school maths teacher who played lawn bowls on the weekend, which is about all the information you need in order to know that he was not a firecracker of a personality. The closest thing Dad had to a passionate pastime was finding solutions to the kind of problems that other people don't think of as problems at all. "Always peel the fat end of the carrot first." I can still recite, verbatim, Dad's spiel about his revolutionary carrot-peeling technique, because once he'd conquered this non-problem, there was never another carrot peeled in Dad's presence without him coaching the process. "When you peel the second half of the carrot, you'll always be holding onto the end you just peeled, which is slippery, because you've just peeled it, but if you peel the pointy end first, when you turn it round to peel the fat end, you won't be able to get a good grip, because you've only got the tip to hold, and the tip is now slippery, because you've just peeled it. That's why you should always peel the fat end of the carrot first."

Dad would impart this instruction so often, and so passionately, that I really wanted to believe he was passing on actual wisdom, like a wax-on *Karate Kid* vegetable-based metaphor on how to live life. But deep down, I always knew that Dad just didn't want anybody to struggle with carrots, because it annoyed him to watch someone do it the wrong way, especially if they didn't even know it was a problem.⊗

Dad's other big love was fixing things. But only temporarily. He was so good at temporary fixes, in fact, that they nearly always ended up being permanent fixtures. For example, when the channel knob fell off our TV, Dad declared he would repair the situation, but the TV was never reunited with its knob and for the rest of its working life we changed the channels with a pair of pliers. When the plastic grip began to fall off the handles of the pliers, Dad repaired them with the red gaffer tape.

The red gaffer tape was Dad's favourite tool in his temporary fixer box. He had snapped up rolls and rolls of the stuff when the local newsagent had a sale, what a big day that must have been. As soon as he could, Dad set about making the red tape an ostentatious feature of our family home. Doors that slammed loudly were silenced, loose pot handles were steadied, and uneven chair legs were levelled—all with the red tape. Our house was practically held together with the stuff and I hated it, mostly because it clashed so horribly with the brown of our carpet.

My dad is not an excitable man. He is slow and measured, and you can always rely on him to be the calm in any storm and asleep in any other weather. For the most part, Dad was the good cop to Mum's bad cop. "You always take your father's side," Mum would often scream at us from the end of her tether. And while I don't want to diminish her frustration, this is not strictly true. We never chose Dad's side over hers; we couldn't, because he didn't have a side.

⊗ A few years ago when I discovered that I could trick myself into drinking enough water if I made it fun by dropping in effervescent children's vitamins, I really thought I was on my way to a Nobel Peace Prize for hydration. But I was horrified to hear myself talking about my vitamin revelation to a stranger at the dog park in a way that was very "always peel the fat end of the carrot first." I could only cringe, because I knew I'd already told far too many people before I'd caught myself being Dad, to do anything about it. And I am mortified to report, that I am still sharing this nugget of useless non-wisdom pretty much every time I see someone drinking regular water, because I can't stand that they don't even know it's a problem.

Whereas Mum could always be relied upon to rustle up a strong opinion on any subject at very short notice, I'm not sure Dad has ever in his life formed any kind of point of view, although I do remember him once suddenly declaring that hummingbirds were pretty impressive, but other than that, he stays out of politics.

A life-and-death crisis was one of the only things that could prompt Dad into decisive action, they really did bring out the best in him; he could suddenly act quickly, but without panic and throw in a joke for good measure. Like the time my brother chopped his thumb off with the axe: "I suppose I better drive you to hospital, doesn't look like you'll be able to hitchhike." Mum, on the other hand, expressed her panic and fear by trying to lower Ben's expectations of life without a thumb and shouted things like "you won't even be able to use a tin opener."

It is beyond doubt that Mum was the personality of the Gadsby clan, but our life was not flavoured by her alone. Ultimately, the character of our family dynamic was forged by the epic tensions that will always arise when you try to combine a chunk of cheese with a stick of chalk.

THE UGLY DUCK

The further away I am from Australia, the more work I have to do to explain the geographical situation of the place I grew up in. While it is usually enough for me to say that I come from a small island off the south of Australia, there are times that I'll need to clarify that Tasmania is not a country in and of itself, but rather a state of Australia. Sometimes I have to go even further to explain that the reason New Zealand is not Tasmania is because it is New Zealand, and on one incredibly exciting occasion I had to break the news to an adult human that Tanzania is not a province of Austria.

I don't find it insulting that not many people know where in the world I'm from. The point of the exercise is not to expose the ignorance of others, but rather, to convey the sense that I grew up a long way away from nowhere. And the reason I do that is because I believe the obscure isolation of my childhood is a key ingredient in the complex recipe of my identity.

I grew up on the very potato-proud, stunningly beautiful North West Coast of Tasmania in a stunningly charmless town called Smithton. To be fair, Smithton was established for no other purpose than to support the industries that necessitated its existence—logging, mining, fishing, farming—so as a town, it has never really had an issue with its own lack of charm. It is a practical place filled with practical people. With a population of just over 3,000, Smithton isn't especially small, but it is exceedingly isolated.

Like most of Tasmania's substantial townships, Smithton was "settled" by white colonisers in the late eighteenth century, although it would be more accurate to say that it started out as a bald patch that had been left behind after all the old-growth forests had been logged and dragged away by boat to help in the settlement of better towns in better places.

Smithton itself was built on the banks of the Duck River, which might sound very picturesque, but as the Duck was a tidal river it would regularly disappear, leaving the fishing boats sitting in mud sludge and the town smelling like a wet fart. The once-thriving Duck River Butter Factory was just a hulking grey shell by the time I entered the worldly equation, but the Smithton of my childhood was still the proud home of multiple timber mills, an abattoir and two functioning factories which sat on either side of the sometimes-mighty Duck.

On the one side there was the fish factory, which was where all the magnificent seafood from the river and coastal estuaries was processed before being taken away and sold elsewhere. On the other side of the river was the McCain frozen food factory, and this was where the fresh vegetables grown in the rich earth of the surrounding farms were all brought to be snap-frozen and then shipped out of town to be—you guessed it—sold elsewhere.

Frozen chips were a particular specialty of this factory, and because the process of chipping a potato for freezing not only involved peeling and cutting but also a partial frying, this meant Smithton could sometimes have a delicious waft flowing through it. But, if the wind was wrong, the tide was out and the mud was farting, then the smell of chips cooking combined with the fish guts from over the road could make Smithton stink like hell, if hell had a hangover from hell.

Although I was born and bred in Smithton, I was never a local. To be a local you had to be from a family that was at least four generations deep, that's just the kind of town Smithton is. Although Dad's family were North West Coasters, it wasn't west enough to grant us any kind of local status, and Mum was from the Southern Midlands, so she may as well have dropped in from Mars. The big kids had all been born in Tasmania's capital, Hobart, which, being on the South East corner of the island, is about as far away as you can get from Smithton without getting your feet wet.

My family had moved to the North West when Dad was offered a job teaching maths at Smithton High School. In an attempt to lure teachers to regional schools, Tasmania's Department of Education was providing housing to assist with relocation. This was enticing enough for my parents, apparently, and so we moved into a lovely weatherboard bungalow with a big backyard, which Dad turned into a very substantial vegetable garden. The most distinctive feature of my childhood home was the massive hedge that served as a fence for two full sides of the block and marked the boundary between our house and the high school oval next door. As places go, it wasn't exactly an oil painting of a situation but there was no denying the convenience of living so close to the school, not least because it meant that Dad could finish work at four and still be home by three-thirty.

Smithton is the sort of place you could easily get stuck in if you're not careful, and my parents were not careful. Isolated on the corner of an already isolated island, Smithton wasn't even the kind of place people would pass through by accident, nor was it the kind of destination you'd ever sensibly go out of your way to visit for the pleasure of it. Other than the spectacular wilderness on the West Coast, the only other destination that could attract any kind of outsider interest was Stanley, a little town about twenty minutes closer to the rest of Tasmania.

I always wished that we'd lived in Stanley instead of Smithton. It had the same wild weather, but it was so much more charming. It is a quaint little fishing village nestled under an impressive volcanic outcrop known as "the Nut." You could easily imagine *The Piano* being set in Stanley, whereas, at best, Smithton could only serve as the production base for a remake of *Deliverance*.

YOU SAY POTATO. I SAY HOW HIGH.

The jackpot of my childhood nostalgia will always bubble up whenever I hear the sound of a horse race being called, especially when it's filtered through radio static. This sound defined most of my childhood weekends so consistently that I seem to be thoroughly steeped in horse-racing culture, despite never having pursued an active thought about it. Most people can remember their childhood phone number, but not me. That memory real estate is occupied by Dad's telephone-betting-account code. I can name more race courses than I can major bodies of water, and I once had a teddy bear called Quinella. The strength of my nostalgia was in no small way anchored by the promise that if ever there was a big win on the horses, then we were an outside chance for takeaway fish-and-chips for dinner.

Most of the time, however, I didn't pay any attention to the races because it was just what Dad listened to when he was in the garden. It was only when his horse started to get repeated mentions as a front-runner that Dad would get emotionally involved, stop whatever he was doing and hurry inside and grab the pliers and switch the TV onto the races before plonking onto his chair and asking for a bit of shush. If any of us kids were around, we would start to gather around Dad's chair, excitedly, but also slowly and silently so as not to interrupt his *shush*. It must have looked like the Children of the Corn had decided to seek out an indoor hobby.

Dad never seemed to get upset if his pick fell back into oblivion, but if it stayed in contention then he would begin slapping his thigh and hissing furiously, and if ever his horse finished a place, we would witness a rare and wonderful thing: Dad expressing joy. When it comes to positive emotions, Dad is more of a nonverbal kind of guy, but you could reliably measure his happiness by the rate at which he rubbed his hands together. If I saw excessive hand-rubbing from Dad, then that was all I needed to inspire a couple laps of the house in an excitable trot. I've never quite been able to express joy as succinctly as I could as a child.

Unfortunately, when it comes to gambling, Dad has never been much of a gambler. His betting style was so cautious that it was rare for a win to do much more than break even, let alone generate enough spare coin to transform our next meal, but you could never really tell because he didn't adjust his level of excitement to the scale of profit. Even when he'd only placed a pretend bet on a horse, his excitement for the theoretical win of his theoretical bet was equal to any monetised result. So even though we knew that a win didn't automatically guarantee us a takeaway treat, it never stopped at least one of us from asking our uncharacteristically excited father, "Does this mean fish-and-chips?"

Compared to Dad's more systematic and careful methods, Mum's approach was far closer to actual gambling. She usually just backed a horse because she liked something about the name. As such, Mum's bets had the potential to be big winners and, although they rarely came in, when they looked a chance the sight of both Mum and Dad hissing and slapping excitedly together, chalk and cheese as one, made the world an infinitely better place, because nothing could bring our family closer together than the chance of a table covered in white food fried yellow.

Despite the rank factory smells that permeated my childhood, the classic fried yellow meal was by far my all-time favourite takeaway food. To be fair, there wasn't much in the way of other kinds of takeaway options in Smithton. There was a pizza parlor, but I was in my mid-teens before I even knew that it existed because Mum hated

Italian food. What can I say, she was low-carb well before it was fashionable? Naturally, there was a local Chinese restaurant, Jade Dragon, and we would, on very rare occasions, have that as a takeaway treat, but I never ate in the establishment itself. I'd heard rumours that there was one table so big it had a lazy Susan the size of a back-end wheel of a tractor. Needless to say, like most kids from regional Australia, I grew up believing that sweet and sour pork was exotic and deep-fried ice cream was witchcraft.

There were at least eight different establishments where you could buy fish-and-chips in Smithton. This is a remarkable statistic given the population was not large enough to support this level of market competition. The only other businesses with excessive representation in town were hairdressers and religion—so us Gadsby kids really never had a chance since Mum cut our hair, we were raised as atheists, and on Fish 'n' Chip Friday we usually made our own.

I don't think it's technically possible to make fish-and-chips at home, but for many years Dad tried to convince us that's what we were eating on Friday nights. But I think if you try to re-create a quick and easy meal at home, and it takes a whole lot of time, effort and patience, then you are not making a quick and easy meal, and you should respect that, and you should call it something else. There was just so much work in homemade fish-and-chips, so the meal became less exciting and more of a chore. The spuds had to be dug up, washed, peeled and cut up into fiddly strips, the fish had to be sealed with egg and breadcrumbs. And in our family, it was a production line and everyone was expected to help—no excuses.

I was never going to complain outwardly, because it was still far more exciting than the meat and three vegetables that usually dominated our plates. But for a treat that promised to be low in fuss there was precious little in the way of instant gratification, and that's why takeaway was such a thrill. Unlike the torture of the snail's-paced homemade version, store-bought fish-and-chips was a far more frenzied affair in our house. Packages would be placed on the coffee table and unrolled to expose their fried yellow guts, and we would all attack like devils would roadkill to make sure we got our fair share.

I had some champion eaters to compete with. Hamish was quick on the draw, and as the eldest, Justin could pack it away pretty quickly. But Ben was the most efficient of all of us kids. He was a machine. I only ever remember seeing him falter once, and it only made me admire him more. It happened during a particularly ferocious attack on a bowl of cocktail saveloys and Ben, who'd been in pole position from the start, snatched the last one and it was halfway to his mouth when he suddenly bent over and vomited. What came out was an absolute marvel, to my mind, and it was difficult to imagine that what came up had ever been down. Most of the little red sausages returned in near perfect condition, and I refuse to believe that I was the only one who thought they still looked good enough to eat.

Despite the savageries that takeaway fish-and-chips unleashed, our family did have one very important rule that we all respected without fail: The fish was sacred. You could steal chips out of someone's mouth but you couldn't touch their fish. We all knew that once your fish reached the safety of your plate, you could relax and begin the mindless shoveling of the chips. But after one particularly memorable win on the horses, there was another fried yellow treat scattered throughout the sea of hot chips that almost gave us all pause, and almost made me pause permanently.

"Squid rings for the squiddly-dids!" Although Dad had often used "squiddly-dids" as rhyming slang for "kids," I'd never imagined he was likening us to anything remotely like these little golden halos of promise. "What are they, Dad?" Hamish asked. "Crumbed calamari," Dad reported proudly. "There's two each and if anyone doesn't like them, give them to your mother." Mum was already chomping into one, and her delight was enough to convince us of the rings' status; we all plucked out our quota and put them on our plates next to our fish.

The meal then proceeded as usual until, in a rather uncharacter-istic move, I decided to sample the squid before the chips had vanished. I thought there was a slim chance I wouldn't like it, so I figured I needed to find this out early so I could trade for fish. My initial reaction was positive. Calamari felt delicious. But then, much to my horror, I found that my teeth couldn't break the rubbery ring, so I reached into my mouth and pulled it out and found that with the batter coating gone, all I was left with was a pale circle of fish mystery. In a hurry to get back to the chips, I gripped the rubbery calamari band between my teeth and yanked it back with my hands to try and break it with force, but when I saw how far it stretched without breaking, I panicked and let it go. As soon as I felt it snap back and lodge into a tight little spot just beyond the back of my throat, I knew I had made a huge tactical error.

I didn't fully understand the ramifications of not being able to breathe and was pleasantly mesmerised by the slowing of time. It wasn't until I tried to eat another chip that I even realised I was choking. My instincts finally kicked in and I stood up and waved my hands in front of my face in a desperate attempt to distract my family away from the chips. Which took longer than is reasonable, but it is hardly surprising nonetheless.

While Mum shouted at me to breathe for the sake of god and other damns, everyone else took turns at thumping me on the back. It was, after all, a chance to hit someone without getting in trouble. It was only when Mum's voice started to fade away that I began to think about dying. My life didn't flash before my eyes. I was too young. All I could visualize was my uneaten piece of fish, as everything else began to fade away.

I was provoked out of my stupor by Dad, who was standing over me. He pulled my mouth open with one hand, jammed the other one down my throat and heroically seized the plug of calamari. It wasn't until he pulled it out and held it aloft that I realised he'd used the TV pliers. It was a good result in that I didn't die, but I was not unaffected. To begin with, I temporarily lost both my appetite and ability to swallow, and then there was the matter of my piece of fish that disappeared into someone else's gullet and for which I was never duly compensated.

CHILDREN OF THE CORN

I'd gotten a little confused over how I was supposed to make friends when I first started school. I'd always assumed that I'd hang out with Hamish as usual, but over the course of the two years that separated our first days of school, Hamish had managed to make himself more than enough friends to replace me several times over. He let me join in the occasional game of cricket, if I promised to stay in the outer field, but I was never welcomed with much in the way of enthusiasm so I eventually stopped asking. I didn't have much experience with people my own age and I didn't have much to say to them. From what I could gather, talking was a good way to climb the social ladder, so my limited small talk skills meant I was not going to break social rank at school.

This is not to say I hated school. I loved it. I loved the structure of it. Every day I knew exactly where I had to be and what I had to do and if I didn't, I was safe in the knowledge that someone would tell me. For a kid like me who was completely devoid of naturally occurring initiative, school was heaven. My problem was that I didn't know what to do during free time. The bark garden was completely off-limits to me, because that was where the cool kids hung out. Sometimes I would lurk around the fort hoping to play but I always felt a little unwelcome, and I didn't know how to go about rectifying that particular situation. After I stopped skulking in the outer fields of Hamish's lunchtime cricket matches, I took to walking aimlessly about or just standing very close to my teacher, Mrs. Smith, whenever she was on yard duty. I wouldn't always talk to her; I would just stand in her general vicinity and watch the world go by.

In the beginning, my apparent inability to procure friends was upsetting, but once I worked out that popularity was mostly preordained, I was able to relax a little. Within the first few weeks of school, I could see that three distinct groups had formed. At the top were the popular kids, who all seemed to know each other already and had smooth skin and heads that weren't abnormally large. There was the grotty group at the bottom of the social ladder, made up of kids who breathed through their mouths and had ugly school uniform variations and bad haircuts. Most of the grotty kids came from the same bleak part of town that sprawled out along the river flat, known as Healdsville, because every second person who lived there either had the surname "Heald" or the telltale red hair of this ubiquitous family.

The third group sat somewhere in the middle and was by far the largest and most complex group of them all, and this was where I found myself. As far as I could tell, the safest place to be was in the middle of the middle. There were some kids who lurked dangerously close to the bottom group, and the stress of maintaining social position must have been tiring for them. Reasons varied for drops in social status, but sudden departures from the school uniform were the usual cause, because it meant you were poor. Mrs. House should have known Monica would never recover from the day she wore her dad's diabetes socks to school. Sure, they remained a safe level of snug around her calves, but restricted circulation would have been easier to recover from. In a school full of white-socked ankles, Monica became a flashing beacon for bullies in her dad's beige and black argyle socks.

Social climbing was possible but, unlike social dropping, it was never permanent. And while everyone seemed to generally agree upon what could make you a bottom-feeder, rising and falling from the top group appeared to be a completely arbitrary process. A charm bracelet might give you a boost, but your sister's fob chain could very well hang you. Despite the dangers involved in getting into the popular group, most of us wanted in. But as I was never a serious contender, I decided that it was safer not to try. This is not to say I didn't dream about it. I was fascinated by the cool kids. I obsessed over them, but I never imagined I would number among them.

Before I started school, my two favourite pastimes were playing games and eating. I was gifted and competitive at both, but the joy was knocked out of me once my formal education began. I blame the gym. By far the largest structure that made up Smithton Primary

School, the school gym was a hulking fortress of corrugated green tin surrounded by a black asphalt moat, an inanimate intimidation that sat at the centre of everything.

The asphalt floor of the gym was a confusing map of lines outlining the courts of a million different sports. I was in a constant state of confusion during sport lessons, trying to distinguish the badminton lines from those for handball, netball and basketball. Adding to this confidence-shredding hellscape was the fact that I seemed to be a magnet for stray projectiles. Given the chaos, it was difficult to tell who was responsible for throwing the balls I intercepted with my head and impossible to know whether they were accidental or not because, courtesy of the relentless echo pinging off the asphalt and tin, all laughter sounded cruel in the gym.

The gym also served as the de facto lunchroom, where all the students in the entire school were herded to sit and eat their lunches all at the same time and all under the watchful eyes of teachers like Mr. K, who would walk slowly through the gym eyeballing each and every child to make sure they were eating. Mr. K was a German man of intimidating proportions, and rumour had it that he was a close personal friend of Hitler and he owned a gun. Whatever the case, he seemed to take it personally if you didn't eat. Whenever he spotted students without food or appetite, his booming voice would echo throughout the gym, saying, *"Food would be the last thing I forget!"* I firmly believe the lunchtime inspections in the gym intensified the already tense state of schoolyard politics.

For a time, I thought the lunchtime inspections were a completely ridiculous notion, it seemed inconceivable to me that anyone would choose not to eat food if given the opportunity. But after a couple of years of substandard sandwiches and nonexistent snacks, even I became unenthused about my lunch-boxed meal. I'd never really questioned my supply of food until I went to school. But once I'd witnessed the steady stream of chips, biscuits and chocolates being pulled from bottomless lunch boxes, I began to feel hard done by.

My sandwich staple was Vegemite. On a good day it came with

lettuce or cream cheese, but in the days leading up to payday it was always on its own with a deteriorating quality of bread. My favourite by far was shit sandwiches—the "shit" was processed luncheon meat, or "Belgium" as I knew it—but I don't know why Dad called them shit sandwiches because they were delicious, and if they were in my lunch box, they rarely survived beyond little lunch.[*] The real shit sandwich was peanut butter. I loved a peanut butter sandwich at home, but after a morning spent drying out it became an inferior product. Other problematic fillings were cucumber and tomato. Again, delicious immediately after production, but after a few hours wrapped in plastic they became unacceptably soggy. This struggle with the textural quality of sandwiches, combined with the stress of schoolyard politics, had a suppressive effect on my appetite, and within weeks of starting school I became a consistent skipper of lunch. I became good at being invisible while pretending to eat, and then, as soon as I got home, I would throw the offending sandwich behind my wardrobe, where it would slowly turn into a pile of mouldy green dust.

Once the school day was over, however, my hunger would return with such vengeance that I would then embark on a near feverish mission to make up for the loss of my midday meal. As it was rare for our kitchen cupboards to have anything other than the sorts of stuff that required time, permission and a recipe to become edible, my afternoon snack would have been a very grim and limited affair had it not been for the good graces of Nan and Pop over the road.

From the very beginning of my school career, most of my visits next door played out the same way. As soon as I'd changed out of my uniform and disposed of my uneaten sandwiches, I would be knocking on their back door. After a quick hello I'd be sent outside to fetch some water from the rainwater tank, and after I'd filled the kettle, I'd call Pop in from the garden while Nan made the tea and plated the biscuits. Once Pop's hands were washed and the sunroom table set, we'd all sit down together for afternoon tea, during which I would

[*] Otherwise known as "recess" to the Americans amongst you.

regale my elderly companions with all the exciting tales from my day at school. My stories were always about things I'd observed from a safe distance, but in the retelling, I would insert myself into the thick of the action.

Like the stories I told them, my relationship to Nan and Pop was one of wishful invention. They were not the parents of either of my parents, they just happened to live next door and were friendly and generous enough to welcome me as their near-daily visitor. As the story goes, my older siblings, who were intermittent visitors themselves, dragged their brand-new sister over the very same day that Mum returned from the hospital after having me. Pop told that story as often as any, and he took great delight in telling me how I'd fallen asleep in his arms as if it were the sure sign our friendship was destiny. Clearly, he didn't know that nearly all newborns are partial to a nap and will take them wherever they can get them. There is no doubt a very special bond did form over time, but it was the biscuits and the calm that first drew me over the road on a regular basis.

Although I loved Pop to bits, I shared the strongest bond with Nan, who indulged me more than anyone else in the world. I think hers are the only eyes I have ever felt comfortable making contact with. They were so calm, gentle, and had a knowing twinkle that made me feel safe even when she was chuckling for reasons I didn't entirely understand. I felt like I could tell Nan anything, and I frequently did. She would always listen to my thoughts and nod along to my stories. But the best part about our relationship was how we could sit in comfortable silence for hours on end.

Nothing ever changed in the world that Nan and Pop lived in. Nothing. Not their home or the rhythms they kept within it. They never changed which day they did their shopping or the groceries they bought, nor did their repertoire of stories ever change, not even the way they told them, the turns of phrases and pauses all stayed the same. Even when daylight savings forced them to wind their clocks back or forth, the one in the kitchen was always kept five minutes fast and the one in the sunroom five minutes slow. Always.

It was impossible to tell how long I spent at Nan and Pop's on any given day, as everything was so consistent it felt as if time warped and stood still as it did. Looking back on all this, I have to wonder if my welcome was as consistent and extended as my visiting habits suggested. I always assumed it was a mutually beneficial relationship, because their daughter lived elsewhere and their real grandkids visited them as rarely as I visited my real grandparents. As far as I was concerned, they were in need of company and I was in need of snacks and quiet time.

Of my real grandparents, our family was closer in both distance and spirit to my dad's parents, who we referred to as the "Grumpy Grandparents" to distinguish them from Mum's parents, who we'd dubbed "Funny." It was only Granddad who lived up to the Grumpy moniker. He was gruff, impatient and always wore the kind of frown that looked like someone had stabbed a potato with a spoon. But I am happy to report that Grumpy Granddad had something of a soft spot for me, even if he didn't tell his face.

Grumpy Grandma was not grumpy at all; in fact, she was a thoroughly brilliant human. My love for her was fostered in the short term by her witch-like ability to cover a table with homemade cakes and desserts, and further stoked by her insistence on second helpings. But it is for less edible reasons that my love endured, because it was Grumpy Grandma who taught me the most valuable of my life skills: how to milk a cow, why to love a garden and how to lose gracefully at cards even when you know how to cheat.

Mum's dad, Funny Granddad, also lived up to his name, but I only knew this from what I'd been told, because he died well before I'd mastered the art of remembering people. All I have to recall him with is one vague memory of feeling very furious at him because he kept calling me Gertrude. I never had much of a relationship with Funny Grandma. It wasn't just the tyranny of distance at play; her personality also helped to push her to the outer edges of my familiar zone. If Granddad was "funny ha-ha" then Grandma was "funny peculiar" and by that, I mean not at all. Funny Grandma was the only old person I ever met who took an instant disliking to me. But that's not why I ranked her last amongst my grandparents—I just didn't like the way she smelt.

Overpowering odors have always informed my feelings about stuff. For example, at school, the tinderbox of lunchtime tensions was probably intensified for me courtesy of the sweaty bread syndrome. All it took was a few uneaten crusts to spend the weekend hiding out in my lunch box and that was it for the rest of the year. I could scrub, soak and leave the lunch box out in the sun as much as I liked, but from thereon the waft of the warm, plastic-infused, musty bread ghost would still greet me every time I popped my lunch box lid. This issue was amplified spectacularly when about three hundred children released their mouldy sandwich phantoms simultaneously under the same tin roof. I liked to blame the lunchtime tension on this smell. It was like we were all looking for someone to blame—an individual scapegoat for a communal contagion.

For the most part I was overlooked for lunch-themed bullying. I only made one mistake, and that was having curried egg sandwiches. By the end of that sulphuric lunch, everyone had taken to calling me Fart Face and I dare say it could have been a lifelong stigma if our teacher, Mr. Bannon, hadn't unleashed the grandest bullying gesture any of us had ever witnessed that same afternoon when he angrily fastened Melody Hastings to her chair with an entire roll of sticky tape to stop her from fidgeting. Melody had the kind of learning difficulties that made her a beacon for bullying, and the kind of gentleness that made it too easy to get away with. It pains me to admit that just like everybody else I dabbled in unkindness toward Melody, but when your teacher leads the bullying charge so brutally, it's hard to know how any kid could be expected to rise above it.

It was not just gross smells that attracted derision during lunch in the gym; anything out of the ordinary could draw a mocking crowd and everything was open to scrutiny: who you sat with, the type of container your food was in, right down to the cut of your sandwich. It was a high-pressure situation with nowhere to hide. And that is why, in the last two weeks of my second year of school, I began to dread the gym so much I couldn't eat at all, not even a pleasantly textured sandwich, because my lunch was wrapped in a dirty secret.

I didn't think the bags were a problem at first. I was even a little bit excited when Dad and I had first discovered them in the boxes stacked neatly on the edge of the main rubbish pile at the dump. We split one of the boxes open out of curiosity, and what we found inside became a part of our family: unused frozen corn-on-the-cob bags from the McCain's factory. Thousands upon thousands of them. They were about the size of a book, made of white plastic, with a photograph of four juicy-looking pieces of corn printed on one side.

This kind of thing could only have happened during the golden age of rubbish tips, when local councils would actively encourage residents to trawl for treasures amongst the landfill of their neighbour's trash. I was always the first to volunteer to join Dad on his scavenger missions, despite the overwhelming pungence of the rubbish pits. I was more than happy to be sent scrambling over mounds of trash to retrieve the random crap and nifty-looking bits of timber Dad had spied from the perimeter of the pile. It never occurred to me that it was anything other than a normal weekend adventure. In fact, I particularly enjoyed the excursions as they gave me the opportunity to build on my collection of broken kitchen appliances.

Dad could barely conceal his excitement as he loaded three cases of the corn-cob bags into the back of the Valiant. "Better leave some for someone else!" he said of the other boxes we left behind. I couldn't imagine that anyone else would experience the same level of joy that Dad did. I couldn't even conceive as to what on earth Dad was going to do with our vast supply. As it turned out, he would attempt to do pretty much everything with the corn-on-the-cob bags. He used them for every conceivable temporary fix, he used one as his toiletry bag, he lined our cutlery drawer with them and tied them to fruit trees to repel the birds (apparently, they don't like corn or irony). He even went through a phase of putting the bags over our shoes and sending us out into the wet in our "disposable gum boots."

I was fine with pretty much all the uses Dad put to the old corn-cob bags. I only took issue the day he decided to use them to wrap up our school lunches. I knew it would only take one kid to catch a glimpse of the yellow and white packaging and an entire year's effort to slip under the radar would've been ruined. I was generally good at not drawing attention to myself, but to be sure, I took to keeping my lunch box inside my school bag and sneaking my sandwiches out one at a time. It was a very successful ploy, and I would've completely gotten away with my dirty secret had it not been for the end-of-year school excursion.

The picnic was at Crayfish Creek, which I was very disappointed to discover was all creek and no crayfish, but still, it was a perfect location for a school excursion as it included a generous picnic area, a tyre swing, and ample drowning opportunities.

I had wandered off during lunch so I could eat alone, and was sitting on a stump amongst the trees on the edge of the playground when I heard Jason Pike and Heath Marshall approaching. They were generally good-natured boys, seemingly uninterested in their own social position, but they took great delight in drawing attention to anyone who didn't want or need it. They often roamed around like freelance bullies looking for trouble, and I knew I would be ripe for the picking, sitting on a stump, alone, eating a soggy sandwich from a corn-on-the-cob bag. I trusted my instincts and shoved my lunch into my bag before scrambling up the nearest tree to avoid their scrutiny. My plan worked until I discovered that, like most children and kittens, I was better at ascending than descending.

Nothing demands your focus like a broken bone. It's a heady combination of adrenaline, swelling, general disorientation and that sickening sound that you can feel throughout your body. I was so focused on the swirl of strangeness and my swelling forearm that I was half-way home before I correctly identified the dominant sensation as pain, and it was only then that I became distressed. It didn't help that Mr. Bannon was driving, but at least I was in too much pain to fidget.

Mum has always liked to indulge in contrary diagnosis, and if Mr. Bannon had arrived on our front porch supporting my right hand in his, proclaiming that I'd broken my arm, then Mum would likely have countered with the diagnosis of "sprain" or "nothing at all." She might've rubbed some Vicks VapoRub onto the "supposed" injury before sending me outside to pick the carrots for dinner. Luckily for me, Mr. Bannon insisted it was a sprain, so Mum decided it was far more serious. "What the hell would he know?" she said as she closed the door in his face.

At first, I took the news of a greenstick fracture badly, because I thought that meant it wasn't broken enough to get a plaster cast. In my mind, an injury that needed plaster was the only one Mum seemed to accept ever since, a few years earlier, Hamish had returned home from hospital sporting a beautiful white cast on his leg after having surgery to correct his "spastic foot" (I swear this is the actual medical term). After witnessing the kinds of privileges it garnered for him—absolution from chores, larger helpings of food, and cuddles from Mum—I'd been determined to get one of my own.

After Hamish's leg cast was removed, he kept it in his wardrobe and I'd often stared longingly at it when I was supposed to be tidying our room. It had been cut down the front to release his foot, but it was still resplendent with all its *get well* sentiments scrawled across it in different colours. So I was thrilled when Dr. Rose dunked the bandage into water and started to wrap the soggy plaster around my broken arm.

I was determined to render my plaster more beautiful than Hamish's, so as soon as I got home, I took to it with a ballpoint pen and tried to draw a horse by a fence. But much to my horror, the pen got stuck in a patch of still-damp plaster and leaked a big blue globule of ink all over my horse. "I told you to wait until it dried," Mum said when I sulked to her about it.

The whole broken bone thing wasn't turning out at all like I'd imagined. My plaster was ruined, I wasn't hungry, and my arm was throbbing horribly with every beat of my heart. I cried myself to sleep that night. Mostly out of pain, but partly out of a weird sensation I will call homesickness. I was snug in the same bed and in the same room I'd always slept in, but I was homesick, sad to the painful bone. I never wanted to go to school again.

Things improved drastically over the next few days. Ben, who was the best of us kids at drawing, fixed my horse by turning it into a jolly man holding a flower with a fat stalk. With the pain subsiding, I began to enjoy the perks of having a plastered arm, which included ice cream, cuddles and just all-round special treatment. The most surprising benefit of the situation was that I was exempt from bathing because the plaster had to be kept dry. For the first few days after the accident, I only ever had to give myself a bit of a wash down at the sink, which I didn't. But I was eventually forced back into the world of showering when Dad came up with the perfect solution to keep the plaster dry: a corn-on-the-cob bag pulled over my arm and stuck down with red gaffer tape.

After a week off school, it was decided I should return, but I didn't see the point. Seeing as there was only a week left until the Christmas holidays, I thought it would be best if I tootled about on my own at home. I had a good thing going on. I was immune to the morning rush to school. I could just sit and watch everyone else get into trouble and then, once they'd all left, I would go out to the golf club with Mum and chat to her incessantly as I "helped her clean." Normally I hated having to help Mum clean because it meant I had to actually make an effort, but with a broken wing I couldn't really be expected to wield a broom or mop, so all I had to do was wipe out the basins and dish out the urinal cakes. I loved urinal cakes. I don't know why I am sharing that detail other than it feels important.

The best thing about it all was that I got to spend quality time with Mum. As one of five children, it was incredibly difficult to get one-on-one time with her. Under ordinary circumstances the best time to gain exclusive access to her focus was to catch her when she was having a bath. This was when Mum was at her most relaxed and receptive, because she wasn't trying to wrangle us all, and the fact that I was vague and slow wasn't impeding or annoying her. I would invite myself in, plonk down on the toilet and have a good old natter. She would drape a wash cloth across her chest or forehead, lean her head back and give you all her attention. And, to top it all off, I was obsessed with the fact that she could turn the taps on and off with her feet. Magic. But this was a rare treat, because Mum only had so many baths and all five of us knew it was a prime time to hang out with her. So, with everyone else at school, I got Mum all to myself.

The decision was sealed on the Sunday night when I was caught playing one-armed cricket. "If you can do that, you can go to school!" said Mum.

"But I'm left-handed at cricket. I'm right-handed at school!" I replied, pointing to my plaster cast and adopting a pained expression. But Mum couldn't be convinced otherwise and I was ordered to have a shower. So, I reluctantly presented myself to Dad and he dutifully sealed off my plaster with a corn-on-the-cob bag.

My main issue with returning to school was I didn't know how my accident had played out in the minds of the other kids. Hamish had said he got some grief about the fact his little sister had fallen out of a tree like a "spastic monkey" (this is most definitely not a medical term), so I was certain I would be relegated to the grotty group and teased for the rest of my school days, and I would have to move to Healdsville.

My worry was for nothing, however, because as soon as I arrived back, I was mobbed like some kind of hero. I was bombarded with questions like "Did it hurt?" "Were you scared?" "Did you actually die? You did? Wow! How long for?" And to my utter delight, everybody wanted to sign my plaster and showed great admiration for the drawing of the jolly man/horse as they wrote their well wishes. If the morning bell hadn't sounded, every available patch of white would have been filled up with well wishes from all my new best friends.

During class time I could feel people looking at me. When I would turn to face them, I expected them to look away, but instead I was greeted with a smile every single time. I'd never known the like. At one point, when we were told we had to pair up, chairs were turned upside down as people on the other side of the room scrambled to attach themselves to me. But they were too late as I'd already accepted my first offer. I always did, because I didn't always get one.

When it came to little lunch, I filed out with the rest of the class as usual, and as usual I wasn't entirely sure where to go, though I was pretty certain I would seek out Mrs. Smith. She liked me a lot even before I'd broken my arm, so I imagined that she'd adore me beyond sober belief now. But I didn't get to find out about any change in Mrs. Smith's feelings toward me because I was invited over to the bark garden to spend little lunch with the cool kids. And just when I thought my day couldn't get any better, I found myself being offered all this food from the lunch boxes of others. Treats I'd only ever dreamed of, chocolate biscuits, cheese sticks, boxes of sultanas and, glory upon glory, chips. By the time I went back into the classroom I was giddily happy and quite convinced I was now a cool kid.

That last week of school was probably the most wonderful time of my entire education career, because I could turn up every day knowing I would be welcomed wherever I went. Brett, the coolest boy, even asked me to marry him and I accepted. He would link his arm through my plaster every day as we walked to lunch. But like all good things, it had to come to an end. And like most endings in my life, I was the last to know about it.

I finally got the memo on the last day of term. I had walked into the classroom thinking everything was still brilliant. I scanned the room and found all my cool new friends sitting at the back, but they didn't raise their eyes to meet mine, and when I walked over to them, they continued to ignore me, and, just to make sure I understood my rejection, each of them turned ever so slightly away from me. I knew it was over, so I didn't put up a fight. I walked away with dignity, found a spare seat next to Melody, and took comfort in her fidgeting.

THE PROVERBIAL GLASS HOUSE

Most people think that there are only two ways to respond to mortal danger: fight or flight. I'm sure they both have their merits but apparently my instinct is to sit very still and just have a bit of a think about things. I discovered this was my survival strategy on the day before my ninth birthday after I rode my bike into the back-end corner of a glass greenhouse. I don't remember the accident itself, other than the sudden and overpowering smell of tomatoes. I didn't scream, panic or cry. I think I must have been in shock. I was certainly very confused, not least because I couldn't work out why I wasn't riding my bike anymore. Without waiting for my comprehension to catch up with events, I just set about extracting my leg from what was left of the glass pane, hobbled clear of the debris, found myself a patch of grass and sat down to have a bit of a think.

The wound on my knee was particularly distressing. Nobody should meet their own kneecap. My older brother Ben had once told me about Rorschach tests and said that if you saw something bad in an inkblot then you were sick in the head, so I tried my best to see a butterfly in the blood pooling out of my knee, but the white of my kneecap kept taunting me and I ended up feeling very sick in the head anyway. I turned my attention to a large shard of glass sticking out of my thigh, which made me feel even sicker in the head, so I decided the best course of action was to lie back on the grass, hoping I would die before Mum could kill me.

Before the accident I had believed with absolute certainty that if I were small enough, and owned a small enough boat, I could've gone sailing all around the wonderful world of my innards. I had thought there'd be plenty of room to navigate between my various bits and pieces, that there would be a nice little bay where I could anchor before climbing onto dry bone-land, where I could swing like Tarzan from veins to arteries, making my way to the land of my belly, a jumping castle of inflatable organs. And when I tired of all the good times, I could climb back into my little boat and set sail for my brain, the comfiest bed in all the kingdom.

But once I met my kneecap and the guts of my thigh, I had to reassess; I didn't like the truth that I was being forced to accept. Not at all. I didn't like the idea that beneath my surface ran a deep river of pain and ugliness just waiting to burst free; that I was nothing more than an unregulated abattoir of blood and guts wrapped up in a far too pervious suit of skin.

It was all a great shame really, as the day had started out so brilliantly. It had been warm and sunny and the preparations for my pirate-themed birthday party were in full swing, Jessica had just made pirate boats out of oranges and jelly and I knew there was a treasure-chest sponge cake she had hidden under a shroud of foil in the fridge, and to top it all off, Mum had agreed to let me draw myself a moustache for the occasion. But the best thing about this particular day had nothing to do with it being my birthday eve. The best thing was that the plaster cast on my arm had finally been removed that morning, which meant that I'd been given the all-clear to take my brand-new bike out for a spin.

I had been more than a little disappointed when I first laid my eyes on the pink girl's bike under the Christmas tree a few weeks earlier. As far as I was concerned, I didn't need a floral basket or a skirt-friendly pedalling experience, I needed a BMX so I could keep up with Hamish. But I didn't dare complain because I knew Mum would not hesitate in taking the bike and feeding it to the starving kids in a television famine appeal, which had become the blanket threat she gave whenever I complained about not having stuff. I didn't understand why we couldn't just sponsor a child already, I was sick of being grateful. But Mum was in charge, so, like an arranged marriage, I learnt to love my new bike.

The one thing that I could easily love about Pink, as I had imaginatively named my two-wheeled steed, was her bell. I had never had a working bell before. The best I'd ever had was the rusted-out number on my old bike that sounded less like a bell and more like a robot dying of emphysema. By contrast, Pink's lovely *ding-a-ring-ring* was a marvellous carnival of sound joy. But ringing the bell was the only thing I had been able to do for the three weeks since Christmas, on account of my arm being in plaster. I hadn't felt any pain for weeks, and in my tiny brain that meant I was good to go. But Mum refused to budge and so I had to endure the interminable wait until the plaster was removed before I could go for a ride. The wait had been nothing short of excruciating, even the *ding-a-ring-ring* of the bell couldn't make time pass more quickly. And so it was, that on this lovely sunny birthday eve, no sooner than I got home from the doctor's surgery,

Hamish and I were both astride our bikes breaknecking it all over the high school grounds like the reckless cop and the nefarious robber we believed we were.

When Hamish eventually found me, he summed the situation up very quickly and succinctly. "Shit!" he said, "Shit! Shit! Shit!" He took in the scene, hands on hips, biting his lip before delivering the news neither of us wanted to hear: "We're gonna have to tell Mum." I looked up and nodded. *Shit indeed.*

As Hamish helped me to my feet, I was surprised to find my leg didn't hurt too much and I was able to stand up, even if I was a little reluctant to stop sitting. I wasn't upset, I had cried no tears, and aside from the stress of discovering the inside of me, I was in pretty good spirits. But that all changed when, over my brother's shoulder, I saw Pink. She was about ten metres up the path, as if she had continued the chase without me. It took a moment before I realised how badly she had fared: her front wheel was bent horribly out of shape, the seat was ripped and the top of the bell was gone, leaving nothing but its buckled guts.

I am not prone to hysterics, but I gave it a red-hot go in that moment, as I tried to convince Hamish to take care of the bike. "Forget about me!" I screamed. "Save Pink! PLEEEEEAAAAASE!!!" Even with the full benefit of hindsight and a mature understanding of priorities, there is still a part of me that is annoyed that Hamish refused to let me sacrifice myself for the sake of my new bike.

I didn't know if I was going to be in trouble or if my leg would be smothered in Vicks VapoRub, and as I couldn't decide which would be the worse outcome, I was well and truly overwhelmed with anxiety by the time we made it back to the house. Hamish was diligently dragging me into the kitchen when Mum leapt out of her sewing chair to cut us off at the pass. "Don't come in here! You'll ruin the carpet!" While it didn't come close to the worst of the responses I'd workshopped in my head as I was limping home, it was still a bit shocking to find out I was less precious than our very ugly carpet.

We stopped in our tracks and waited in the kitchen as Mum pushed past us and grabbed a Tupperware container off the sink and told me to put my foot in it. Judging by the look on her face when she stood back, I think Mum was quite shocked to discover that she had not applied an actual tourniquet. The next thing she tried was at least in the ballpark of first aid, even if it was equally ineffective. No sooner had Mum applied a Band-Aid than it began sliding down my leg. Undeterred, she put another one on, then another, and then another. I watched, mesmerised, as they all surfed their way slowly down into the Tupperware, which was slowly filling up with my blood.

By the time we got to the doctors for the second time that day, Mum was well and truly on her own roller-coaster loop of emotions. I just sat. My leg was throbbing, as it was wrapped a little too tightly in a towel and I could feel the glass digging in. But I wasn't about to complain. I knew Mum was stressed about my birthday party, and she didn't even know about the bike. So, I just sat and had a think about things.

Dr. Rose was a jovial man who had been our family doctor for years. Mum liked him so much that when he left town, she refused to replace him. I liked Dr. Rose too, except that he wasn't very gentle. You want gentle when it comes to removing glass from open and bleeding wounds. You certainly don't want big fat sausage fingers digging around your insides with carelessly wielded needles and tongs.

I could feel every bit of every needle, every bit of glass being removed, every bump of Dr. Rose's not so gentle approach and yet, each and every time I flinched he would just chuckle as if he'd made some sort of a joke. The whole process was exactly as excruciating and distressing as it sounds, but I did my best to keep my mouth shut and my eyes dry as Dr. Rose fumbled his way in and around my wounds. But eventually it all got too much, and my stoicism crumbled. Dr. Rose didn't seem to notice when I began to blubber uncontrollably, but Mum did, and she abruptly stopped her moaning and pacing about and came over and stood behind me. I was sure I was about to get some kind of telling-off, but instead she just leant over and gently said, "It's OK, little one. I'm right here. You're going to be OK."

As much as I wanted to and as hard as I tried, I couldn't stop crying—I had seen too much, I had seen my kneecap and, for the first time in my life, I saw that Mum was not in control of the world around me. I saw that she knew this and that it frightened her, and so it frightened me. Out of desperation, Mum leant in even closer and, with her eyes right over mine, she cupped her hands over the sides of our faces, blocking the world out and then, when it was just the two of us, in a whisper she said, "Count the red lines in my eyes."

I shut my eyes. I did not like what I felt at such close range of Mum's gaze, with all the crackling of her shot blood filling the whites of her eyes, but I did not need to see, I did not need to make a tally, the cocoon of her care was enough to help me find a bit of calm. As the youngest of her five children, I think I had quietly assumed that I was disposable, a backup sprog at best, and less valuable than ugly carpet. But that assumption dissolved whenever Mum pulled me in like this, and I was always left with irrefutable evidence that I was loved, and that I was very precious in the bloodshot eyes of at least one person on earth.

THE MORAL OF THE STORY

They say that a girl can see her future by looking at her mother. Skin-wise, I have a very bleak future. Shortly after Hamish was born, Mum suffered a breakout of boil-like pimples and they were responsible for leaving her face pocked and scarred. This story should have raised sympathy, but all it raised from our family were jokes. I remember one time I asked Dad to give me a clue during a game of trivial pursuit. I don't remember the question, but I'll never forget his clue: "your mum's face." The answer was "the moon." He used the same clue to help Hamish with the answer "the plague."

I spent much of my childhood dreaming of an alternative mum for myself. My imagined replacement mother always made more of an effort to hide her greying hair, took better care of her teeth, and wore perfume. She still had holes in her face, of course, but only the necessary ones, like ear holes, nostrils, and not necessarily a mouth.

When I was a kid, I used to feel sorry for Dad. We all did; and sadly, Mum knew this and that must have been painful. Dad's preference for fence-sitting has been a near-constant source of frustration for Mum. As a child I couldn't at all comprehend why, but now, as an adult, I can see the immense pressure she must have been under. Essentially, when it came to emotional labor and decision-making, Mum was operating as a single mother of six (five children and one adult man). But whenever things went wrong, which they frequently did, Mum would suddenly be married again and having the anatomy of her mistakes explained back to her by the very man who'd refused to help in the first place.

In terms of fodder for my comedy, I am ashamed to admit that I have positioned my mum at the butt of my jokes to a far greater extent than I have my dad. This is unfair to both of them. Dad was the calm to Mum's storm, and so it was just too easy for me to believe that it was my mum, alone, who was responsible for packing my emotional baggage. It is only now, after a significant chunk of life has passed since, that I can recognise that Mum was not always the right target, she was just the easy one. So, I would like to ask that if you find yourself judging my mother harshly, just keep it in mind that I can be a lazy hunter and Dad is a parental gazelle.

In truth, Mum is a stronger bit of human machinery than either Dad or I. She has never been one to keep her grievances to herself, sure, especially when they relate to Dad, but she has always made sure we knew how lucky we were to have a father like him. And we were. He was gentle, consistent and his world revolved around his family. He adored Mum and, for the most part, he respected her as the leader of our pack.

Mum is hands down the funniest person I know. She is loyal, honest and kind. She is also someone who, despite all the struggles life has thrown her way, is doggedly determined to find the joy in both the big and little pictures of life. She is earnest, and as such she can be easily wounded, and as such, she can just as easily wound you back. But she has never, ever been cruel. She also loves me the most fiercely out of all the humans on earth, and it is unconditional love too, and always has been.[⊗] But, as she was fond of saying to me when I was a teenager, "I will always love you no matter what, but I don't have to like you."

In this book, I am not offering a full portrait of Mum, I can't do that. Her story is her own, and she, being a much more dignified human than me, is not a public-facing story teller. What I am offering is a portrait of our relationship, and, like any parent-child relationship, ours is an incredibly complicated, ever-evolving thing, that no one side can truly render completely. So, it is with a huge amount of trust that she is giving over to me in these pages, to represent our relationship. And it is with a huge amount of trust that I ask you to trust that I adore my Mum and that she adores me, even though there are times where it might seem that we really do not like each other.

My parents were both very resourceful people, evidenced by the fact that I didn't really know we were poor when I was growing up. I clocked that things were always a bit tight in the days leading up to payday, but it never really occurred to me that this was a reflection of where we stood in relation to the world. I assumed we were well-off simply because our teeth were a good fit for our mouths. But in reality, I was just too vague to recognise the special flavour of stress that is forged when making ends meet is only ever a perpetual struggle. My parents managed to shield us kids from this reality not only by making sure all our basic needs were met, but also by raising us to believe we had no right to expect anything more and allowing us all to believe that we wore homemade clothes, drove a broken-down car and shopped at the rubbish tip, simply because they had decided that was how they wanted to do the living of life. This can't have

[⊗] Out of all the humans on earth, I love my mum the most fiercely. This will be a bit shit for my spouse lady to read, but I will remind her here that she is definitely number two and that Mum is 78 years old and there is a succession plan in place.

been easy for them, because by choosing to shield us from their stresses, they made themselves a target for our resentment.

As far as I am concerned, their strategy paid off, and I am so grateful to be able to look back at my childhood and find this pocket of my memory filled with knowing I was safe, that I belonged, and that I had a right to exist. Because these are the memories that were to become my tether once life began to pull me deeper and deeper into a world where safety and belonging were not things I was capable of achieving on my own.

THE FORMATIVE YEARS

STOP! CONTEXT TIME!

I hope I have already impressed upon you that Tasmania in the 1980swas a fairly isolated pocket of the world, but I think my story would be better understood with more context than just that of my own very limited and childish life experiences.

I think you ought to know that Tasmania had once been a particularly wretched convict colony, set up specifically as a place to re-home the worst of the worst criminals that Sydney did not want ruining the respectability of its own convict colony. I want you to know that Tasmania was a devastatingly brutal settlement that decimated the Indigenous population in what can only be described as attempted genocide. You also need to know that I am a direct descendant of those white settlers and convicts who so violently carved out their new life on that forsaken little island.

You need to know that when I was a kid, Tasmania was a joke to the rest of Australia, and Tasmanians were considered the ignorant, inbred, backward homophobic descendants of criminals and other feral types. You need to know that to this day almost half of the 550,000Tasmanians are functionally illiterate. One in five children in Tasmania begin school developmentally disadvantaged and remain behind national averages in high school, with one in four not completing their schooling at all. An estimated quarter of Tasmanians currently live in poverty, with a third of the population receiving the majority of their household income from government payments. Around 40 percent of the state is in part-time employment and the Tasmanian workforce is the oldest in the country, which is another way of saying that poor young people are not winning in Tasmania.

Like in all the other messes left in the wake of colonialist expansion, Tasmanians can be very divided about who we want to be. But those divisions were openly hostile throughout my childhood as environmentalists clashed with the logging and mining industries, gay rights activists fought for law reform, and Indigenous groups struggled for land rights—even though most Tasmanians continued to refuse to acknowledge their right to exist at all. And that right is still dangerously in jeopardy today—which is not unique to Tasmania—with the child mortality rate for Indigenous infants approximately double that of non-Indigenous; and across Australia around 45 percent of Aboriginal men and 34 percent of women die before the age of 45, with over 70 percent dying before the age of 65. And if you aren't great at contextualising statistics, that is fucked.

You also need to know that Tasmania only decriminalised homosexuality in 1997 and not without a decade-long fight. You also need to know that Tasmania is breathtakingly beautiful. Really.

This isn't how I would've described Tasmania when I was a kid, because I wasn't particularly conscious of these tensions and histories, they were all just happening in the background of what I assumed was a completely normal and unremarkable childhood. I suppose it was normal, given that these kinds of tensions were playing out all over the world. And sadly, they still are.

In many ways, I had an incredibly happy start to my life because my world was defined by a wonderful consistency. I was rarely bothered by new things, people, or ideas, which allowed me to grow up in a state of blissful ignorance. My adolescence changed all that, however, as the outside world began to crash over me, relentlessly, in a way that did not burst my bubble so much as it slowly and insidiously poisoned the already vulnerably thin veneer of my existence.

1988

1988 was a big year for me. I saw *Crocodile Dundee II* at the cinema, it went completely over my head, not least because I hadn't seen the first movie, but I sure did love all those hats and knives. This was also the year Milli Vanilli was formed, I turned ten, and Australia celebrated its bicentennial, marking the European invasion of 1788. 1988 was also when I learnt that there was an alternative way of saying "two hundred years." In other news that would not affect me for another decade or so, Prozac hit the market in 1988. Like I said, it was a big year.

My celebration was a little bit more subdued than my country's. My sister made me a swimming pool cake and then, on theme, I went to the actual pool for a swim. Australia, rather ostentatiously (and insensitively) if you ask me, reenacted the "first fleet" of 1788 that sailed uninvited into Sydney Harbour, but without the convicts, scurvy and attempted genocide. This was followed by fireworks and a whole entire year of government-funded jubilations, such as gifting every single school student in Australia with a bicentennial commemorative coin.

I was very sceptical of this so-called "gift," because I didn't have any use for a coin that couldn't be exchanged for chocolate and/or more chocolate. And given that the coin is now worth a whopping twenty dollars on eBay, I feel quite vindicated in my youthful cynicism. It's not that I was a regular Elon Musk with a savvy (read: *slavish*) enthusiasm for made-up currencies that made me doubt the value of the bicentennial coin; my issue was that I'd already been burnt by another government-driven excitement ruse: Stamp Explorer.

The 1980s was a decade defined by collectable fads. Perhaps that's why the Australian postal service thought they could successfully invigorate a passion for stamps in children. In hindsight, it's hard to believe that anybody could've ever thought it possible to lure kids away from collecting Cabbage Patch dolls and slap bracelets with something as dishwater dull as envelope art. But someone did have that idea, and then even more people must have agreed to it, because that's how shit ideas get spun into reality.

I was hooked the moment Stamp Explorer was unveiled at morning assembly. How could I not be? What with the promise of binders, monthly newsletters about stamps, free stamps to put in your binder, and the fact that it would all be sent to you by mail. All we had to do was fill in a form and send it off with a self-addressed stamped envelope. It was all very meta.

Hamish had also signed up for Stamp Explorer, and we talked giddily about it on the bus home from school. Our excitement boiled down to just one thing—and it wasn't the accumulation of stamps—it was the promise of mail. Our own mail. Mail that we could open. Mail addressed to us. We were so utterly thrilled by this prospect that as soon as we got home, we ran straight to the mailbox to check to see if the first instalment of Stamp Explorer mail had arrived. We did not understand the mechanics of the postal service because we were millennials before our time.

Ben quickly caught on to mine and Hamish's eagerness and turned it into a sport. He made sure he got to the mailbox first so he could greet us with the mail after school. He'd draw out our anticipation for as long as possible, flipping through the mail slowly, one bill at a time, examining each envelope with exaggerated intensity. "No. No. Nope," he would say, shaking his head each time before throwing his hands in the air. "Not today!" This went on week after excruciating week until one day, halfway through the ceremony, apparently unable to conceal his own shock, Ben held an envelope aloft: "It's here!"

After ripping the envelope open, Hamish confirmed it. I didn't dare take my eyes off the one envelope still in Ben's hand. He peered at it closely, for too long. I made a grab for it, but he whisked it out of reach.

"It's not for you!" he said. I couldn't believe it. I was gutted. *How is this possible?* "Yes, it is!" I said, with more certainty than I felt. "Sorry, Miss Hannah Gadsby," Ben said mockingly. "There is no mail here with your name on it." My heart sank. "But there is a letter here for a 'Ms. Hanwah Godslay.'"

I wish I could blame my childish handwriting for the misspelling of my own name, but the application form was designed to be read by a machine, the page filled with multiple rows of alphabet that required you to colour in the circles around each of the letters of your name. Apparently, I'd gotten bored or confused during the search and had taken to colouring in a few random ones. Mum had warned me to ignore all the taunting of my siblings, but I couldn't, and so I really only have myself to blame for making my new nickname stick so thoroughly that to this day I am known as "Godslay" or "Gods" to the rest of my family.

To compound the humiliation, Stamp Explorer turned out to be every bit as boring an enterprise as you could imagine. It really is something when you can make collecting and organising objects boring to a young kid with autism spectrum disorder. But that's exactly what Stamp Explorer managed to do. Then, to compound all that, Stamp Explorer proved as impossible as a gym membership to terminate, which meant that I was still getting their very disappointing monthly newsletters addressed to "Ms. Hanwah Godslay" by the time the bicentennial rolled around three years later.

I was not a particularly proud Australian heading into 1988, probably because I didn't have an alternative experience to compare it with. But as the bicentennial year progressed, I began to absorb some of the "Australia Is So Great!" fever. How could I not? We won the women's field hockey gold medal at the Olympics. And then there was the ad—the bicentennial ad—that asked me directly to help with the "Celebration of the Nation." I loved that ad. It was a simple premise, a gaggle of Australian television identities standing in the desert in front of Uluru, linking arms with a bunch of people who were not celebrities, and who were, incredibly, not all white, or able-bodied, and singing their guts out about how great Australia was and that I should help them celebrate. How could I not?

I loved the idea of "multiculturalism," because it made sense to me. I'd always struggled to feel as if I belonged, and so I thought that everyone should be made to feel welcome—because by this logic, then I would be welcome too. Who said selfishness can't lead to human rights advocacy?

This was obviously a few years before I was capable of understanding the devastating racial divisions that lay at the heart of the Australian story. And well before I was able to take the hint that colonisation was actually a very hostile takeover situation and not the story I'd been taught at school about all the wonderful white men in ye-olde boats who brought their cool ideas to every corner of the globe. I was completely oblivious to the protest movement headed by Indigenous leaders at the time, but I know about it now and I feel comfortable signposting my ignorance, not in the way of an excuse but as an acknowledgment of being part of the problem.

Sure, I was experiencing 1988 with a ten-year-old brain that lacked the capacity for critical thinking. But the reason it was so easy for me to believe that everybody was living together in harmony was the colour of my skin. I am white, which meant the same thing then as it does today—I don't have to think twice about it, if I think about it at all.

I am sure my own ignorance was not helped by the fact that adverts were by far my favourite TV shows in 1988. And most ads in Australia in the 1980s had hairy white men grunting about beer and sport, so please forgive me for not understanding that other people were a thing. To this day I can still sing most jingles and quote verbatim most ads from my childhood, probably because I'd discovered quite early in life that quoting ads out of context was a great way to make people laugh and avoid answering difficult questions at the same time.

"How'd you get so fat, Hannah?"

"The same way liquid gets into this chalk."⊗

⊗ From 1976 to 1991, Colgate ran an ad campaign for "Fluorigard" featuring the endearing schoolteacher "Mrs. Marsh," who dipped a piece of chalk into a cup of dyed blue water and then broke it in half to demonstrate to her pupils how deeply the liquid had seeped into the edges of the chalk's cross-section. A tidy metaphor for the way Colgate's toothpaste would permeate the enamel of their teeth to protect against decay. If only all things so suffusive were also so palatably wholesome.

or:

"What time is it, Hannah?"
"Stamps!"

I particularly enjoyed community service ads, like the bicentennial one. And not just because they all had incredibly fun and catchy jingles attached to them, and were repeated incessantly because they were often funded by the government. Although I am sure these facts did help them sink their hooks into me, I think the most likely reason I went in for these ads was because I could afford to pick up what they were putting down. I had no chance of ever being able to purchase even one Transformer toy or pair of Nike shoes, but I could definitely "do the right thing" and pick up other people's rubbish and put it in the bin.

My favourite of all time was the ad campaign designed to encourage people to be sun-smart, in which a seagull with a speech impediment sang a jaunty little tune telling me to "slip on a shirt, slop on sunscreen and slap on a hat." I had no idea at the time that an increased chance of death by melanoma was the real-world ramification of being sun-naive, I just followed the advice because I loved the song. That was the way most community service ads were angled when I was a kid, motivating positive behaviour through the art of a jolly jingle. But then along came the Grim Reaper.

Imagine you're a nine-year-old Australian kid, you're sitting with your family and watching the *Sale of the Century* quiz show on TV, and then your regular programming is interrupted by this:

A cloaked reaper stands in a foggy landscape, his tattered robes fluttering about him, as a very ominous soundscape sets an appropriately grim tone. Scared? Good. Once the scene has been established, you then get briefed with some horrific statistics, but you are too young to understand what is being said and why. But you are scared, because you are always scared when a solemn disembodied voice is matched with an image of literal death.

The fog clears and you see that the Grim Reaper is at Hell's own bowling alley—at the other end of the lane, a group of human people are lowered down as his ten-pin targets. It is clear to you that these people are wholesome family types, because the men have tucked their shirts into their slacks, the women all have feathery hair and the children are all blond. They are exactly what you have been taught to identify as "ordinary" Australians, unlike that ragtag group singing about the bicentennial.

As you would expect, the Grim Reaper gets a strike on his first bowl, scattering his terrified pin people every which way to their presumed death. Then, to drive home the terrifying point, the camera tracks through the fog, showing you glimpses of the strewn dead bodies. It's a regular pet cemetery. But for humans.

Another rack of terrified white pin people is then placed down, and the Grim Reaper grabs a second giant bowling ball and sends it hurtling toward them with his usual deadly intent. Embarrassingly, he fails to strike all ten this time, leaving a terrified mother clutching her baby (yes, it is a blond one). I'm not sure if they represented one pin or two, but either way, the Grim Reaper manages to collect them both with his next delivery, which sends the baby flipping out of its mother's arms and scoring the Reaper a decent spare. As the ad ends, we are treated to a wide shot of Hell's own bowling alley and you can now see that there are dozens more Grim Reapers striking out "ordinary" Australians ten at a time.

Before the Grim Reaper first appeared on Australian television screens in 1987, the only thing I knew about HIV and AIDS was that it was very frightening to adults and had nothing to do with me. But after I saw this ad, I became very, very concerned and utterly afraid. The advert gave me the distinct impression, you see, that if I had a small cut on my little finger when I was within a three-mile radius of someone who'd heard about a friend of a friend whose cousin knew someone who'd caught AIDS, then I would most likely catch AIDS myself. And that was apparently the correct response.[⊗]

Some people, most particularly the guy who came up with the concept, will tell you that "The Grim Reaper" was a work of genius,

⊗ The internet did not invent the concept of misinformation.

a revolutionary approach to television advertising. But I'm here to tell you that it was, and remains, a total and utter shit stain of an idea. And you don't need to go any further than the first line of the ad to understand why:

"At first, it was only gays and IV drug users being killed by AIDS."

It is the word "only" that pisses me off. "Only gays and IV drug users." That is to say: *"Only" people who don't matter. "Only" people whose suffering should be of no concern to you.* Like I said. A total and utter shit stain of an idea. Defenders of the ad might argue that the "only" was simply about identifying those whom the AIDS epidemic was affecting, and not a statement of this demographic's value to the community. To which I would say: If you're such a genius at mass messaging then you should be aware of how the word "only" would work in the minds of those who are already looking for ways to subjugate the humanity of the people who are listed after the word "only." Take the early framing of the COVID-19 pandemic as a case in point: to say that at first it "only" affected old people is both wrong and wrong.

The Grim Reaper ad campaign was supposedly cut short because it gave children nightmares. That nobody predicted this outcome at the pitch meeting is thoroughly astounding to me. Despite the fact that it only ran for a few months, this ad is seared into my mind alongside all the other ads, but for very different reasons. Unlike the community service ads before it, this one was not designed to motivate any kind of action, positive or otherwise. It was designed to urge people to take AIDS seriously, and to protect themselves accordingly, and it did that by way of creating a sense of abject fear. Which is a very easy thing to create when you drop a B-grade horror film onto TV just before the Fast Money round of *Sale of the Century.*

I have no doubt that the Grim Reaper ad motivated many a sexually active adult to slip, slop, slap on all the condoms, but I question whether fear was the right way about it. Fear is good for a shock, but it is not known as an effective gateway to healthy or nuanced conversations. At the time, I don't remember ever having a conversation with an adult about AIDS, but other kids filtered what they'd heard down to me, and the gist of things as I understood them was that gay men were the Grim Reapers. And as I was the kind of kid who trusted television adverts, I didn't see any reason to doubt that conclusion.

STOP! POLITICS TIME!

I have to give you some local political context now, and this is where hiring a ghostwriter would have come in real handy. Politics is one of those things that I find blood-boiling and bloody boring in equal measure, and the only other topics that have that kind of effect on me are the men's rights movement and Gwyneth Paltrow. But while I can ignore that pair of human tautologies and their streaming spumante of redundancies—I cannot escape politics. Blergh.

The same year that "The Grim Reaper" dropped, the Tasmanian Premier, Robin Gray, travelled to the mainland to try and convince people to move to Tasmania, because, apparently, our stagnant gene pool was becoming a bit of an own-goal problem courtesy of Tasmania's incredible success at repelling all things "foreign." So, our ever-charming elected leader bravely crossed enemy lines to let people know that Tasmania had clean air, low house prices, and no "drug problem," and then he buffeted these supposed facts with a declaration that Tasmania would welcome absolutely everyone to its shores. Everyone, that is, except homosexuals. "Homosexuals," he said, "we are not interested in."

Given that Robin's biggest achievement in office had been the printing of a series of bumper stickers that encouraged the violent murder of environmentalists,[*] it is not surprising that he was prone to tacking caveats of hate onto everything he said on his constituents' behalf. It is unclear as to whether his attempt to woo mainland-

[*] Australia's environmental political party is called the Greens and I'm sure they were thrilled to receive Robin G's invitation to Tasmania in 1988, following his propagation of catchy slogans like "Keep Warm This Winter: Burn a Greenie." A nice bit of charm from a real piece of smarm.

ers to Tasmania was successful, but it is safe to say his blatant display of homophobia worked to confirm Tasmania's reputation as being an island full of bigoted, inbred, backward, red-necked bogans, and proudly so. Cool chat Robin G.

Back then, Tasmania's homophobia was nothing but a casual joke to the rest of Australia.[⊛] But in 1988 things began to change and Tasmania's homophobia went from being just a butt for the jokes to becoming a lightning rod for political debate on the global stage. And, also, a joke butt. What was so special about 1988? Well, to nutshell it, that was the year that it really dawned in a meaningful way to most that Tasmania's criminal code gave Tasmania's homophobia a rather firm legal foothold, courtesy of two laws each worth a potential twenty-one-year prison sentence.

In short, Sections 122 (a) and (c) and 123 of the Tasmanian Criminal Code together rendered homosexuality illegal by prohibiting, among other things, sexual acts "against the order of nature" between consenting adults in public or private, with a particular vehemence toward any acts between two males. They were largely dormant laws in Tasmania—the last prosecution took place in 1984, and most of the ninety-six cases that were ever brought forth were prior to the late '70s—but they were still apparently representative of Tasmanian ideals. In 1988 around 70 percent of Tasmanians were against gay law reform.

STOP! FUN FACT TIME!

Robin Gray was not a thorough Tasmanian. He hailed from the poshest suburb in all of Melbourne: Kew. So . . . what do we make of that? Nothing new. Robin Gray still qualifies to be called a shit in a biscuit. I just wish we hadn't made him feel so welcome.

[⊛] Sadly first-hand experience taught me time and time again that there were even many mainland gays who saw us as living beneath them and were no less fond of engaging in the cruel mockery.

STOP! HISTORY TIME!

In 1988 a group of law students from the University of Tasmania formed the Tasmanian Gay and Lesbian Rights Group (TGLRG), and in August of that year they quietly established a stall at Hobart's weekly Salamanca Market and began to distribute leaflets and gather signatures for a petition supporting gay law reform. Only a few weeks into the life of the TGLRG stall, the Hobart City Council intervened, deciding there was no place for homosexuals in their family market—because apparently artisanal sourdough, moon cups and wall art made out of spoons are the absolute opposite of all things gay. The stall was banned, and the TGLRG was threatened with police involvement. As many of them were law students, they were in a good position to see the ban for what it was—legally dubious—so they continued to turn up. The council did follow through on their threats, however, and on October 22, 1988, nine people were arrested for trespassing. The next week it was thirteen. The following week it was twenty-seven.

It was big news in Tasmania at the time, but the conversation was largely being played out above my ten-year-old head. I had no idea that 130 people were arrested, no idea that the council eventually backed down and all the charges were dropped because the arrests were unlawful, or how this civil disobedience galvanised the gay and lesbian community in Tasmania, bringing them together and, for many of them, out of the closet. All I knew was that names like "pooftah" "poojabber," "faggot," "AIDS merchant" and "grim rapers" were what the cool kids were calling the not-cool kids. And I was desperate to be a cool kid in the same way that liquid gets into chalk.

1989

The world had a lot going on in 1989 My wife was born, spoiler alert. The year also saw the Berlin Wall torn down in jubilant scenes that sealed off a decade of Soviet collapse and thoroughly negated my project on East and West Germany.⊗ In local news, Australians watched Prime Minister Bob Hawke cry live on TV in response to the Tiananmen Square massacre and later offer asylum to 42,000 Chinese students. And I became an athlete. No, really.

There was no theatre in Smithton, no cinema, no gallery and no museum. If it wasn't for the McCain's factory mural, there would be little evidence that any kind of artistic endeavour had ever been pursued in Smithton. Outside of the vagaries of what I understood to be "church stuff," there were only two extracurricular hobbies for the youths about town to choose from: sport or delinquency. Only the really talented were able to dabble successfully in both fields. My parents were on the pro-sport side of the debate and, as such, they made sure we all got ourselves involved in at least one sport or another. Jessica did gymnastics, Ben and Hamish played football, and Justin and I chose field hockey.

My first, true, choice of sport was Australian Rules football. I had grown up kicking the ball around with Hamish with great competitiveness and I loved playing football to the point of giddiness, but as girls were not allowed to play, I kept that dream to myself. The closest I got to sharing that dream was begging my parents to let me wear my brother's football shorts when I played hockey. I was supposed to wear a skirt, but, as I appealed to my parents, I had to wear one of those dreadful things all week at school, so surely I should be able to wear what I wanted outside of that. Dad said yes. Mum said no.

Mum understood how bullying worked and wanted to protect me from being shamed, but Dad, who did not understand the crueler side of the social dynamics of children, didn't see any problem with my wearing my brother's shorts. Looking back, I believe that they were both correct. But Mum being Mum meant that I did not wear the shorts; and the world being the world, I still felt all the shame anyway. And so began the rupture between who I felt myself to be

⊗ Full disclosure, I did the project in 1992. Research was not my strong suit.

and who others thought I ought to be. That rupture has a name—dysphoria—and it has an effect—pain. I wanted to be a boy so bad it hurt.⊗

I was a slow-moving kid, not to mention thoroughly vague, and I proved to be a poor reader of play, so I was very quickly relegated to keeping goals for my hockey team. The goals suited me. I had good eye-hand coordination and quick reflexes if I was paying attention, and I showed such early promise that I was selected to play for the North West Coast under-sixteen girls' hockey side in the Tasmanian regional championships. I didn't do particularly well. In one game I think I let through seventeen goals, while my counterpart on the other side of the pitch saved every attempt that came her way. None of this is surprising given I was only eleven years old and defending against girls twice my age whilst wearing protective gear on my legs that also obscured my vision.

Despite being the worst goalie at the tournament, I was the one chosen to have my photo taken with Maree Fish for the local paper. Maree was part of the Australian field hockey team who'd won gold at the Seoul Olympics in 1988, and she had turned up to inject a bit of razzle-dazzle into what would have been otherwise a fairly lacklustre affair. In the photo I stood beside my Olympic hero, holding her Olympic medal between my teeth—the first but not the last time a photographer coerced me into looking like an absolute twat for public consumption. Not surprisingly, given this brush with athletic excellence, I left the tournament feeling like a star. I'd been actively encouraged by everyone involved, giving me the impression that they truly believed I had real talent, despite all the evidence to the contrary. But I was eleven years old, so I was still young and gullible enough to believe them.

Holding an Olympic gold medal between my teeth was not the most significant thing to happen in my life in 1989 That honour goes to my getting a dog for Christmas: Ronnie Barker.

⊗ I'm a regular Pinocchio. Except instead of lying, I just imploded. And also, I am not a fictional puppet.

Ronnie replaced our Pekingese Corgi, Porgi, after she went to live on "the farm," or, as we knew it: got run over by a log truck. She had been a truly lovely little friend to me, but Ronnie Barker more than filled the void she left behind. He ended up being with my family for over fifteen years and was my constant companion until I moved out of home. So, needless to say, he was mightily important to me, but if this book was being written by a ghostwriter, I don't think they would put Ronnie at the top of the significant events list for my life in 1989 because that was the year I was molested for the first time.

I am not interested in giving you a portrait of my abuser, but you should know four facts: he is not mentioned anywhere else in this book, he was not related to me, he is no longer alive, and I had nothing to do with that last fact. You should also know that when he was alive, and at the time he was abusing me, he was considered to be an upstanding citizen. A churchgoing man. A married man. A father.

He groomed me with praise, attention and, I won't lie, a little bit of sugar. It didn't take much. It is very easy to pick kids with ASD off their pack because we tend to lurk around the edges anyway and we trust very, very easily. It would be great if more people in the world understood just how trusting autistic kids are, because at the moment, outside immediate families, it seems like the only people who see the link between vulnerability and easy trust are predators. This is not so safe.

My abuser claimed that he wanted to teach me how to kiss and unfortunately, I was just beginning to appreciate, with dismay, that my worldliness was lagging compared to most kids I knew. So, I trusted that this adult man was offering to teach me something I should have already known. My parents were busy people and it was completely possible in my childish logic that they'd forgotten to teach their youngest about this kissing business—or worse, I hadn't been paying attention when they had. So, in the spirit of closing every ignorance gap I could without bothering anyone, I earnestly presented myself for the lesson with my head raised, lips puckered, and eyes closed.

I don't know what I was expecting, but I will never forget the immense shock I felt by what did happen. I could not move. He pressed himself against me, his arms and hands were roaming everywhere and his whole, open mouth sucked at my face, his tongue forcing my mouth open. It was all just so earth-shatteringly horrific. But, of course, I went back for more because that's how grooming works, like liquid gets into chalk.

The kissing lessons were always followed by him pleading with me to keep "our little secret." Strangely, I found this significantly more distressing than the physical abuse. The secret I was being asked to keep thoroughly repulsed and frightened me, but it was the grown man who had rendered me completely powerless who was the one to cry like a baby, appealing to my good graces while at the same time threatening me with a list of possible retributions. I just couldn't understand the power dynamic. I could not find any logic in it whatsoever, but I kept his secret for him anyway. He seemed so sad.

STOP! CONTEXT TIME!

In June 1989 a pro-homophobia rally was organised in the North West city of Ulverstone by "concerned citizen" Rodney Cooper. During his speech in front of about seven hundred people, Cooper declared: "The moral rot of this country has gone on for long enough, and the silent majority has been quiet for too long!" Homosexuality, he and other speakers insisted, threatened the family unit and lowered moral standards "unacceptably."

Some members of the TGLRG hired buses to travel north to protest the meeting. They took a decidedly non-rotten approach to voicing their opposition and just stood outside the rallies with candles and banners that read, talk to us. not about us. But some kind of moral rot was nonetheless detected (read: *projected*) and the peaceful candlelight vigil was met with large groups of people, many holding cricket bats, chanting, "Kill them. Kill them. Kill them."

I had no idea. I was too busy taste-testing Olympic gold medals and becoming best friends with a puppy, and, as a ghostwriter would most likely prefer to emphasise, I was also being groomed and abused.

1990

The '90s kicked off with a recession in Australia. In its wake, our own treasurer described us as a "banana republic," which I thought made us sound like a "dessert island," which may have prompted my first-ever dad joke. On the more optimistic side of 1990, the Hubble telescope was launched, as was the Human Genome Project. Plus, MC Hammer released "U Can't Touch This"[⊗] and we were intro-duced to a new species of marsupial from Papua New Guinea called the golden-mantled tree kangaroo, so that's a good news day for ev-eryone.[✎] And to answer the question you did not ask, yes, I was also forced to retire from hockey in 1990.

When the orthopaedic surgeon asked me to describe my pain, I thought he was an idiot. Pain was pain. "It hurts?" I ventured. I didn't have the sophisticated pain vocabulary that I now have, so all I had were synonyms. "It feels sore?" I ventured, when I saw that he was dissatisfied with "hurts." I was about to add "painful" to my list of pain descriptors when the doctor changed his line of questioning.

"Tell me what happened."

I looked at my mum.

"Was your mum there?" he asked.

"No," I replied.

"Well then, there's no use looking to her to answer your question. Tell me what happened!"

I suddenly felt very homesick talking to this adult my mum didn't

---

[⊗] STOP! Hammer Time!
[✎] Everyone, except maybe the golden-mantled tree kangaroo, which is now criti-cally endangered due to hunting and deforestation.

even know. I wasn't sure what kind of doctor he was, and I wasn't sure I liked him.

"I fell off my bike," I said.

"How did you fall off your bike?" I mustn't have answered this question to the doctor's satisfaction either because he just sighed, shook his head and gave up. He then stuck a syringe into my knee and extracted something that apparently didn't belong in a knee. A week later I underwent a total knee reconstruction.

I often think about that question. *How did I fall off my bike?* And the best I can come up with was that I just fell off my bike weird. Aside from the distressing gunshot-like snap that my knee had made, I've never been able to work out why this fall was so different from all those that came before it. When I was lying on the ground in the wake of the spill, I didn't even know that I had hurt myself in a new and exciting way. I had no clue as to the existence of ligaments; I had assumed that our bones simply clung to each other for dear life. But I quickly learnt all about a ligament's function when I tried to stand up and my right knee cracked sharply, rotated and then buckled beneath me.

When I heard that same terrible gunshot sound again, about six months after my surgery, I decided not to mention it to anyone. For a start, I couldn't face the trauma of trying to find another word for pain while explaining to an impatient doctor how *exactly* I'd jumped over a log.

About halfway through 1990, Jessica moved to Devonport to study at the "technical and further education" college (TAFE). When Ben had left for university the year prior, I'd hardly noticed—he was so quiet—but Jessica's departure would have a little more impact. I remember being very excited about the prospect of having my own bedroom for the first time in my life. With my own space I wouldn't have to hide in cupboards anymore to get some solitude. Jessica and I had been sharing a room for a few years, and it had gotten to the stage where she would just barge in and say, "What are you doing?" with such suspicion that I would feel guilty no matter what I was up to. If I was reading a book, I would drop it and say, "Nothing." If I wasn't doing anything, I would pick up a book and say, "Reading." On one occasion she woke me up to ask me why I had been pretending to sleep.

Before she moved out, Jessica had given me a pep talk while I watched her pack up the vanity unit we shared. "You're the only girl now," she said. "Mum's going to treat you differently than the boys. But don't worry. I want you to know that you can call me anytime you want."

I didn't think there was any need for that, I was practically a boy, wasn't I? I was certainly more like Hamish than I was Jessica, so it stood to reason in my mind: I should be treated the same way as Hamish.

As Jessica's pep talk continued, I walked over and started drawing faces in the dust on the now-empty vanity unit. Jessica had always had way more trinkets than me, and I wasn't going to miss them at all. I hated dusting around them so much. It's not as if Jessica was a girly girl. Like me, she'd grown up with three brothers and knew how to stand up for herself. We were just . . . different. As my finger circled the dust, I began counting all the ways we differed. Jessica wore earrings, she liked trinkets and shoulder pads. She cared about things I simply didn't understand. She brushed her hair and showered regularly. She had boobs. She liked them, in theory.

"I don't wear earrings," was the best way I could translate my thought process.

"You'll be able to one day!" she said, holding my hands and looking at me with a kind of intensity I found unsettling. Her eyes, magnified by her glasses, were tearing up and I had no idea why.

I understand now that Jessica was consciously carving out a moment, a connective memory, with her little sister. I'd grown up slowly, ineffectively, and could barely look after myself whereas she had grown up quickly, very effectively, and looked after everybody. She wanted to be my big sister, to make my life easier, help me navigate my way through high school, boys, and the biggest challenge of all: Mum. But what she didn't know was that I had been watching and learning my whole life, making copious mental lists on how the living of life was done. I thought Jessica was being overly dramatic and so I said, "Okay" and left her to pack.

If I could go back in time, I would make myself give my sister the biggest hug I was capable of giving before I left that room. It never occurred to me at the time that sixteen-year-old Jessica would have been terrified in her own way about leaving home. It also never occurred to me that she may not have known how much I loved her. I never told her, because I had always thought that loving someone was just something you did, not something they needed to be told or shown.

After being so excited by the prospect of having a bedroom all to myself, I felt far less sure about the whole situation when the time came for me to retire for the evening. With my cheer quickly fading, I climbed into bed and took comfort in the familiar squeak of the springs and the fact that I now had two pillows, which was a luxury I'd only ever dreamed of. But with the lights out, all my good feelings began to drain away, replaced by those with a flavour closer to despair. It wasn't unusual that I was going to bed alone. Jessica and I had different bedtimes, after all. But this time was different because she wasn't coming to bed later, and the finality of that was spelt out by the empty space where her bed had once been.

When I'd watched Dad dismantle it earlier that day, I'd been thrilled by the space being created. *Finally,* I thought, *I can do cartwheels in my room.* It had never crossed my mind to do cartwheels in my room before, not least because I'd never been able to do a cartwheel. But faced with an uncluttered expanse of floor space, the possibilities seemed limitless. Maybe I could become a circus dog after all.

But with the lights out, my performance space looked unfriendly so I turned onto my back and tried not to think about the void where Jessica's bed had been. A raft of questions began to flood my thinking: *Will I always feel so alone? Where will I go when I leave home? How can more pillows be more uncomfortable?*

The wardrobe door didn't shut properly. I thought about climbing in. I knew I was too old to sleep in the wardrobe, but even with my back turned and my eyes shut tight I could feel the empty space, its cold and lonely emptiness threatening to overwhelm me. I turned onto my stomach and buried my face into my pillows. It felt better despite my breathing being severely restricted.

Jessica and I had once shared bunk beds, and I remembered how her foot would dangle over the edge of the top bunk and talk to me. The day after it first happened, I had quizzed Jessica and I was satisfied that she was completely ignorant of the nighttime chat I'd had with her foot. The next time it happened I asked the foot directly if she was Jessica. When the foot responded, "Who's Jessica?" with a cluelessness I found utterly compelling, I was satisfied that the foot was a separate entity from my sister. With no reason to doubt her autonomy, I began to talk a lot to "Footsie," as I came to know my sister's disembodied foot. I told her everything. I talked more to Footsie than I did to anyone else in the world, and I was bereft beyond my own comprehension when she eventually stopped visiting me in the night.

The night Jessica left was the first time I'd thought about Footsie in a long time, and as I did, it dawned on me that it had been my sister all along. My trust in both the foot and my sister had been so complete that I never made the connection that Footsie's sudden disappearance happened immediately after our bunk beds were disengaged and placed side by side. I sat up in bed, incredibly frightened by the uncertainty of my future. What hope did I have in the world if it took me this long to figure out the trust I'd put into a magical foot was misplaced? I wasn't crying, but I was gasping. There was a weight in my chest. I couldn't move, and drawing breath suddenly seemed impossible.

If I could go back in time, and if I could be certain that my presence wouldn't compound my terror, I would go back to that night and sit beside myself. I wouldn't say anything. There was nothing to be said and there still isn't. I would just rub my little back the way my dad had once done. I'd just returned home from hospital after having the major reconstructive surgery on my knee, and when everyone else went outside to play cricket, I became so upset I hobbled into my bedroom screaming banshee-like, threw myself down on my bed and howled inconsolably into my pillow. Dad followed me in a few moments later, prompted by Mum, and sat beside me on my little bed and started rubbing my back. I can remember twelve-year-old me desperately wanting him to tell me something to make it all feel better, for him to say the right thing, but all he said was, "Never mind, Gods," and kept awkwardly rubbing my back until the worst of my feelings went away on their own.

As of yet, I have not been able to travel back in time to the night that Jessica left, and neither of my parents had any idea that I needed to be consoled, so as it happened, I did end up climbing into the wardrobe with my pillows and waiting to die. I hardly need to tell you, but I didn't die. I woke up sometime later, peeled my shoes off of my face, made my way back into bed and I was fine. I'm always fine eventually. I just find it incredibly difficult to cope with change.

STOP! HISTORIC HOMOPHOBIA TIME!

In December 1990,the Ulverstone Municipal Council passed a motion opposing the decriminalisation of homosexuality, formally declaring that it had "no duty or obligation to its gay or lesbian constituents." The Ulverstone council was no doubt motivated by the proposal of a health bill in the lower house of the Tasmanian Parliament which included gay law reform as a strategy for HIV prevention.

The proposed "HIV/AIDS Preventative Bill" argued that gay men were a high-risk group and the laws were driving them underground, making the epidemic difficult to manage. This was met with vocal opposition, many calling it a contradiction; how can legalising homosexuality be a solution when it is gay men who are the primary cause of the disease spreading? A rebuttal that effectively elevated any homophobic subtext to the level of text: If you had AIDS and were gay, you were entirely at fault and your government was not inclined to care.

The debate seemed to gleefully drag pretty much every anti-gay theory into the public forum. It was a sin. It was a crime. A sickness. Childish wilfulness. A sinister conspiracy. A genetic deformity. But the one that stuck in my mind was the connection between homosexuality and paedophilia. I was not confident I understood much at that time of my life, but to that point I was certain: gay people hurt children. Enough of the zeitgeist had worked on my comprehension for me to "know" that. Like liquid gets into chalk.

Despite the hostile opposition, the bill was passed by the Lower House with 17 in favour and 17 against, with the chair providing the casting vote, and then sent on to the Upper House for further deliberation. Had I read about it at the time, I undoubtedly would have assumed the vote was made by an actual chair. But I did not read about it. I was too busy badly managing my sister leaving, trying to hide the fact that I had badly re-injured my knee and, as my imaginary ghostwriter would insist on putting at the top of any list: I was still being intermittently molested.

STOP! CAVEAT TIME!

The reason I am not like my imaginary ghostwriter, and do not wish to prioritise my abuse in the telling of my story, is because it was not a luxury I could afford at the time that it was happening. You see, when you are forced to keep a trauma secret in order to survive, you need to actively avoid incorporating the traumatic event into your official version of self. You don't forget it, you just don't put words around it. And when there are no words, there is no sharing. And when there is no sharing, you can't find your way back to safety. And with all that comes a deep and dark dose of shame.

I was abused for two years, and by the second, the kissing had escalated to the kind of acts that, even if I had been a consenting adult, would have been a crime according to the Tasmanian criminal code. As the very naive twelve-year-old that I was, I failed to grasp that what was happening to me was genuine paedophilia, nor did I understand the implication of that fact: that I was not legally, or otherwise, capable of consenting to the sexual acts I was being coerced into. I was under the distinct impression that it was entirely my own fault. That's how shame works.

1991

I became a teenager the same year the Cold War was declared officially over and the Gulf War officially commenced. Coincidence? Yes. It was also completely random that Freddie Mercury died the same year I got hips. RIP Freddie. But fuck you, puberty. It really cramped my entire existence. It's very hard to be gender-contrary once puberty hits, especially if it hits you in a way that gifts you with sudden-onset childbearing hips, debilitatingly painful cramps, unpredictable periods and massive mood swings. How could I possibly be a boy if, at a glance, I looked and behaved like a perimenopausal woman? Apart from my body changing in all the ways I found utterly distressing and uncomfortably incorrect, I also gained the ability to produce acne and lost the ability to speak under duress. And 1991 was the year I took up golf and went to the mainland for the first time, where I was unceremoniously dubbed a "dirty lezza." Oh, and I started high school. It was a very big year.

The transition from primary to high school should have been easy for me. The high school landscape was very familiar, it was practically my own backyard, so I knew it like the back of my hand, give or take a relocated greenhouse here and there. My dad was a maths teacher there and my siblings had all already tested the water before me. But I still cried twice on my first day. The first, a brief panic-induced weep before the school day had even begun, and then, at lunchtime, when I was safely alone, I let a much deeper and uglier sob burst forth.

My mistake had been to assume that high school would be exactly the same as primary school, just transplanted to the new location. I hadn't taken into account the influx of farm kids who'd transferred from all the little primary schools scattered about the region. My other mistake was not made by me, but I still had to wear it. The high school uniform was exactly the same as my primary school one—a green check dress with a forest green jumper. But I had outgrown my school jumper over the Christmas holidays and Mum had replaced it with a white one. I will never understand her logic. It was bad enough that everyone else wore a machine-knitted V-neck and I wore a homemade round-necked windcheater. But why did she choose white material over green? Not only was I taller and wider than most of the girls gathered by the gym, but I was also substantially less green. I was like a cauliflower in a field of broccoli. This did not sit well with me. Blending in is of great importance to someone who needs to work out the lay of the land before making a statement, preferably one I had prepared earlier. But I was not granted such comfort. I stood out at first glance and that made me very anxious. The other kids with uniform anomalies were probably still the grotty kids, and I did not want to be grouped with that lot.

I leant on the fence and watched everyone babble about excitedly. I had ridden my bike over the patch of concrete at my feet thousands of times, but on my first day of high school it suddenly felt hostile and foreign, and so my first little cry began, before the first bell had even sounded, as I looked from one face to the next trying to work out where and how I fitted into the new world disorder I had unexpectedly found myself in.

We were ushered into the gym to be divided into our home groups, and a bearded teacher took to the stage. I loved this gym. Dad had occasionally let me in to play basketball on my own, and I'd loved the squeak of my shoes on the polished floorboards and the rhythm I could make with the bouncing ball and its own echo. I knew you could go up the stairs at the side of the stage and climb a ladder in the wings and hide on a satisfyingly dusty shelf. I also knew there was a back door in the boy's toilet where you could escape out onto the tennis court. I knew that under the stage was a perfect place for a picnic of quiet, with or without snacks, and I knew you could get in there via a tiny door half hidden by a rubbish bin. I knew this gym incredibly well, but I didn't feel so comfortable anymore. I didn't move straightaway when the unknown bearded teacher called my name to go stand with the rest of class 7-4. I waited for a few others to be called so that my white jumper was not associated with my name.

After calling out the six different classes, the bearded teacher introduced us to our homeroom teacher and told us to follow them. As I dawdled at the back of my group, I caught a glimpse of Dad standing in front of a class of older kids. Only a few hours earlier and less than a few hundred metres away from where I now stood, I'd heard him trudge his usual way past my bedroom door, popping out his nighttime wind as he made his way to the bathroom. But as I walked past him now, even my ever-benign gaseous dad felt like a frightening intrusion.

My disorientation had reached fever pitch by the time the lunch bell rang. Finding out that we had to move classrooms for every different class, and that every different class was to be taught by a different teacher, was too much for my change-resistant brain. I wanted one room, one teacher. I wanted familiar faces and I really wanted to cry. I knew lunch was the best time to establish alliances but I needed to go home for some quiet time. I made my way across the oval feeling highly conspicuous courtesy of the white of my jumper and the brooding grey of my isolation. As I got through the hedge, I went straight to the wood heap and started in on my bigger and uglier cry.

The wood heap had replaced the hole in the hedge as my favourite place to be. It had a corrugated roof and a dirt floor. It was dusty and damp but homely. Dad had built it next to the shed, which shielded it from the house. The wood was stacked neatly against the back wall, and I would make myself an armchair by taking a few logs out of the pile and setting them to the side. I would park myself in the gap and chat to myself. I knew that I was too old to be talking to myself, and I was becoming self-conscious about it as I felt the expectation of maturity bite into my flights of fancy. It had become a battle of wills between my imagination and my developing inner voice. To be fair, my inner voice was still largely external, but it was already starting to take on the negative attitude that was to be its trademark for most of my life. "What is wrong with you?" was all I could manage to ask myself that day in the wood heap. "What is wrong with you?" I asked, again and again.

If I could go back in time, I would love to have a cup of tea and a chat with my sad and sorry self in that wood heap. I'm not sure what we'd talk about, but I wouldn't bring any hindsight-born wisdom from the future to share. I'd keep it light, natter about nothing at all, just so I would know that we would never lose the habit of talking to ourself, and that young me shouldn't waste any more energy trying to fight it.

The effort to navigate school resulted in a complete collapse at the end of the day; navigating the layers of both written and unwritten rules left me shattered. That I had a room of my own is probably what held me together. I would go straight there and decompress. I still climbed into my cupboard from time to time. I just wish I had known how to draw on the resource that was my sister's love. I never did call her.

My first year of high school wasn't just a gauntlet of social anxiety, it was also a crash course in teenage sexuality. After the Easter holidays, I found out that the most popular couple in high school had sex in the bath. This was deemed safe by many in my year—because of the hot water. So, it must have come as quite the shock when she fell pregnant. Then there was a guy in my year who was paid five dollars to jerk off into a Mr. Juicy bottle (a brand of orange juice). He collected both the money and a surprising amount of respect. Then there was the other kid, in the year above me, who was hailed a hero after the rumour circulated that he'd masturbated into a bread roll and made some "faggot" eat it.

I was personally brushed twice with teenage sexuality that year. The first brush could more aptly be described as assault, as it involved one of the most popular boys in school grabbing me from behind in a bear hug during a PE class. He pinned my arms to my sides and pushed me up against the bricks of the changeroom walls and "dry humped" me, pushing his erection into me repeatedly until both he and it were apparently satisfied, at which point he let me go, slapped me on the back and said "thanks champ" before jogging off to join the rest of the class, who were throwing balls at each other's heads on the football field.[⊗]

The second brush occurred at a junior golf tournament in Ulverstone when I walked past one of the junior boys and he offered me twenty dollars for a blow job. I must have looked confused, as he clarified *a blow job* as "a gobby," which didn't help my comprehension, so he made it very clear by saying, "Suck my dick." Twenty dollars represented more than a fortune to me, but I did not need to deliberate before I declined. I was mildly repulsed by the idea of touching a boy anywhere, let alone wrapping my mouth around one of their little fellas. Perhaps that should have been the clue I needed to understand my sexuality, but given everything that you know about me and my circumstances, it should be unsurprising to know that I did not make that connection.

It had been Mum who suggested that I take up golf. I had been sidelined from nearly all sports since my knee had taken to regularly and painfully buckling out of much of its load-bearing responsibility. I wouldn't have chosen golf, but as Mum sold it to me as slow hockey, I decided to give it a go. I'd barely been playing for a year when I received an invitation to play in the Jack Newton Junior Golf Classic. I thought Jack Newton was just a one-armed golf commentator who wore a bow tie, but after being selected to play in his tournament I soon discovered that he'd once been a very successful professional golfer, until he walked into an aeroplane propeller at age thirty-three. Although the accident destroyed his golfing career at its height, Newton chose to dedicate his life to the future of the game.

The tournament was held in a town on the mainland called Cessnock, which meant I had to fly to get there. This was the first time I had ever been on a plane, and I had the most wonderful time. I got tingles in my belly when we took off, and I exploded with excitement

---

[⊗] I am not going to name the boy, who is a man now, but I did google him recently and was very relieved to discover that he did not go on to become a Supreme Court justice.

when I was presented with the in-flight snack. Drinking orange juice at a great height constituted the most exciting thing I'd ever experienced, and the flight ended with another tingle in my belly as we landed, leaving me exhausted with sensory overload. I couldn't talk for hours.

Cessnock's motto was "Wines, Mines and People"—a recipe for a good time if ever there was one. I was billeted out with a woman who spoke at a shout, drove on the wrong side of the road to avoid potholes, didn't believe in cutlery and served a side of bacon with every meal, even if the meal itself was a slab of bacon.

Jack Newton made a point of watching every kid in his tournament tee off on the first hole. It was daunting to see him standing there with one arm behind his back and the other not there at all, and the pressure to impress him was enormous. I was not at all confident I was going to rise to the occasion, because I was premenstrual. And during my short career of hosting an active uterus I had noticed that besides the significant swings in my mood, the other reliable effect of my monthly hormonal fluctuations was that I completely lost my ability to coordinate my hands with my eyes.

The three girls I was grouped with all coped admirably with the pressure, pinging lovely little shots up the centre of the fairway. By contrast, I hit a terrible shot, sending the ball scooting sadly along the ground. It was the kind of shot that I'd overheard the old man poets at the Smithton golf club describe as a "snake rapist."

I played awful golf. The other girls in my group were nice enough, but I could tell their kindness was born of pity. They were going places. In fact, one of them had even quit school to become a professional golfer. I knew I was a different species to these girls, who all had ponytails, short shorts and silky-smooth legs.

I couldn't take my eyes off their legs, wondering how they'd got such nice ones and if it was too late for mine. I also began to wonder why I was so obsessed with their legs, but I was far too deep in the closet to answer that little riddle. So instead, I tried my best to make them laugh while I pretended not to care about the terrible game of golf I was playing. I might have charmed the girls I was playing with, but that was about it. After my round, I went to join a group of juniors standing behind the eighteenth hole watching the rest of us play. As I approached, I heard someone call me a "dirty lezza" and the rest of them laugh in agreement. To have another person reveal your secret to the world is humiliating enough, but it's so, so much worse when it happens before you've worked it out for yourself and then to hear everyone laugh. I walked past without saying a word. I would love to say my silence was dignified, but in all honesty, due to the duress of the humiliation, I couldn't say anything because I couldn't form a single word in my head, much less aloud.

That night, when my billet asked me how my round had gone, I told her I'd played okay but I didn't hold out much hope of bringing home the trophy.

"I didn't think so," she said with a sigh. "They never give me the good golfers."

I stared at her openmouthed but she paid no notice and just kept tearing strips off her bacon as the tributary of wrinkles around her mouth slowly filled up with liquefied pig fat. I didn't say anything either. I couldn't. I just looked down and picked gloomily at my food. I was ashamed of myself; I knew I was never going to be a good golfer, and as such, I was never going to have nice legs, good hair or a billet with a fork.

STOP! POLITICS TIME!

In the very fine year of 1991, the HIV/AIDS Preventative Bill was debated in Tasmania's Legislative Council, which was the upper house of Parliament—and the last step before the anti-homosexual laws could be overturned. Spoiler alert: this attempt at reform, like so many others, failed, but it was a lively debate, by all accounts. There were calls for homosexual activists to be imprisoned or forced into expatriation, and even a bit of chat about the reintroduction of the death penalty. There were also "jokes" made about the possibility of the stoning of gay men.

Of course, an obligatory barnyard analogy was tabled. Hugh Hiscutt, the member for West Devon, commented: "If we had a bull like that, I know where he would end up if he would not serve the females—he would be in the mall tomorrow among those eight thousand sausages."

The specificity of how many sausages get exhibited in "the mall" is the least striking element of that argument. But it is still striking nonetheless.

Speaking of sausages, Independent Parliamentarian Dick Archer added, "When I hear a minister of the Crown making reference to the decriminalisation of homosexuality, I feel sick in the guts—when I hear these people talking about human rights, my blood boils. More money should be made available on policing the law. We must wipe out these addicts, we have to catch it, wipe it out the same way we catch murderers—track them down."

That debate trickled heartily into the letters to the editors, which was the only part of the newspaper I was reading at the time. I don't recall the specifics of what I saw as a young person, but when, later in life, I decided to research the events, the contents of those letters did not surprise me: not the celebrating of the decision to uphold the law, and not the detail with which some letters described the kind of punishment that should be meted out to homosexuals. I was also not at all surprised by the headline in *The Examiner* which declared that the debate to decriminalise homosexuality would herald in a new era of poofter bashing.

1992

It's hard to believe that I could top 1991. What with it being a palindrome year and all. It's a tough call, but if I didn't top it, I certainly gave it a nudge. And certainly, the whole world was giving it a nudge in 1992. George Bush Sr. visited Australia at the same time as Billy Ray Cyrus topped the charts with "Achy Breaky Heart." Cool stuff. And for a brief moment, white people were forced to contend with the systemic injustices of their making, as images of the Rodney King trial and protests were shared the world over, as was the horrific genocide that was taking place in Bosnia. In good news, the Australian High Court handed down the Mabo decision,[⊛] and light-up sneakers were invented, which, to be clear, is not at all comparable. In big news, I saw my first full sex scene on TV and made the Tasmanian Junior Girls golf team (unrelated). And finally, I bought a piece of jewellery. But wait, there's more! Here, let me offer you the free steak knife of all free steak knives: I came out to myself. Kind of. Oh, and I took up smoking.

Without a doubt the most intriguing item of this list would be my purchasing of jewellery, so, naturally I will begin there. I sincerely hope I have already impressed upon you that I was never much of a jewellery gal. But you might be surprised to learn that I did have a jewellery box. It was the only thing that lived on my dresser after Jessica had moved out.

My next-door neighbour, Pop, had given it to me for my tenth birthday and I loved it, but I loved it for very complicated reasons, and none of them had anything to do with the object itself. It was mottled black plastic adorned with beige and tan parquet inlay, and once opened it was a clusterfuck of mirrors—you could see yourself on every surface: the lid, the pull-out wings of the lid, the floor and even the insides of the tiny drawers. And, providing it had been wound up prior to the lifting of the lid, a perky little plastic ballerina would pop up and spin jerkily around the floor mirror to a tinny and dissonant rendition of Tchaikovsky's *Swan Lake*. It was my personal hell in a tiny box, but I loved it because I was supposed to.

The year before he gave it to me, Pop had given me a knock-off Barbie doll. No sooner had I unwrapped it than I'd yanked off her head and all of her limbs. I didn't even bother undressing her. I got

---

[⊛] This landmark case overturned Australia's *terra nullius* doctrine, which was essentially the English colonialists saying, "No one was here when we arrived, so this entire continent is ours now." The Mabo decision legally acknowledged that, actually, many Indigenous communities had been living there for many, many thousands of years, and it formally laid the groundwork for the pursuance of Indigenous land rights. Yes, please.

one hell of a lecture from Nan about it. She told me that even if I didn't like it, it was very rude to do what I did. I felt deep shame about the whole episode. I wanted to explain that I didn't pull it apart because I hated it, although that was true, I did hate it, I had no use for a doll. But that was beside the point, I had pulled it apart because I liked seeing how things are put together.

So, when I got the jewellery box, I was determined to love it. I wasn't thrilled to get it, but I did my best to look pleased and was sure to wait until I got home before I pulled it apart and studied the mechanics of it. It was fantastic. Once I worked out that the ballerina was moved about by a magnet, I swapped her out for the Monopoly dog, to the bottom of which I had glued a coiled paper clip. And I stuffed the ballerina into one of the drawers. Next, I disengaged the "music" so my little dog could circle about in peace. And last of all, I wallpapered the mirrors with scraps of material I'd been collecting from the piles of offcuts that gathered under Mum's sewing machine. I was exceedingly proud of my renovations. Although, now that I have described it, it does sound like I turned it into a tiny David Lynchian funeral diorama.

Aside from the retired ballerina, the only thing I put in my jewellery box was a blue copper sulphate crystal I'd made in science class. Other than its stunning shade of blue, it was not a particularly pretty situation, and, as it hadn't occurred to me to cut the string I'd grown it off, it looked more like a jagged little tampon than it did a precious stone. But it was still the closest thing I had to jewellery until I bought myself a necklace.

For reasons I still do not understand, I decided the best use of my birthday money was to buy a gold locket pendant. As I didn't get much in the way of cash for turning fourteen, the necklace I invested in was an appropriately cheap-looking thing, and if there was any carat involved in its composition, it was most likely to be of the misspelt root vegetable variety. But it was very special to me, and so I had my own initials engraved on the front—yes, that is worth repeating, my own initials engraved on the most visible surface of a very cheap necklace.

As soon as I got home with my freshly self-monogrammed piece, I put a picture of Nan on the inside of one door of the locket and one of Pop on the other, so they could hang around my neck all day and look at each other really closely in the dark. Yes, that is also worth repeating but I am tired from a lifetime of being an unfortunate personality, so how about you just reread it to yourself whenever you are in the middle of a bout of low self-esteem.

I had had every intention of wearing the locket at all times but I found it to be something of a constant irritation, like I was being lightly strangled by a sharp hair all day long, and whenever I wore it, I couldn't not think about it. The problem with not wearing a cheap necklace, however, is that without my neck to keep it tidy, it would magically self-knot to such an alarming degree it would look like a fancy cat threw up a gilded fur ball on my nightstand. After only a week of intermittent wearing and constant untangling, I decided to retire it permanently and I tossed it unceremoniously into the jewellery box with the tiny ballerina corpse and my blue crystal tampon.

As difficult as it is to imagine that my life could get any more exciting, I went and got myself onto the Tasmanian Junior Girls golf team. My selection came after playing in my first State Championships. And no, I didn't transform myself after the Jack Newton Classic—I didn't go out and get me some shiny hair and nice legs and the kind of golf skills that come with them. The truth at the heart of my success was that there were barely enough girls playing golf in Tasmania to make up a team at the time. The dearth of talent was such that it was almost guaranteed that any girl under the age of eighteen caught holding a stick within a ten-mile radius of a golf course was going to be selected, and I'm not even sure that it mattered what kind of stick.

After the team was announced, I was pulled aside by Mrs. Barrington to get my uniform sorted. Mrs. Barrington was a kind and gentle woman, well into her seventies, and she spoke as if there was a clod of mashed potato permanently stuck in her throat. But as silly as her voice sounded to me, it did little to detract from the thrill I felt at being treated as if I was important.

When Mrs. Barrington asked what size uniform I would require, I just shrugged. My mum had always made my clothes, so the closest thing I had to a measurement was how much Mum complained about how big I'd gotten since she'd made my last round of clothes. So, when Mrs. Barrington asked again what size I would need, I dutifully responded with the very matter-of-fact "My size is very big."

Apparently, that was a satisfactory answer for Mrs. Barrington, and she moved the discussion on to the more serious matter of decorum. I was told that, as a representative of the Tasmanian Ladies' Golf Union, I was to behave in a ladylike manner at all times. And this was when my enthusiasm took a real nosedive, because I was all too aware that I was not a natural lady.

The grace of developmental flourish that early childhood allows had been replaced by the fear-filled guidance most adolescents tend to get as they are stewarded toward adulthood. As such, since becoming a teenager, it had been impressed upon me by everyone—my family, my teachers, my peers, my culture, and the whole zeitgeist of my existence—that I was not allowed to be boy-like anymore. So, driven by my deep desire to belong, I'd been studying the ways of the "natural" woman for years, both in real life and on television.

Despite my best efforts, I was really bad at it. I could never manage to sit with my legs together or have nice hair that bounced. Makeup seemed like self-torture; jewellery, as you well know, was beyond me; clothes interested me but for all the wrong reasons, like warmth and pockets.[⊗] I'd never understood that tan lines were something that you not only had to think about, but also make an effort around. I'd noticed that most girls consistently wore anklets that were barely visible above the shoe line, but I wore an array of sock lengths and every day it was potluck as to where on my leg they would pull up to. This meant that every day I spent in the sun got its very own tan line, which made my legs look like a geological sediment experiment.

My lack of ladylike potential went far beyond the surface. I be-

⊗ Hands are so heavy.

haved wrong. My gait was not graceful, as was required of a lady carrying books on her head. Another problem I had was that the only time I could laugh at menfolk was on the rare occasion I found them genuinely funny. Their mere presence was not humorous to me in the same way it seemed to be to "natural" women.

Furthermore, whenever I felt as if I had any kind of knowledge, I was inclined to share it, whereas natural women rarely seemed to want to do the knowing of things out loud. They could be so smart, charming and funny then lose it all as soon as they hit the orbit of larger groups and/or boys. It was confusing to me. I decided that if ever I stumbled into the ability to be smart, charming and funny I would never turn it off. Not for anyone. But back then I struggled to form spontaneous speech. Everything I said during that time of my life had been prepared earlier.

I had observed a reliable exception to this hiding of personality amongst women who had been married for years. I noticed that these women very much liked to share the knowledge of how little their husbands knew in large groups, but only if those large groups were devoid of men. Especially husbands. This behaviour was way above my age bracket, but still, the restraint looked somewhat disingenuous to me. I couldn't understand why women would want to keep this information from their menfolk. Surely a man would want to know if he was stupid, so he could self-correct. That's how I liked to do the living. Obviously, this observation was made before I had a grasp on the concepts of toxic masculinity and male fragility and the near constant threat of violence they harboured. I suspect that was due to the fact that my dad was a very gentle soul who would take a nap over an argument, and my mum had never been shy about knowing things out loud, no matter who was within earshot.

This may seem like a sarcastic riff that adult me has cobbled together for your enjoyment, and while I'll admit there is some truth to that idea, I need you to know that it is also a genuine reflection of my adolescent style of observation. I'd been studying people my whole life, collecting clues on how to behave, and I'd been earnestly compiling lists on this subject ever since starting high school. There were two main categories: what made people popular, and what made people unpopular. My theory was that if I could take on the characteristics of the former and lose the habits of the latter, then I would look like I belonged, and I would not feel so profoundly alone.

One of the most obvious conclusions I made during my early observations of natural women was that they had lots and lots of feelings about boys that tended to lead to very erratic behaviour. Naturally, I felt obliged to at least try and manifest similar feelings about boys, so I did the only thing I knew how to do: copy the behaviour of other girls. Let's call it reverse-engineering normality.

I gave up on that course of action very quickly because being a boy-mad teenage girl meant having to giggle at boys, and that felt like a total bullshit waste of energy to me. Outside of my family, boys were just never observably funny in my presence. Their whole repertoire revolved around just two basic concepts: being mean (about girls and teachers, and to each other), and bigging-up all things dick and dick-related.

I am not suggesting that this is the sum teenage boy repertoire, but it was all I witnessed at the time, and pretty much ever since, if I'm being absolutely honest. What I didn't understand until much later in life was that boys changed their behaviour around me, because they could not sexualise me and that was confusing to them. To be fair, I had the same problem with them. I could not sexualise them even though I knew, as a girl, I was supposed to. But if you are a man, don't be dispirited. If you manage to make me laugh, and many of you have, at least you know you did it on merit alone.

Once I figured out that the reason I found girls to be much funnier than boys was because I much preferred their company, I realised that I had lots and lots of feelings about girls. And, although it didn't necessarily lead to erratic behaviour, it was very disorientating. So perhaps what I was feeling was the same thing girls felt around boys. The thought process was as simple as that, and no sooner had I stacked these ideas on top of each other than they clicked very satisfactorily into what I understood as truth. I was gay.

It really did dawn on me as matter-of-factly as that. I don't remember where I was or what I was doing, but I remember the sequence of thoughts very clearly. And as soon as I had the thoughts, I tried to un-have them. I really did not want to be a paedophile. They sounded like terrible people. Fortunately, my river of ignorance still ran quite deep, so I was able to completely repress my sexuality without too much effort. All I had to do was stop actively participating in life.

Thankfully, despite my lack of ladylike qualities, it didn't take me long to work out that in order to be a "lady" in the world of teenage girl golfing, all I had to do was not be a "slut." So, given that I was shy, deeply closeted, fat, had selective mutism and undiagnosed autism, I was never going to be caught straying very far from "appropriate" behaviour.

The only issue that could potentially "slutify" me was the fact that I was a smoker. My entry into the world of tobacco was made in the spirit of fitting in. Everyone around us smoked, so it was only going to be a matter of time before Hamish and I stole one out of Mum's packet and had a go. I am happy to report that it only took one drag on one cigarette for me to work out that smoking was total bullshit. It tasted terrible, it smelt worse and made me feel very nauseous. I didn't reject the idea immediately, however. Too many people around me smoked for me to just put it aside, so, in the interest of a thorough investigation, I continued to dabble for a few months. Still, I kept coming to the same conclusion—smoking is bullshit. Sadly, what is not bullshit is just how addictive cigarettes are. And that was that. I became a smoker, and just about every day of the twenty years that I smoked, I was trying to quit.

The worst thing about smoking was that I could never afford to do it. Especially when I was an unemployed child. The only way I could indulge my habit was by stealing Mum's, which compounded the stress of it all. Though, as much as I hated it, smoking did come with the unexpected benefit that it completely dulled my sense of smell and taste. This may sound like a drawback, but it's a real gift for someone with extremely strong sensory sensitivities, something which almost everyone with autism experiences. My sense of smell often crosses too far into the lane of my sense of taste, which tends to trigger my already distressingly overactive gag reflex. I'm not exaggerating when I say that even the memory of a bad smell can conjure a taste so bad, it'll trigger a fit of retching. Smoking all but stamped out this dreadful phenomenon, which freed up a lot of energy that I could dedicate to dealing with the fact that sounds could trigger feelings, many of which my body registered as pain. But more on that later.

Smoking would eventually help me cheat away a portion of my social anxiety, in that I could appear to be participating in a conversation when all I was doing was blowing smoke in its general direction. But at first I was not in it to be a social smoker; it was entirely an antisocial pursuit. Sneaking off to talk to myself in the wood heap became so much more acceptable to me when I did it under the guise of having a sneaky cigarette.

STOP! STATISTICS TIME!

By 1992, Tasmania was the only state where sodomy was still a crime. South Australia had decriminalised homosexuality in 1975, followed by the Australian Capital Territory in 1976, Victoria in 1980, the Northern Territory in 1983, New South Wales in 1984, and both Western Australia and Queensland in 1990. And while these decriminalisations did not necessarily indicate the cessation of active homophobia on the mainland, Tasmania was tangibly and unequivocally behind. So, on Christmas Day of the previous year, when the United Nations Human Rights Committee (UNHRC) made it possible for Australians who felt their civil rights had been violated to submit appeals directly to them, Nick Toonen, a young gay man from Hobart, immediately lodged an application, arguing that Tasmanian Criminal Code Sections 122 and 123 violated his right to privacy. And on the fifth of November 1992, the UNHRC accepted the Toonen case as admissible. The struggle for Tasmanian gay law reform was about to get global.

1993

Even white people began to notice racism in 1993, when the Native Title Act in Australia had farmers convinced that their land would be forcibly taken and given to the Native Title owners. Sadly, not a lot of white people seemed to know that racism wasn't something to brag about. America was having a time of it too, with the Lorena Bobbitt trial getting sensationalised egregiously in the news. Apparently there was just no time to spare for a respectful dialogue about domestic violence, because there were too many dick jokes to make. There was also the Waco siege of David Koresh's Branch Davidians compound, which did not go great. On the other hand, the *Cheers* series finale did go great, when 93 million viewers tuned in, making it the most watched television episode of the decade. Norm!

Back to me, you will be pleased to know that 1993 was a quiet year for this little guy, but don't get too excited, it was still a big old slog. The year began with me playing my part in Tasmania's coming last in the Australian Junior Girls championships. At school, my grades, which had already been in steady decline, plunged dangerously close to failing at the same time the incessant shaming of my body kicked up another gear or two. There were a few positive developments I can report; I got funnier, and I discovered a joy that was to become a lifelong passion: art history. In other good news—well, "good" under the circumstances—I managed to keep my sexuality a secret, to both myself and the world at large. The drawback was that for all the effort it took to double-closet myself, I paid the price with an increased sensitivity to everything even vaguely gay-related. And in very sad and bad news, there was a lot of "gay" in the zeitgeist of 1993 to be sensitive about, and it was rarely vague and never positive.

Apparently, some kind of sports scientist was enlisted to help the Tasmanian Junior Golf Team prepare for a more winning performance at the next National Championships, and I was sent an exercise program to follow and encouraged to make a habit of eating bananas. The exercise program required all sorts of complicated equipment, and so it was that I met my first-ever "personal trainer," Mick, who was the proprietor of the imaginatively named "Mick's Gym," which was situated on the outskirts of Smithton.

Mum said she would drive me there every Wednesday after school until daylight savings started, but after that, I was to ride my bike over. When we pulled up in front of a little bungalow with a large corrugated-iron shed out the back, I wasn't convinced we were at the right address. But when I saw a small wooden sign with the words mick's gym burnt into the timber, I had to concede we were close. Mum didn't get out to check that the shed backed up the claims on the sign, and practically pushed me out of the car and drove away, leaving me with Mick at his not-so-salubrious gym. I can't see this sort of scenario happening anymore. There's an enormous amount of trust involved in leaving your fifteen-year-old daughter with an old man who will be taking her into his shed and working on her body. Thankfully, it was a gym and Mick was great.

We stood alone in the gym while Mick studied the exercise program, and as he did, I studied Mick. He was a lean, wiry old man with grey hair, deep wrinkles and very gnarled hands, and his outfit of canvas work trousers and a pilled woollen jumper made him look more farmer than fitness guy. The gym didn't look very fresh either. It had brown carpet and corrugated iron walls, which were mirrored along one side. But it was definitely a gym. There were benches, free weights, and the air was thick with the smell of rotting onions and other issues of the foot. Eventually Mick screwed up the program and tossed it in the bin, patted my belly and grunted, "We'll get rid of it." For the assigned hour, Mick set about finding out just how weak I was. If I could lift a weight, he gave me a heavier one. If I couldn't lift it, he yelled at me. I discovered three things during my time at Mick's Gym: If someone yells at me, I do as I'm told; I can produce my very own onion smell; and when I'm straining to lift something my top lip twitches.

The following week I met another couple of members of Mick's Gym. They didn't register my presence at first, focused as they were on flexing in front of the mirror. They had obviously lifted a lot of weights in Mick's Gym, because their arms looked like Rottweilers, but not as friendly. Their massive chests forced their massive arms so far away from their body, it was as if they were perpetually frozen in a partnerless hug. Mick saw me staring and asked me if I would like to look like them? I politely declined, and they all laughed really hard and slapped me on the back like I was one of them. I wasn't, though. I had no idea what the joke was. I still don't.

I got stronger very quickly. And within two weeks I doubled both the weights I was lifting and my confidence. By the third week I could do crunches without assistance or asking what they were. I am incredibly jealous of how rapidly my fifteen-year-old body reacted to exercise, and I often wonder what would have happened if I hadn't been forced to stop going. Could Mick have changed the course of my fat-filled life?

I will never know the answer to that question because daylight savings started, which meant I had to start riding my bike across town to Mick's Gym. I wasn't thrilled by the prospect of riding my bike. It wasn't just the fact that I had two quite traumatic bike accidents under my belt, it was also the matter of the helmet.

In 1991, helmets had become mandatory and Dad, who so rarely offered an opinion, had lots to say about that, pointing out that a helmet wouldn't have saved my knee or protected me from the greenhouse. Ultimately, I think Dad's resistance to helmets was financial. I am not sure where our family helmet came from, but as it was the only one that we had, riding bikes was no longer a thing us kids could enjoy doing together; and because it was made of unadulterated Styrofoam and completely devoid of any of those fancy patterns that the 1990s were so famous for, we never fought over it. As I set off to Mick's Gym, I saw my reflection in the front windows of our house, and saw a fat girl wearing a pink and blue homemade tracksuit with an argyle harlequin pattern topped off with the poverty chic of a Styrofoam lid. There was no escaping the fact that I was a bully magnet on wheels. I had barely recovered from the "adipose test" from a few months earlier.

After ordering the class to stand in a line against the wall, our physical education teacher went from one child to the next, pinching each student with a metal pincer in a few places before informing the entire class what percentage of their body was fat. It was a compulsory test because apparently, in the midst of life's most traumatic bodily transformation, it was important that children be told how badly they compared to a "normal" body. Whatever the fuck that is.

By the time my teacher got to me, my dread levels had reached impossible depths. I didn't need data collected from a pincer to tell me I was fat. I understood very well by then that I was both overweight and disgusting. How could I not know that, given that I'd been body-shamed by adults and children alike for years. Adults tended to say things like "dumpy" and "doughy" and liken me to "the side of a house," whereas kids preferred to use much more playful terms like "thunder thighs," "fat moll" or "Hannah the Heifer." I was also beginning to wonder if people might believe I was deaf, because they always said the cruel things about my weight by either yelling them or talking about me as if I wasn't there.

I failed the adipose test. Apparently, I had too much fat for the pincers to cope with. I am not entirely sure how my teacher phrased it, but the whole class laughed heartily. I went home that night and weighed myself. The resulting ten-stone verdict would be most welcome today, but at the time, I panicked. I didn't even know what stones were, but I assumed they were fat, and most likely ugly, and that I had ten of them.

I felt like Mick and his gym were helping me break out of my flesh prison, but I wasn't ready to be witnessed in public exercising. As I slowly rode my bike down the main street, I saw a group of girls standing outside the milk bar and braced myself for some kind of jeering. I was not disappointed. Then I rode past a group of kids from Hamish's year by the recreation centre. They didn't see me pass but as I got further down the road, I heard them all laugh. I couldn't be sure they were laughing at me, but I owned it anyway. It pained me to think I was a joke.

I enjoyed my unwittingly last-ever session with Mick, and at the end he slapped me on the back and said, "Well done." And I felt pretty good. I remained feeling pretty good until I got to the main road on my bike and saw people. I didn't want another anxious ride home, so I turned left and took the long way back.

I've since used Google Maps to work out that I turned a three-kilometre ride across town into a twenty-kilometre back-road suicide mission. I was oblivious of that fact, but by the time the road turned into a dirt track, I knew I'd made a very bad decision. I should have been home an hour earlier and I was only about a third of the way there. Mum would be getting worried, and I started worrying about Mum getting worried. But there was nothing to do but keep riding. It was a quiet country road with cows as my only witness. Thankfully, cows don't mock fat girls. Us heifers like to stick together.

By the time I got home, everyone was on high alert. They were on high alert because Mum was worried about me, and the way she dealt with that was by yelling at everyone else in my absence. I was happy to be home, but I was scared of Mum. I could feel her wrath from about a kilometre out. And she did not disappoint.

I found her out by the washing line being angry at the pegs. She spun round when she heard me drop the bike down and immediately began shouting. I felt the lump in my throat before I could explain myself. I knew she was right, anyway. It was dark and I should have been home hours earlier. For all she knew, I'd been fraternising with boys, getting myself dead in a ditch or, worse, pregnant.

I tried to explain myself to Mum but distress clamped my voice. "I didn't want to . . . People were laughing. I took . . ." I gasped.

This was enough information for Mum to round in on me afresh. Why would I do that to her? Why would I cause her so much worry? They were good questions and I had to take a deep breath to try and plead my case with an accusation of my own. "I didn't want everyone in town laughing at me. They all laugh at my stupid clothes and my trademark helmet!" I yelled back.

It was very tense for a moment and then Hamish said, "It's probably your 'trademark' arse they're laughing at." I hadn't expected that, and I certainly didn't expect it to be the perfect icebreaker. But

Hamish had managed the impossible. He made Mum laugh at the height of her fury and the air cleared almost instantly. Relief and merriment took over the backyard as everyone started laughing really hard. Except me, of course. It didn't feel good to find out I was a family joke. I knew why the kids at school took the piss, and I had an inkling that strangers in the street thought my unusual shape was worth a laugh, but I thought my family was a safe place. I wasn't allowed to go back to Mick's Gym after that.

This thwarting of my potential for brawn was made all the more painful by the failing of my brain. But there wasn't much to be done about it, because I was no longer making an effort at school. I didn't decide to become lazy on a whim born of a bad attitude. I was tired. I was tired of all my earnest and concentrated scholastic efforts being met with not just dwindling grades but also my teachers' lowering estimation of me. My report cards were almost exclusively filled with sentiments like *Hannah does not apply herself* or *Hannah is falling well short of her potential*. Sometimes the sentiments were more bluntly expressed: *Hannah is lazy* or *Hannah has a bad attitude*. Sometimes they were contained within genuinely insightful observations, and far more interesting language: *Hannah's participation in class is spasmodic* or *Hannah brings a rather ethereal presence to class discussions*.

The truth is, none of my teachers seemed to notice how hard I was trying. Instead, they would invariably conclude that laziness, mine, was the root cause of the ever-widening gap between my perceived intelligence and my poor results. None of my teachers were inclined to wonder if it was their teaching methods that were falling short. But as is often the case in small, isolated, under-funded and under-resourced schools, the application of critical thinking amongst the overburdened teachers was, at best, spasmodic.

The main stumbling block to succeeding at school was how difficult I found it to do the learning in class. Halfway through a lesson, my brain would switch off: *No, I've had enough. I don't want to do it anymore.* It wasn't melodramatic about it, it would just hit its threshold and shut down, leaving me helpless to take in new information, and sometimes unable to speak or even think. As the school year progressed, my learning window would get smaller and smaller, and by the year's end it would be closed tight by morning break, if it opened at all.

This had always been the case, but in primary school I had a chance of keeping up because there were significantly fewer variables to my day. High school, in comparison, was a clusterfuck of environmental shapeshifting, with no day ever looking the same as the one before, and, as you've probably picked up by now, change was not my friend any more than my classmates were. To me, high school was a war zone of sound: the squealing, the laughing, the yelling, the plastic wrappers, the chalk on chalkboards, the snapping of gum-chewing, the clicking of pens, the dragging of metal chair legs on concrete. All the noises would reach my ears at the same time with the same intensity and my brain refused to tune any of them out, let alone try and put them in any kind of helpful order.

Sounds have always had the ability to make me feel things: audible chewing elicits anger, loud noises can bring on sudden anxiety, and high-pitched sounds resonate in my spine with something akin to physical pain. It's not all bad. A satisfying key change in a song brings on all the sensations of cresting on a roller coaster, but stripped of the terror. It's lovely. But a lot of noises all at once, even if they are exclusively pleasant sounds, will always feel like an assault. So, the relentless cacophony of high school was constantly and unbearably overwhelming. And don't get me started on the smell of it. Body sprays competed with hair sprays, which competed with the always over-deployed deodorants that still somehow managed to lose the war against the toxic bouquet of teenage body odour. Thank god I was a smoker; I might've perished otherwise.

The other hurdle high school threw up at me was homework. I am not morally opposed to extracurricular curricula; I just didn't have time for it. As in primary school, I needed my evenings to catch up on the things my brain had been unable to take on board during the day, not to mention recover from the sheer exhaustion of trying to subtly navigate a sea of hypercritical teens for hours on end. On top of that, the closer I got to being an adult and the further away from being a baby, the more chores I was expected to get done at home. These extra burdens, as reasonable as they were, led to my brain shutting down more and more, and, without my brain, learning became impossible. I was also dealing with another new and particularly excruciating educational experience: having my own dad for a teacher.

Dad had a reputation for being a grump, and it was well known that he did not tolerate fools. Well, it was well known by other people. The Mr. Gadsby I knew was a different person—he was not grumpy, he was placid, and I knew for a fact that he absolutely did tolerate fools. Having my dad as my teacher gave me the kind of visibility I'd been trying to avoid my whole school career. I didn't know exactly how the other kids would respond to the reality that sitting in their midst was the daughter of the man they really hated who was grumpily teaching them a subject they ultimately resented. But I knew enough that the situation was not going to elicit anything approaching good feelings toward me.

My fears played out at the end of the very first class when, as we were filing out, bottlenecked at the door, a girl, let's call her Karen, muttered, "Your dad's fat." She had said it loud enough for group effect, but it did not hang in the air for long enough to gather much tension because as soon as Karen's taunt had been issued, I fired back, "At least we know who my dad is."

Everybody within earshot laughed and it was a sweet, sweet moment. I had entered the classroom with a target on my back and had emerged a hero—even if it was for just a nanosecond. What nobody else knew was just how much work I had put into the preparation of that quip. I had spent the whole of my Christmas holidays imagining the worst-case scenarios and thinking up the best ways to deflect them.

This was how I had always approached my social anxiety. Heading into any kind of new situation, I'd run through all the scenarios I was able to imagine and then prepare my responses ahead of time. The older I got and the more experience I gathered, the more complex the situations I was able to imagine and the better I got at responding. But below the surface, my brain was always doing intense levels of manual labor, the duck legs of my thinking whirring through the Rolodex of possibilities I had prepared earlier. It was as exhausting as it was distressing. No wonder I was burnt out by fifteen.

If I was struggling with my grades, then I was failing dismally at all things social. By the end of primary school I had worked out how to be friendly, which was enough for a while, but once I hit the tweens, shit got messy really quick. As the social networks at school became more and more complex, I found it impossible to make the jump from friendliness to being a friend. I understood that I had a rich inner life, and I swam in it as often as I was able. I assumed everyone around me also had a rich inner life, but I was at a loss as to how to connect my world to theirs. I thought I was doing all the right things, the same things as everyone else, but I was always made to feel odd, apart from the crowd. What I didn't (couldn't) see were all the rivers of intuitive connections that other people make with each other.

Free time continued to be my worst subject. I thought it was bad in primary school, but at least back then it was enough to hang around the vicinity of kids having fun. Loitering was no longer tolerated in high school. And rightly so, it's creepy. So, I made a habit of going home for lunchtime respite. I'd have a cheeky cigarette in the wood heap, make myself a sandwich and then park myself in front of the television and let my mind zone right out for as long as possible before toddling off, back into battle.

If I couldn't go home for lunch for some reason, it was my habit to head to the library. This was not my habit because I was a nerd. Libraries have never been places I've been able to think clearly. Apparently, books and I have a different optimal environmental temperature and the hum of fluorescent lights fills me with despair. I went because it was a place where I could reliably be left alone. I only pretended to be a nerd, and I think I fooled a lot of people that I was a big reader, but if anyone had bothered to observe closely, they would have noticed I was just studying the indexes of history books. I found scanning the lists of subjects in the back of books somehow calming.

I'd stumbled upon the little book on modern art when I was pretending to look for another one, scanning the shelves and plucking out random books I'd judged by their covers. I didn't like to admit it then, but I will freely do so now: to this day, I still like my books to have pictures in them. I was so confused by the intensity of the stuff the little art book stirred in me. I couldn't understand the jargon that attempted to explain the art. Words like "juxtaposition" and "curvilinear," phrases like "forced perspective" meant nothing to me. But as soon as I flipped it open, I became completely absorbed. I lost all sense of myself in the world. I am sure my curiosity was piqued in some part by the proliferation of nude female bodies that littered the pages, but on a conscious level, I swear I was only there for the articles.

I hadn't borrowed a book for years, because my overdue status was terminal. So, I stole it. Took it home. Made it a secret. Absorbed it. Within the year I had relieved the library of every single one of its art history books. All three of them. The books were small, the writing was impenetrable, and the pictures were mostly little black-and-white reproductions, which for a book about modern art is only marginally better than having no pictures at all. This didn't matter to me, because it wasn't the art itself that spoke to me. It was the relationship between the words and the images.

I would read all about a particular work of art and then try and make the meaning fit the image. How exactly did the artist's brushwork "transform dabs of flat colour into a vibrant conversation"? That was a tough one to answer when looking at black-and-white reproductions. That I failed more often than not in my quest was the hook that dragged me into the world of art history. I thought that if I could bridge the gap between the words and the images, then perhaps I could find the key to the hows and whys of other people's thinking.

I was not frustrated by my inability to make the same connections in my own observations. I would assume I was missing a piece of the puzzle and go in search of it. The books were generalist—so I had to go in search of a lot of missing pieces elsewhere. I began to spend so much time at the library collecting all the information I thought I needed, I wasn't even bothered by the fluorescent lights anymore. I stopped caring about fitting in at school, I stopped worrying about what I looked like, I stopped worrying about who I was. I had faked it until I made it, and I became a nerd. It was heaven. It was the closest thing to joy that I understood in 1993.

My bourgeoning obsession with art history did not translate into an improvement in my grades. In fact, my brain began to resent the time that school was taking away from thinking about art, and the negative tone of my school reports got even worse. But I didn't care, my brain was alive. If making people laugh was my lifeline, then thinking about art became my pleasure, it calmed my thinking in a way that nothing else could. I would take all the puzzles and questions it threw up at me and roll the fingers of my thinking over them, searching for possible answers and solutions. I didn't care if I couldn't find any. It was the thinking that gave me joy. Thinking about art history made me feel safe, because, unlike the real world, it felt like a puzzle I could solve. It gave me a window into the world that terrified and confused me so much, like little air vents in my trapped existence. And I was indeed trapped. Trapped in my body and trapped in a very small town. I was so well trapped that I believed my pain was a natural law, like gravity.

STOP! BIGOTRY TIME!

It was a well-known joke in Smithton that you couldn't call yourself a "real local" unless your parents and grandparents had all been born and bred in Smithton. It was a joke everywhere else that you couldn't call yourself a "real local" unless your parents and grandparents had all been born and *inbred* in Smithton. Funnily enough, swap out *Smithton* and replace it with *Tasmania* and you have two more jokes that were very popular all over Australia during the 1990s.

The prevalence of the conspiracy theory that outsiders were destroying Tasmanian identity played no small part in the heightening of homophobic sentiment. There were many who believed that homosexuals had infiltrated every level of government, as part of carrying out the nefarious "real gay agenda" which was to corrupt the family unit and to dominate Tasmanian identity. In the north of the state, my neck of the woods, local leaders made it clear that they believed the south of Tasmania had already been contaminated and, by extension, was no longer authentically Tasmanian.

Very little was done to dignify the discourse, and too often those who used the most violent language were given a much bigger platform than they deserved. The latent fear of gays that sat just below the surface of too many small-town folk all over Australia became easily politicised and weaponised in Tasmania. This is what turned homophobia from a thing that was condoned on the quiet, like in most small towns, into something that could be freely and openly justifiable, a duty born of a God-given right.

Meanwhile, the UNHRC pursued its investigation on behalf of young Nick Toonen. As the case of *Toonen v. Australia* progressed, the Tasmanian Government supplied a series of defences for their anti-gay laws. I think it is worth noting the reasons they gave, because it is always interesting to see how people justify bigotry in legalese:

1. *Toonen's rights had not been violated, since these sections had been enacted democratically. Thus, it could not constitute an "unlawful" interference to privacy.* This is a very bold defence to offer an international governing body that had been formed after World War II specifically to safeguard against a repeat of the gross, catastrophic and murderous human rights violations that had been enacted by the democratically elected Hitler, leader of the democratically elected Nazi party of Germany.

2. *The law had not been used in the years prior to Toonen's complaint.* I am not very well versed in law, but I don't understand why you wouldn't want to close a legal loophole through which human rights could be legally violated, unless, of course, you wanted to reserve the right to exploit said loophole.

The third reason laid out by the Tasmanian Government goes some way toward explaining why they would want to leave any and all loopholes exactly where they were:

3. *The laws were justified on public health and moral grounds.*

Although they were careful to make a distinction between "homosexuals" and "homosexual acts" (stating that the laws pertained only to the latter), by evoking morality in this defence it is clear that the Tasmanian Government was hell-bent on keeping homosexuals subjugated to a criminal class. I don't know how this relates to privacy, but it is an unequivocally appalling idea to actively want to defend. It was fiercely defended in 1993, however, particularly along the North West Coast of Tasmania.

In the North Western town of Burnie, the self-declared "proud" homophobe Richard Gibbs set up a support network for people who objected to homosexual and bisexual behaviour: the Homophobic Activists Liberation Organisation, or, HALO. Good on him. In his statement to the press, Gibbs proclaimed that it was "natural" to feel "repulsed" by homosexuality before declaring that it was time "for homophobics to come out of the closet." It is always offensive when victim status is claimed by the very people who are actively advocating for legal limitations on the human rights of a marginalised and vulnerable group within their community. But the vileness of this tactic goes through the roof when they do so by co-opting the vernacular of the very group they are so proud to hate and oppress, legally or otherwise. How can "all lives" possibly "matter" in a world where people just keep doing this kind of horrific shit?

Where did I stand on all this in 1993? Well, to put it bluntly, I was homophobic. How do I know? I was afraid of homosexuals, even though I was sure I had never met one. (Fact check: I had met gays, but closets be closets.) I remember hearing an old bloke at the golf club saying that "AIDS was cancer for faggots and they all deserved to die," and I remember the only thing that I took issue with was the fact that cancer was not a virus.

I overheard a lot of openly violent homophobic riffs at the time. I liked to collect them, remember them and revisit them. I never repeated such things out loud. I would just turn them over in my head, wondering about the hatred they spelt out and pulling at the threads of fear they were wrapped in. I thought about them with almost abstract fascination, believing they were a curiosity that had naught to do with me. It took many years of revisiting them before I understood what such ideas really meant. It took me even longer to understand that the reason I'd taken to collecting ideas that had nothing to do with me, was because they had everything to do with me, and I must have known it, even if I didn't understand it.

1994

1994was the first year that Australia Day was celebrated by all states at the same time, which, to be clear, is nothing to celebrate, unless the uniform erasure of Indigenous culture is your thing. Speaking of America, the Beastie Boys gifted us with a new vocab word for the ubiquitous hairstyle in their 1994song "Mullet Head." Australian cinema gave us *Muriel's Wedding* and *Priscilla, Queen of the Desert* and Nelson Mandela was elected president of South Africa. Which is not a film, just an unrelated fact tacked onto the end of a poorly constructed sentence I decided to keep in as an ode to my failing grades of the same year.

In other news, I turned sixteen and there was nothing sweet about it. School continued to be an exhausting struggle. I hated my body more and more each day, and it, in turn, tried to kill me. More on that later. And guess what else? Australia's national broadcaster—

the ABC—aired the Sydney Gay and Lesbian Mardi Gras. I did not see the flaunting of gay lifestyle myself, as I was in hospital having my gallbladder removed. Again, more on that later. What made 1994 all the worse was Justin leaving home (to be a bus driver in Queensland) and Hamish moving to Launceston (to be a trainee supermarket something). Good for them, but bad for leaving me all alone with Mum, Dad and talk-back radio.

My only safe havens in 1994 were thinking about art and visiting Nan and Pop next door. I was still venturing over every day after school, drinking cups of tea, sharing carefully curated summations of what I would like to have experienced at school, citing crushes I had on boys by quoting from conversations I had overheard, adding a little buoyancy to my sinking grades, but not too much, because being too smart in a town like Smithton was way worse than being as dumb as bricks. I like to think I struck a good balance in my falsified report cards to Nan and Pop.

Their house was the only place in the world that felt safe from all the change that threatened me from all other angles. Every year since I could remember, Nan would undo a knitted jumper and knit it again. I don't know what it is about that fact that fills me with serenity and satisfaction, but it does. I used to love helping her unravel the jumper, winding it around the little space heater to rid the yarn of its old kinks, and balling it up for her so she could knit a brand-new jumper that, to my untrained eye, looked exactly like the old one.

Life at home was so much more fraught. Without the buffering of siblings, I had become confused by Mum to the point of paralysis. I wanted nothing more than to be a good kid. It never made sense to me to mount any kind of rebellion as a teenager—life was already a supreme struggle, I couldn't see the sense in agitating for more. But I was apparently terrible at communicating my good intentions to Mum, whose attitude toward me seemed to swing between suspicion, fury, frustration and sweetness for reasons I could never understand, even in hindsight.

There was always going to be a tension in being my mother's

daughter. That is her love language. But it became all the more strained once I hit puberty, because the blooming of my hormones coincided with the dwindling of hers. I was frustrating to Mum. I was vague and quiet, slow-moving, shy, and my body seemed to trigger some deep-seated issues of her own, so, like most parents tend to do, she transferred them over.

Mum was, and is, a much more dynamic spirit compared to me, and she worried that the teenage me was too sullen. Personally, my life felt as if it was dancing with chaos every waking moment and a fair chunk of the slumbering ones. But as most of the action was taking place inside my head, with very little of it managing to manifest itself externally in any easily observable fashion, I can see how, to the outside world, I might have looked functionally inert.

That is the best excuse I can offer up as to why Mum refused medical intervention when I was diagnosed with gallstones. To be perfectly fair—it is peculiar to the point of unbelievable that a sixteen-year-old would suffer a condition most associated with people who are straddling middle age. But instead of erring on the side of caution, Mum doubled down on denial—telling the treating doctor that I didn't have gallstones and that I was "just trying to get out of doing any work."

The problem with gallstones is that between attacks you can be pretty much okay. It was only the digestion of food that caused the problems. So, in the morning I would be fine but somewhere during my first or second class my body began to violently reject the digestive process and I would be sent to the library, which, as far as sick rooms go, was as unhygienic as it was illogical. I would be parked behind the trolleys of returned books, and left to rock back and forth, the pain so blindingly intense that I couldn't even spare a care to preserving my hard-fought invisibility. Once the attack had passed, I was sent home to Mum, who, upon seeing no evidence of any kind of malady, would promptly send me back.

This fun cycle of pain and wilful neglect was broken only when Mum witnessed an attack herself. I was eventually taken to the local hospital, but not before Mum gave me a swig of sherry in a last-ditch effort to prove herself an adroit health care professional. I was put on a regimen of painkillers and jelly and told that my body should sort itself out, but when one of the stones made its way out of my gallbladder and blocked my liver duct, I was rushed to hospital in Launceston. I don't know how I got there, the pain was so violent, but I do remember being very yellow.

I needed to submit to an enema and undergo a cholecystectomy, which I was told was a big old operation to remove my gallbladder. I was not, however, told what an enema was. But as soon as my butt cheeks were parted, I knew nothing good could come of it, and I clamped myself back together again as tight as I could. I was surrounded by nurses at that stage; two stood down the bed, a cheek apiece, outside of my field of vision. They were not holding me down, but I couldn't move.[*] A third nurse was patting my head and telling me everything was going to be all right. I was not at all convinced. And I did not, as she suggested, relax. Instead, I did the only thing I am capable of doing when under duress: I clenched my butt cheeks together and said something funny.

"Isn't this sort of thing against the law?"

Now, to be fair, I did not understand that what I had said was funny until after all the nurses laughed. I was just being factual. Laughter is not the best medicine, but it did help me submit to taking a syringe full of soapy water up the arse. I was then told to hold it in for as long as possible before taking myself to the toilet. I like a challenge, so I clenched my butt once again, this time in the spirit of achievement and not fear. After the nurses left, the surgeon came in to talk me through the procedure. He pointed to the five places I was to have a keyhole incision. He barely touched me, but with each slight jab of his finger I writhed uncomfortably. "Yes," he said, "I can see you are in a lot of pain." He told me to relax, there was nothing to worry about, and then he left the room. But I did not relax, not for pain or fear, but because there was a dose of soapy water very ready to make a hasty exit.

---

[*] Nurses really are miracle workers.

I swung my legs slowly over the side of the bed and made my way over to the bathroom door. All of which was possible with the tightest of pressed butt cheeks and a ziplocked sphincter. But what was not possible was pushing the bathroom door open—the heavy, heavy hospital bathroom door. I tried again, with just a little bit more oomph. But that little bit of oomph was all it took. You know that scene in *The Shining* when the elevator doors open and a river of watery blood fills the hotel corridor? Kind of like that.

At this point you may be wondering, *Hey Hannah, I thought you were poor. So why is it that you had a private hospital suite?* I didn't. There were witnesses. There were many, many witnesses. And none of them could be convinced that holding in an enema for upward of fifteen minutes constituted an achievement. None of them. It's so embarrassingly clear in hindsight that when the nurse told me to hold onto the enema for as long as I could, she was not issuing me with a challenge. The humiliation of my naivete and literal thinking is painful in the admission, but I would like to remind you that I was a goddam child, and not only should I not have been expected to understand complicated medical processes, I also should not have been left alone in the middle of an enema procedure, and, last of all, hospital bathroom doors should not be heavy.⊗

I woke from the surgery alone in the recovery room. And, as is often the case when a bunch of people have rummaged amongst your major organs, I was unable to move. As I darted my eyes around the room trying to make sense of it all, a nurse bustled in to check on all the beepings and whatnots around me. She was humming to herself, lost in her thoughts, and I wasn't sure if I should talk or not, so I waited, watching her. I think I should have said something, because when she turned and saw that I was awake, staring at her, she jumped with fright. I retaliated with my usual startle reflex and was met with a world of pain. And then I went into shock.

I'm sure the shock had everything to do with the anaesthetic and major surgery I had just emerged from, but as I lay there shaking

⊗ Seriously.

uncontrollably, chilled to the bone and burning up all at once, all I could think of was the look of terror on the nurse's face. The nurse did not hold it against me, and without hesitation she began wrapping me up in a foil blanket and saying all the comforting words in very comforting tones. She was soon joined by others, and I found my shaking freezing hot self suddenly surrounded by very serious, very caring, very concerned adult people who were all actively invested in my well-being. I kept apologising through the chattering of my teeth, and a young, softly-spoken man bent down and gently took my hand and told me it was the furthest away from my fault as is humanly possible. I had never known the like. He kept holding my hand, and I passed out.

The procedure went only marginally better than the enema. The gallbladder is supposed to be the size of your thumb, but mine was about as big as a pear and ready to burst. The keyholes were abandoned in favour of a three-inch incision, through which my gallbladder and its eighteen stone babies were removed. My digestive capabilities have not been pain-free or entirely effective ever since that operation, but I didn't know that was to be the unfortunate case way back in 1994, so I was pretty happy with the outcome. Why wouldn't I be? I had a great big scar, a jar filled with gallstones, and a really great story about shitting myself in hospital.

Mum has her own story as to why she mistrusts doctors and is angrily sceptical of ill health, but it's not my story to tell. Suffice it to say, Mum had plenty of her own painful demons to deal with, and I truly believe she did the best she could. That's not to say that her best was always enough, but it was still her best and that is all you can ask. I was not so mature in 1994, and I mined her guilt mercilessly. Every time she told me off, I would deftly remind her that she'd almost killed me. In fact, to this very day I can still use the "great gallbladder neglect" card to fill my mum up with instant guilt. That it can still so reliably wound her is all the proof you need that she really did do her best, and that she knows all too well that it wasn't always enough. Which in and of itself, is enough.

Mum's small-town claustrophobia was hitting a suffocating peak in 1994. She was done with Smithton. It was too small for her, in terms of both physical size and mindedness. Next to drinking, the two most popular pastimes in Smithton seemed to be gossip and misogyny—and the pursuit of these hobbies, especially when combined, could never reasonably be characterised as casual. My mum was not afraid of a drink or two, but she had something of a zero tolerance for misogyny. In terms of gossip, Mum didn't exactly teetotal—she had a lot to say about other people—she just tended to serve it up right-smack-bang in their face. Which is not the best tactic for a not-local to take in a town like Smithton.

I don't want to gripe about a town that a good many people are happily inhabiting as I write (and, I can only assume, as you read), but I couldn't live there as an adult human either. I was struggling enough with the place as an adolescent in 1994, by which time the bubble of blissful ignorance of my childhood had long burst and so, like my mum but for very different reasons, I could barely breathe.

I didn't understand my sexuality on any kind of conscious level, but I understood that there was something *wrong* with me. I'd witnessed Smithton's intergenerational rumour mill in action my whole life, and I'd seen all the ways it could be a very bad place to make a mistake. Forgiveness was rare, and forgetting was rarer still. I understood that it would be catastrophic to *be* a mistake in a small town like that.

We were not alone. Even I could tell a lot of people struggled to flourish in Smithton. Over the years, Mum had taken to mentoring quite a number of outliers. They were usually young people, friends of my siblings who found her to be a kind and open-minded confidante who encouraged them to reject shame and feel pride in who they were, especially the parts of them that were the very reasons they had drifted to the other side of belonging. It was not lost on any of her own children that this openhearted mentoring was not at all the same spirit she applied to parenting.

I remember, when I was really little, Mum had taken to helping an old lady I will call Daisy. This is not her name but it suits her. I don't remember much about Daisy except that I loved her. I was the only kid not yet at school, and so Mum would pay Daisy to clean our house and watch over me every Monday while she went to clean the golf club. Like all empathy-driven endeavours, it wasn't a financially savvy arrangement. Daisy would bring me a small packet of out-of-date and very stale chips—which I loved—and I would follow her around and chat to her the whole time. I always looked forward to seeing Daisy, and then one day she just stopped coming. I was bereft. I was also very confused, but Mum never offered me a reason. In fact, she never spoke of Daisy again, so I assumed it must have been something I said. I said a lot.

Years later I learnt that Daisy had become suddenly ill and died shortly thereafter. I pressed Mum: "Why didn't you tell me?"

"Well," Mum replied. "You were only four years old; I didn't think you were ready to grapple with traumatic things like death and disease."

To this day I don't understand her logic. Death and disease are facts of life, and as such can be explained, even to a child. Or, she could have lied. Kids can swallow a lie! But a sudden disappearance of a friend left completely unexplained? How could any child hope to wrap their head around that without rising distress?

Like most tiny children, I did not collect many correct facts about Daisy. For a start, Daisy was not old. She was younger than I am now. She was impoverished. She was an alcoholic. She drank methylated spirits and she was the mother of her own father's child. But she was so kind and gentle and I loved her, and I love my mum for the dignity she offered the woman I will call Daisy.

In 1994, Mum was providing support to a young woman who, at a guess, was somewhere around my oldest brother Justin's age. I will call this woman Lilly. It was clear, even to my untrained eye, that Lilly had a problem, a very big life problem, and my mum was helping her through it. Every Friday night, she and Mum would talk and talk for hours, drink lots of wine, then sherry, inevitably eschewing dinner for all the cheese and kabana Dad could serve up to them.

I liked Lilly a lot, but she wasn't elderly enough for me to be able to talk to. I had no idea what she and Mum were on about, and if ever I got too close to them, they would suddenly turn the conversation into something benign and Mum would eventually tell me to go away, at which point I understood that I was not welcome.

This was frustrating because I was obsessed with Lilly. I was so drawn to her, and I would watch her like a hawk every time she visited. Before long, I had decided that I wanted to be like Lilly in every way. She wore jeans, a belt and, invariably, a checked shirt tucked in. Her hair was pulled back into a no-nonsense ponytail, and she had a big watch. There was little hope for me to take on her look, given that Mum was in absolute control of what I wore and the cut of my hair. I pestered her for a brief time, but I gave up as Mum deftly ridiculed the idea. Even the simple act of tucking my shirt in was mocked, and as I was as sensitive as any teenager, it felt too dangerous a point to rebel against. And I couldn't wear my hair in a ponytail, because my mullet was not yet long enough.

The only thing I had control over was to try to be like her. I loved the way she sat: she would cross her legs, not knee to knee like most women, but more like a bloke, ankle over her knee. I began to do it myself whenever I'd go over to Nan and Pop's after school. I tried to communicate like her, talk with my hands, jump out of my seat to laugh with my whole body. But, ultimately, I felt my attempts fall pitifully short. Sure, I could sit like a bloke, but I couldn't seem to mimic Lilly's energy. She had the kind of vim and vigour that was at complete odds with the sluggish life force that was animating my body at the time.

It was decades later before I got the clue to the riddle of our opposing levels of intensity—beyond genetics and age, which were clearly a factor. Lilly was coming out of the closet whereas I, with barely a conscious thought behind my decision, had just pulled the closet door shut tight and locked it thrice from the inside. Lilly was experiencing distress, anxiety and grief, all the feelings that come with the blow of a profound rejection. I know those feelings. I would go through my own cocktail of that trifecta of woe seven years later when I came out to my own family. But unlike Lilly, I didn't have someone like my mum to help me navigate the pain of it.

STOP! CIVIL DISOBEDIENCE TIME!

In May of 1994,the same month that Nelson Mandela was sworn in, Tasmanian gay men began turning themselves in to the police with details of their illegal sexual activity. They were drawing from a tactic pioneered by Sydney gay activists in the early 1980s as a protest against the raids on gay sex clubs—the idea was to highlight the hypocrisy of the anti-homosexual laws and try to embarrass both the federal and state governments into either enforcing or repealing the laws.

The potential twenty-one-year jail sentence was clearly laid out in the criminal code, but it was not the risk of serving time that made the Tasmanian gay law reformers so heroic, it was the risk of the outright and often hostile withdrawal of love and safety from the communities into which they had been born. Coming out often meant facing unmitigated rejection from their families, or harsh ultimatums, such as being sworn to secrecy, committing to conversion therapy or, at best, getting themselves a one-way ticket to the mainland. In the unlikely event that their family did stand behind them without any qualms or conditions, it often meant the whole unit would be subjected to a merciless community shaming.

Fortunately, as testament to the prolonged bravery of the activists and their supporters, public opinion in Tasmania was starting to shift in 1994in favour of gay law reform. But if there was anybody in my world who supported the reform, they didn't speak up within my earshot. Ever. Not even Lilly or Mum.

At school, a pamphlet began to circulate promoting the "Say No to Sodomy" campaign and was met with the general attitude of "As if we needed to be asked!" Although it didn't seem to galvanise the anti-gay sentiment amongst my peers, it did encourage an uptick in general expressions of homophobia—ranging from the "playful" to more blatantly horrific and violent rhetoric. I made my own contribution by telling my story about the enema in a way that downplayed my own humiliation and emphasised the supreme grossness of all things butt-related. I knew what I was doing.

In June the "Say No to Sodomy" rally was held at the Burnie Civic Centre. If I ever knew anything about it, I don't remember, but apparently it drew a crowd of about seven hundred people. As something of a veteran of touring in regional Australia, I can report that this is a massive turnout, especially when the only talent were the not especially charismatic homophobes of the likes of George Brookes and Chris Miles. The reasons they, and other speakers, gave as reasons for saying "no to sodomy" at the rally were similar to those outlined in the pamphlet: the real gay agenda being the complete removal of the legal age of consent, which is the classic tactic you should now be very familiar with: equating homosexuality with paedophilia.

It is perhaps not surprising, then, that when the Sydney Mardi Gras Parade hit Tasmanian television screens, it quickly became less of a cause for celebration and more of a destructive and divisive event. The little bits of footage I saw of the parade didn't work to awaken my repressed sexuality, it all looked like a very foreign spectacle, but the debate that it ignited all over Australia was incredibly confusing to me, because until then I had been operating under the assumption that everyone on the mainland was cool with the whole gay thing, and Tasmania was the last refuge of the dumb and stupid homophobe.

But apparently, seeing the Mardi Gras on television had roused a lot of feelings for a lot of people. Naturally, ABC Radio callback was flooded with opinions. My dad listened to talk-back radio, and because he did, so did I. I was by no means a savvy consumer of the media in 1994,but even I understood that talk-back radio was a pretty gross universe. Sure, it offered a platform for isolated voices to connect to a wider world, much like Twitter does now, but really, it was, and is, just like Twitter, used far more consistently as a way to elevate and disseminate toxic and hateful ideas. Because, for some baffling reason that can only be explained as an evolutionary backward step, we human beings just love, love, love to fling and eat our own shit in the name of entertainment.

This was most likely the time that all the classic homophobic catchphrases were burnt into my easy access lexicon. They included "Flaunting their lifestyle," the infamous "[insert pejorative term] gay agenda" and the ubiquitous and, to my mind, most destructive defence of homophobia in the history of the English language, "Think of the children!"

The barrage of negative "talk-back" included this gem from a federal minister, Wilson Tuckey, who told ABC Radio's *AM* program with all the pizzazz of the Tasmanian Criminal Code: "I just think it's an outrageous situation that the ABC should select this time to promote a Mardi Gras which is out encouraging people, basically supporting something that is an unnatural act. I don't want to give the children of my electorate the thought that it's all a great idea and their great chance to be on TV is to be homosexual."

STOP! MOTHER TUCKER TIME!

Charles Wilson "Ironbar" Tuckey was a deliberately antagonising and hateful figure in Australian politics. Just so you have the measure of the man that is Tuckey: in 1967 prior to his political career, when he was a thirty-two-year-old hotelier, Wilson Tuckey was convicted of assault and fined fifty dollars. Just so you have the measure of Australia: Wilson Tuckey had beaten an Aboriginal man with a length of cable—an "ironbar," if you will—and on top of his conviction and feeble fine, he continued to be reelected as a federal minister in the Australian Government for thirty years. I don't know why adults don't ever seem to want quality humans doing their bidding in government. Perhaps it's because of our fondness for the flinging and eating of our own shit that pushes us to so recklessly conflate leadership with "entertainment."

STOP! MARDI GRAS TIME!

Closer to home, the talk-back radio homophobic whinge-fest fallout from the broadcast of the Mardi Gras merged with the furious grass-roots backlash in North West Tasmania that had blossomed after the United Nations' Human Rights Committee's unanimous decision that Tasmania's laws breached their international agreement on human rights. Above the fray of talk-back, Tasmania's attorney general at the time, Ron Cornish, had his own take on the ruling:

The law cannot make people sexually pure, but it can restrain sexual perversity. Even if it cannot restrain such perversity, it ought to try. Further, even if it can do nothing else it ought to identify evil for what it is.

In a letter to the *Mercury* newspaper, the religious group HALO asked, "Can the UN prevent God's wrath falling on those who reintroduce the practice of Babylon?" Good question. But it is doubtful that the editorial board of a regional newspaper could hope to answer that question with 100 percent accuracy. The UN's ruling set an important international precedent; but this wasn't the end. We are talking the UN here. They make toothless recommendations all the time.

The decision required that either Tasmania repeal, or the Commonwealth government override, the specific laws. Spoiler alert: The Tasmanian laws were eventually changed. But the process was not swift—three more years—nor was it graceful, or respectful—it involved an even greater slew of hate and bigotry, in high and low places alike. And sadly, the toxic debate was met with a considerable and sharp rise in suicide rates of young gay men, particularly on the North West Coast.

In October, the decision was made by the Tasmanian attorney general that it was not in the public interest to charge all the gay men who had turned themselves in. A decision which pretty much rendered the anti-gay laws about as useful as an infected gallbladder. This was around the same time that Mum, after years of lobbying, finally convinced Dad to put in a request for transfer out of Smithton.

While I'd understood my fear about leaving town very early on in the uprooting process, I didn't feel anything I could honestly call sadness. To be fair, I couldn't identify any of the emotions swirling about me as we sent Ronnie Barker to stay with my grandparents and packed up the house for the big move to Launceston—Tasmania's second largest city a few hours away. Completely stripped of our furniture and the guts of our life, my old home had warped into an alien landscape. My empty bedroom felt like a stranger's shell, and there was nothing left to mark my life save for the loathsome brown carpet and all the mouldy green stains left by the stack of old sandwiches we'd discovered behind my wardrobe. Even the locket I'd invested in had been unceremoniously consumed by its blue crystal jewellery-boxmate.

I was borderline cheerful at the prospect of leaving until the moment I heard the familiar sound of the latch catching on Nan and Pop's garden gate as it sprang shut. That's when it finally occurred to me that I did not know if or when I would ever be drinking tea with them again. I had not known a time without the comfort of their reliable company. The grief hit me like a psychic shovel, and with the shock of it I made an involuntary, sharp, hiccup-adjacent sound. I guessed it was a sob. But it was just one. A little one, a baby. And that was it.

I paused before crossing the road back home and turned back toward Nan and Pop's house. I began scanning it for all of its familiars so I might be able to bring it to mind whenever I needed, and that's when I saw Nan framed by the white sill of the little diamond window by the laundry. I waved, and she waved back to me with one hand. She was holding the other one over her mouth. I could see the cup of her palm and I knew that hidden beneath it was the tissue she'd been using to dab away her tears while I chatted away, telling her all about the next exciting chapter of my very amazing life while we slowly sipped what would be the last cup of tea we would share as neighbours. Of all the wonderful details I stuffed my memory bank with on that last visit, the most precious by far was the sound of Nan's teacup finding the groove in its saucer.[⊗]

1995

By 1995, the damage to the ozone had become dire enough that it could no longer be ignored. Australia was right under the hole and we were getting sunburnt the most, despite all of our diligent *slip-slop-slapping*, so in a rare act of environmental unity, the government banned the use of destructive CFCs. And in geopolitical news, voters all over the world united to elect Blue the newest colour to be added to the M&M mix. Meanwhile the Soviets began their withdrawal from Afghanistan and Osama bin Laden formed Al-Qaeda. In Tasmania, twelve parcels of land were handed back to their rightful Indigenous owners. The Northern Territory became the centre of a national debate about euthanasia, and, not entirely unrelated, I found myself filled with new levels of despair in Launceston.

There are three reasons I can point to as the root causes of my misery in 1995. The first was that I basically failed every subject at school, except one. The second was that I had my first serious dawning that I might be a lesbian. Since 1992, I'd had many not-so-serious dawnings, with which I had always played denial whack-a-mole whenever they popped up. But this time my sexuality breached so thoroughly into my consciousness that I couldn't deny it anymore. Nor could I deny the abject fear it brought with it. The third reason

⊗ *Clink.*

for my misery was the tsunami of social anxiety that crashed over me after moving to an entirely new home, new town and new school. Transition has never been my friend. Although, there was one aspect of my new world order that delighted me: nobody knew who I was.

I'd never been an unknown entity before, because everyone in Smithton knew everything about me before I'd even been born, which was suffocating to say the least. As soon as I arrived in Launceston, I felt a relief I didn't even know I was desperate for. It felt so good that I began to lie for no good reason. It was never about big stuff because I didn't have much of an imagination. I just found it strangely exhilarating to tell the world I'd had Weet-Bix for breakfast when in fact I'd started my day with Vegemite on toast.

Despite my fun new hobby of harvesting deceit, I had a very awful time going to school in Launceston. It was too big and too full of people I'd never met, who all seemed to have swagger, confidence, friends and style. I was still awful at adapting to new environments, still wearing homemade skivvies, and more anxious than ever, so I decided to eat lunch on the toilet until I worked out how to negotiate my new world. In my defence, I didn't eat a lot of lunch, I would mostly perch on the closed toilet seat, hold my sandwich and eavesdrop on the bathroom world of girls, wondering how the hell I could possibly join in.

There was talk about makeup, broken hearts and crushes, all topics I felt hopelessly out of touch with. But the thing that put the most fear into my heart was the way they gossiped about absent friends. I didn't know who they were or who they were talking about, I didn't know a single soul in the whole school. But what I did understand was that they were talking about people they knew and, apparently, were friends with. I could never be part of a group of friends, I thought. I trusted that what people said to me was a true indication of what they thought; but listening to these lunchtime conversations, I saw that there was a whole world that happened out of earshot. When people spoke of a clique, I imagined there was one *click,* one emotional connective mechanism that bound the group to each other. Now, sitting alone on the toilet holding a sandwich, I got my first inkling that friendship groups were a myriad of clickety-clacks of unknowable threads ceaselessly weaving themselves together, all the while threatening expulsion to anybody who dared fray from the group. The complexity was not in the topics but in the way the bathroom diplomacy was conducted. And it was complex. I'm not kidding. I didn't understand half of it. If you were to compare its dynamics with the basic-level chat that apparently happens in men's locker rooms, it's utterly baffling as to why women have been excluded from positions of power for so long.⊗

A few weeks into starting at my new school, I worked out that because nobody knew anything about me, they didn't care to keep tabs on me, so suddenly just being friendly was enough again. Nobody knew I was alone, so I figured I could forgo the toilet-stall lunching and be outside as long as I kept moving with purpose. To the casual observer it would look as if I was on my way to catch up with all my friends somewhere over there. Nobody had to know how profoundly alone I felt and how hopelessly lost I was on my way to nowhere at all.

Smoking helped. That took me out of the school grounds and into the world, where even fewer people cared if I was coming or going. I had started to walk the few miles to school in the morning, as a way of saving my bus fare to put toward the purchasing of cigarettes. After I finished my lunchtime smoke, I would head out further into the world, wandering the streets, exploring the few blocks around the school to kill time. I didn't dawdle. I had to look like I knew what I was doing, because I would frequently pass groups of students sitting in cafés doing that socialising thing that they did. Whatever that was. It was on one of these walks that I discovered the Launceston Art Gallery. I walked past it the first few days, unsure if

⊗ Disclaimer: I do not know what really goes on in the boys' loos, I am just going off of the "locker room talk" defence that men so often use to explain away the horrific speech of their "bros." If that's anything to go by, then it is dim-witted nonsense in comparison to the high-stakes diplomacy that gets negotiated by most adolescent girls in bathrooms across the globe.

I was allowed to go in. Then I walked around it for a few more days, unsure of how I was supposed to get into the place even if I was allowed in. The day I finally got the courage to walk inside my first-ever art gallery, I was met with the closest thing to heaven I could imagine.

It was as quiet as a library, but, unlike books, art needed to live in conditions that suited my constitution wonderfully. The air flowed freely, the lighting was calming, and I could sit alone and not have to pretend to do anything. I was allowed to do what came naturally to me, to sit quietly and observe. The collection was mostly made up of colonial art, which suited me fine, as it sparked my curiosity about Tasmanian history, a topic I soon realised I knew very little about. Each time I went, I would collect questions and then later go to the library to try and find the answers.[⊛]

Much as they had done the year before, my grades suffered. My anxiety no doubt played a role, but my choice of subjects was also a fault line. It was probably a mistake to enroll in a subject called "athlete development" in year twelve. But in my defence, I was very overwhelmed by the rupture of moving from Smithton, so when the Launceston College careers counsellor said I should absolutely take the subject, citing my "exceptional golfing abilities" as a reason, I agreed. In his defence, he still gave far better career advice than his Smithton equivalent, who'd advised me to never become an electrician and just left it at that.

And thus, in my final year of school, I spent three hours a week focusing on my golfing career in an attempt to develop athletically. My game didn't improve at all, but I did learn a terrible lot about how terrible a game golf was, especially for a teenage girl in the mid-1990s. If you want your daughter to learn about her place in the world, I would highly recommend you steer her toward that wonderful game. To boil it down to its bare essentials, golf is a game of considerable skill, elitism, white supremacy and sexism all wrapped

[⊛] What kind of creature would I have become had I had a smartphone in 1995?

up in a genteel walk, and I'm so grateful that I had the opportunity to learn, so early in life, that having a decent level of skill means fuck-all in life if you're a girl, and especially so if you're of the fat and poor variety.[⊗]

I didn't really need to be formally educated about all this, I'd had more than enough practical experience to understand that golf was not riddled with intentional intersectionality. At the Smithton Country Club, women couldn't join as members—we were "associates," which meant that we could only play on weekends if we teed off early enough so as not to interrupt the men's competition. Whenever Hamish won a competition, he would be awarded prizes designed to encourage him to play more golf, like new golf balls or a fluffy shark wood cover, whereas I would only ever win loot for my dowry. My very impressive collection of homemaker paraphernalia is still sitting under my parents' house collecting dust, full of crockery, crystal and a clock made out of Huon pine carved into the shape of Tasmania. The only useful thing I ever won was a vase so ugly that Mum still uses it to keep the toilet brush in.

The main assessment criterion for athlete development was to organise sponsorship for myself. I was to do this by approaching a local business to ask them if they wanted to buy me a tracksuit, so I could embroider their company logo on it as big as they wanted. After one rejection, from an accounting firm my cousin worked for, I gave up. I also found the whole enterprise ridiculous. I played golf, and golfers were supposed to wear smart casuals, so tracksuits were entirely inappropriate. However you would like to name the reason— laziness or belligerent logic—the result remains that I thoroughly failed athlete development.

At the time, it felt absurd that I could be the best player in the Tasmanian Junior Girls golf team but still fail golf because I couldn't charm a businessman into buying me a tracksuit. These days, I can

---

[⊗] It wasn't until later that I learned how being white meant fucking all of the privilege.

see how right it was to fail me. You need to attract sponsorship if you're going to make it in sport. And if you're a woman, you have to be attractive to attract sponsorship.

The one subject I did well in during my year at Launceston College was art, but let's face it, most brooding teenagers with a penchant for internalised morbidity do well at art. There was very little in the way of formal lessons in art class; you were just encouraged to turn up and create whatever art floated your idea boat. If there were any class discussions, they were very loose occasions, with everyone sitting around drinking instant coffee and talking about stuff that went so far over my head I have no hope of guessing what they were on about now. The thing that struck me was the way in which the students drove the conversations to the point of being equal to the teachers, who seemed very happy to sit back and be on a first-name basis with their students. It was a very disorientating power dynamic for me, not a scenario I had rehearsed or anticipated, so naturally I didn't participate at all beyond holding a cup of coffee and watching everyone, creepy-like.

According to my anthropological efforts during these "lessons," I worked out that there were two types of people who gravitated toward being arty: there were the quiet, intense, off-kilter kinds, and the more flamboyant, outrageous types. I belonged to the former, but I was fascinated by the latter, drawn to their dramatic performance of life and the often over-the-top quality of their animation— because I had no idea what made them tick.

There was one guy in particular I took to watching rather intensely for a while; an untrained eye might have thought I had a crush on him, but it was closer to revulsion that drew my scrutiny. I will call him Greg. Greg was loud, petulant and aggressively right in any argument. He had long hair that would hang over his face, I assume so he could sweep it back for dramatic effect. He was also incredibly sensitive, and not in the "that flower is so beautiful I might just cry" kind of way; it was the "Today is Wednesday" flavour of sensitivity. Reacting to facts like they were personal insults is just not something I had any chance of wrapping my head around.

My fascination with Greg ended abruptly the moment I engaged him directly with a fact that he returned with a lot of feelings. It happened during an instant coffee session which had been unfolding as usual, a handful of students talking way above their pay grade with the rest of us sidelined as either witnesses or, in my case, a totally confused and utterly disengaged bystander. Then things took a turn when the conversation moved to the topic of homosexuality, and without my meaning it to, my attention snapped into sharp focus.

I don't want to waste your time by rehashing a conversation had by a bunch of ill-informed teenagers, most of whom were probably on the cusp of becoming hobby socialists, so I will cut through the crap and give you the broader context. The Tasmanian Government had just banned a bunch of gay and lesbian films that had been set to be screened at a film festival, explicitly identifying the anti-gay laws as the justification for the censorship. It could be argued—successfully, in my humble opinion—that the film festival would have gone completely under the radar had it not happened in the middle of the rabid conservative backlash brought on by the UN taking on the *Toonen v. Australia* case.

The Tasmanian Government's act of cowardly retributive censorship played only a small part in the class conversation, but I bring it up because it was the part when I happened to join in. Most of the conversation had centred on just how supremely stupid and ignorant people from the North West Coast were. I hadn't taken offence to this assessment of me and my people. I felt only shame, and not the kind of shame that makes you want to react and push back, but the kind that makes you want to pretend you are someone else. Fortunately, this was something I was well practiced in doing.

But there was still a part of me that wanted to join in the conversation, just to prove that I wasn't the same as the people they were hating on; but as soon as I felt I had something relevant to say, the conversation had already moved on twice over. It felt like I was trying to join a jump rope routine in cement boots. So, naturally, I tried to engage in the only way I knew how: by saying something funny. I had observed the group dynamics closely enough by then to be able to guess at how best to land a laugh. I waited for the first lull in conversation, which happened when talk turned to the government's censorship of the film festival, and then I pounced in to share the only relevant facts I had on the matter: "I've only been to the cinema twice in my life," I deadpanned: "*Milo and Otis* and *Crocodile Dundee Two*." This was not strictly true; I had also seen *Bedknobs and Broomsticks* but I didn't want to overwhelm them with the literal tragicomedy of my life. I was right to hold back, because everybody laughed anyway and I felt good.

I used to think it was just the facts that made this a funny thing to say, but that's because I had no idea how to see the context of me in any given situation. Now I know that facts don't do much on their own; the thing that carried the funny over the line was the jarring effect that happens when a person who nobody has registered as being in the room suddenly speaks up and says something borderline random. As far as garnering a laugh, it's a very reliable technique. I highly recommend it.

My mistake was not what I had said, but when I had said it. For someone who watched conversations as intently as I did, I was still a poor reader of the room, because what I had thought was a lull in conversation turned out to be a dramatic pause in the middle of one of Greg's impassioned speeches. I might as well have shot his favourite Wednesday in the face.

"Do you think this is funny?" he asked angrily, before the laughter even had time to run its course. All eyes were on me and so naturally I lost the ability to speak, it was all I could do to shake my head and look at the ground, which was not the answer Greg was prepared for, but that didn't matter; he launched his counterargument as if I had said, *Yes! It is the funniest thing I have ever heard!* I mean, I did think it was pretty funny, but I kept my eyes to the ground as he lectured me, for the benefit of all witnesses, on just how wrong I was to laugh at the gays. His brother was gay, Greg railed, his life is hell, Greg wailed, his rights have been trampled on, Greg cried. He was like a white woman in 2020. I wanted him to stop yelling at me, my body was burning, my ears were drumming. I wanted to rock back and forth in my chair but I didn't dare, I was already on the cusp of total humiliation. Greg's soliloquy droned on, but I could no longer turn the sounds he made into sense because my head suddenly filled with a fact I didn't want to believe and couldn't say out loud, even if I had known how to speak: *I am gay. I am gay. I am gay. I am gay. I am gay.*

I left class and did not go to my next one; instead I walked all the way home. I walked faster than my fitness levels would usually accommodate, hoping beyond hope I could outpace the burning shame I felt. I knew I couldn't take it home with me. Mum and Dad were already struggling enough with the move to Launceston, so I couldn't imagine any scenario where it would be appropriate to add to their stress by bringing any of my stuff into the conversation. Not even if I made it funny. All I knew was that I was gay, and as badly as I didn't even want to know that much, I couldn't banish it anymore. I chose not to think about it and just held it in my head like a hot potato, which is a terrible metaphor for a terrible feeling.

Halfway through the first term, I was given my own corner of one of the painting studios, which gave me somewhere to hide from everyone, which I was very grateful for. And I began spending much of my final year at school sitting in a darkened studio producing muddy compositions filled with tortured figures. I was a terrible artist, but I did have a terrific talent for spinning interpretive significance to explain my lack of actual skill. In other words, I was a budding conceptual bullshit artist. Even as I did harbour a half-formed wish to be an artist, if I had paid any attention to my own mind, it would have been clear that it was the theory and history of art that appealed to me, more than the physical practice. So, when we were given our one written assignment for the term, I dropped everything else and devoted all of my energies to it.

We could write about anything we wanted pertaining to the history of art. Ordinarily this kind of "anything you want" assignment would fill me with a paralytic dread, but a purpose came to mind as soon as the class had been issued the assignment. And while most everyone else tossed it aside and focused, rightfully, on the *practice* of the subject at hand, that is to say "art," I threw myself headlong into my magnum opus. I was going to map the evolution of the depiction of the human body in Western art. Ambitious? Very much so, yes. It makes me laugh to think of how confident I was that, despite being a seventeen-year-old with severely limited life experience and woefully poor research skills, I could absolutely sort out the whole Western history of human self-representation.

The three little books I stole from the Smithton High School library served as my starting point. One was on the concepts of modern art, one was specifically on Cubism, and the third, rather uselessly for this project, was about Fauvism. If you don't know what I am talking about when I say things like "Fauvism," don't worry! The history of art tends to play out over most people's heads. I believe it is designed that way so that elite wankers can spin their superiority complexes into something measurable, and hopefully (for them only) marketable. But to catch you up . . . Fauvism is what you get if you take Post-Impressionism and put it on Expressionist steroids through a Technicolor lens. And that sentence is what you get when you have dabbled in enough wank to get by, but not enough to participate elegantly.

From what I could understand, modern art was the thing that smashed "realistic" depictions into smithereens, distorting the human body into a million different directions until it disappeared altogether. I was most interested in modern art, but I felt I should make an effort to understand what came before it, so I could understand what exactly was revolutionary about it. So, I began to work my way backward from the twentieth century, reverse-leapfrogging from one art movement to the prior one all the way back to the Ancient Greeks, because that's as far back as our myopic canon can shoot.

I had never worked so fervently and passionately on anything, and yet, again, I barely raised my head above the pulpit of a passing grade. Throughout my magnum opus were angry red lines struck through every time I had written "figurative art," which was a lot, as it was the central theme. It was struck through with red because I had spelt "figurative art" incorrectly every time as "figural." Yes, it would appear that I had made up an entirely new word, and I was appropriately embarrassed by that oversight, but I still couldn't understand why that meant my assignment was only worth a C-plus. So, I plucked up all the courage that I had, and borrowed against a future amount, and approached my teacher to ask what I had done so wrong. Surely my making up an entirely new word is not outside of the boundaries for art history (*see* Fauvism).

My teacher was not exactly dismissive, but he was firm in his belief that incorrect spelling showed a poor grasp on the subject matter. I begged to differ. He responded by telling me it was not the main issue, and complained that what I had turned in was barely more than a list of facts, before adding that having encyclopaedic knowledge about a subject was not the same as creatively engaging with a concept. He told me he was more interested in hearing me talk about the way that art made me feel. I had never been more excited by anything than I had been about compiling that list of facts, and I told my teacher as much. He invalidated this idea so confidently that my own certainty completely crumbled.

I felt ashamed that I hadn't understood what had been expected of me, and even more ashamed by the fact that art on its own apparently didn't make me "feel" anything. I understood that art made other people feel things, and I thought that if I could understand what it was that made the feeling happen then I would be able to have the feelings too. I could join in. I continued my lunchtime visits to the gallery, but I stopped asking the usual questions, I stopped trying to contextualise the paintings within broader histories and just stared at them, trying my best to feel something, hoping my hardest to be filled with some kind of emotional resonance. The closest I got was feeling frustrated by my lack of appropriate feelings.

My next assignment was to write about one piece of work. Any piece of art that I wished. Again, such an open-ended question should have terrified me, but I did not hesitate. I chose the painting that adorned the cover of my book about Cubism and which had been a source of intrigue ever since I stole it, probably because it was that book's only colour reproduction: Pablo Picasso's *Les Demoiselles d'Avignon*. It was both a good and bad decision. Bad in that *Les Demoiselles d'Avignon* was not a title I could spell correctly with any kind of consistency. Good in that there were a lot of books about Picasso in the library. Don't worry if you don't know the work itself. No shame there. To give you a nutshell of an idea, it depicts five nude women in various states of sharply angled distortions standing in front of a bowl of angry, too dangerous to ingest, fruit. Painted around 1906, it shattered both the beauty and pictorial norms of the day and is the work most often cited as the beginning of modern art, which, if you are unclear on that as a concept, is the art that tends to look like your kid could do it, but your kid couldn't do it and your kid didn't do it, so it's probably best if you let go of that cliché and just think about how it makes you feel.

As a way of combating my apparent void of appropriate human response mechanisms, I decided to co-opt the way that other people felt about Picasso's "seminal masterpiece." I found everything I could that had been written about it, then I split the information into two parts: facts and feelings. I then took the latter and synthesised the sometimes conflicting, often pretentious and always, to me anyway, nonsensical ways that other people described their emotional responses. Then I culled it down to those that made the most sense to me, feelings I could at least imagine having, casting aside all erotic readings and every phallic reference, and there were a hell of a lot of them. I then took my co-opted feelings about the painting—the dynamic, the fervent and so on—and reworded them—the energetic, the impassioned, etc.—so that they almost made sense to me, and then I hung these feelings onto the sequence of facts I'd chosen to best tell the story of *Les Demoiselles d'Avignon*. I got an A, and I barely even looked at the painting itself. Which is good, because, to share some genuine feelings of my own, I fucking hate that painting with a passion. More on that later.

My one and only A of the year had very little effect on my overall performance, and the real reason I managed to scrape through my last year in school with a passing grade was because of a medical certificate. During the appointment I'd told the doctor I'd been feeling unnaturally tired, which she took at face value and then filled in the appropriate paperwork excusing me from having to sit my final exams. I felt like a fraud, as if I had cheated my way out of at least trying to do my worst.

It took another twenty years to get the diagnosis of autism that would explain most of my struggle and dissolve nearly all of my shame about it. Given that girls on the autism spectrum were criminally underdiagnosed at the time (and continue to be), it would be too much to expect of a general practitioner to have succeeded where most specialists failed, but if only she had asked me a few more questions, or if only I'd thought to tell her how distressed and isolated I had felt, then I might've been diagnosed with depression, maybe even anxiety, which would have gone a long way to helping me understand that I wasn't lazy, obstinate or deficient. But instead, I was told I had a virus and that I should rest up and then get on with "normal" life. Despite my woeful results, I did manage to learn one incredibly valuable lesson in my final year at school, and that was just how easy it was for a girl like me to slip through the cracks unnoticed. And because I am who I am, that was neither good nor bad; it was just a fact.

STOP! HIGH COURT TIME!

The banning of the twelve films that were to be screened as part of Tasmania's first Queer Film and Video Festival were mostly documentaries or features about lesbians. Even though Sections 122 and 123 of the criminal code did not technically include acts of lesbian sex, the Tasmanian attorney general, Roy Cornish, cited them as justification for this act of censorship, saying "certain sorts of conduct are not acceptable in Tasmania. These films all relate to homosexual and lesbian lifestyles, and therefore after careful consideration it was decided we wouldn't give that exemption."

As all twelve films screened at festivals across the rest of Australia, it was not a good look for Cornish. In fact, his argument served to undermine the government's claim that the laws were not a threat, due to their lack of enforcement. In November 1995, this opened the doors to activists Nick Toonen (our same friend from *Toonen v. Australia*) and Rodney Croome, who lodged a new case against the Tasmanian Government in the High Court of Australia on behalf of the TGLRG, arguing that Sections 122 and 123 of the Tasmanian Criminal Code were inconsistent with the Federal Human Rights (Sexual Conduct) Act (1994) and thereby invalid in Tasmania.

The High Court recognised that even if the two provisions were not enforced, they existed as a constant threat, overshadowing the lives of gay men in Tasmania. This decision meant that the High Court now had the authority to determine whether or not the Tasmanian laws were invalidated by the overarching federal laws. The end was nigh.

1996

In 1996, high school was over and so was Charles and Diana's marriage. The Spice Girls introduced the world to "zigga, zig ah," children everywhere shed inconsolable tears when they let their Tamagotchis die, and the 1996 Atlanta Olympics hosted a bombing by an anti-abortion, anti-homosexual domestic terrorist—but an innocent security guard who lived at home with his mum was incorrectly dubbed the culprit. Speaking of innocent people living at home with their mum, Hamish organised a job interview for me at a local supermarket, and so marked my grand entry into the world of underemployment. 1996 was also the year I learnt about workers' compensation and, funnily enough, unemployment.

I arrived to the job interview wearing a chambray shirt tucked into an elastic-waisted pair of green and blue striped trousers. Although I should be grateful that Mum was still bothering to make my clothes and indeed that the stripe was vertical, I still felt a bit self-conscious about turning up to a job interview looking like I was ready for bed.

David, who, according to his name badge, was the store manager, gave me the job almost immediately, and while I'd love to have you believe I nailed the interview, I think it's more likely that David was not a particularly astute hirer.

"How would you describe your work ethic?" asked David.

"Good," I mumbled, and elaborated no further.

I didn't realise I was supposed to at least try and be charming, but even if I'd known I doubt I would've been able to turn it on. Since moving to Launceston I'd been faced with so many new situations that I'd lost the ability to reliably string fully-formed sentences together, and on top of that, I was finding it nearly impossible to separate my teeth on the rare occasions that I could speak. Luckily David took me at my—one—word and gave me a job in the delicatessen.

Working in a supermarket deli was never going to be a great job for a fat tomboy with a queasy stomach and a sensitivity to sound and light, given the white dress I had to squeeze into, the cold meats I had to handle, and all the hard surfaces that sound and light bounced off all over the place. But I tried. I was punctual, and I worked steadily if I knew what I was supposed to be doing. I served customers when they approached the counter and I cleaned up any mess if it was obvious enough. I was even happy to clean the fish cabinet out at the end of the day, and by "happy" I mean I tolerated it and managed not to vomit. By the same token, I never approached a task I hadn't been introduced to, and I didn't always notice when the shaved ham was at dangerously low levels or the coleslaw was about to turn bad.[*] The worst of my skill deficits, however, was that I had no idea that I might need to hurry.

Jodie, the head of the delicatessen, seemed to take an instant disliking to me. And I can understand why. No doubt she was under a lot of pressure managing people, budgets and cold cuts, and so she didn't

[*] pro tip: Coleslaw is always about to turn bad, because it is nothing but vomit larvae.

have time to babysit a slow-moving virtual mute with absolutely no initiative. And so, I very quickly became a thorn in Jodie's side. It drove her to distraction that if I didn't know what I was supposed to be doing, I'd stand uselessly until someone enlightened me. At the time I felt very confused by Jodie's clear frustration with me. As my boss, I thought, surely it was her job to boss. She wrongly assumed I would both notice and care about dwindling ham. I do understand her frustration, I really do: the delicatessen was her life, after all, and the source of her personal pride, whereas for me it was merely a hiatus in a much bigger hiatus, because the end of school had pressed pause on my life and nobody had told me what to do next.

Falling down is rarely a dignified thing, and there is absolutely nothing I can do to glamourise this particular tumble. For a start, I was wearing a white dress and a paper hat, not to mention carrying a tray of coleslaw. I'd been working in the delicatessen for two weeks when the accident happened. I had just been told off by Jodie in front of numerous customers for being too slow and was trotting out to the back when I stepped in a hot pool of liquified chicken fat. My foot immediately responded to the laws of slippery surface physics and shot out sideways while the rest of me dutifully obeyed the laws of gravity and took the fastest route down. Caught at the crossroads of my conflicting momentums, my right knee snapped.

The only way to rectify such an undignified fall was to stand up and continue with what I was doing. Sadly, getting up wasn't a fluid manoeuvre I could achieve, but I did manage to resume an upright stance of sorts just as my colleagues, drawn by the clanking of the coleslaw tray, rounded the corner. Other than the severely displaced salad, I presented them with a reasonably dignified scene—that is, until I tried to walk and my knee, which was already swelling, rotated unnaturally and then buckled. With agony as my new overlord, I returned to the floor in a hurry, oblivious to my dignity or otherwise.

I don't know who was more relieved after my accident—Jodie or me. She didn't have to continually guide me through all my obvious duties, and I got the rest I had been needing for years. It seems strange to call it a restful time, given that I had to undergo another total knee reconstruction and months of rehabilitation, all the while living at home with Mum, who was beyond frustrated that her youngest could not be thrown out of the nest so she could also get the rest she'd been needing for years.

I understood I was a burden, but I didn't know how to go about lightening the load that was me. I couldn't drive, and I struggled to read the bus timetable and coordinate myself to be at the stop in time, even though it was right outside our house, but I didn't want to ask my parents for help. I didn't want to be so dependent. So, as soon as I was able, I began to walk the five kilometres to my physio sessions. Despite the inevitable exhaustion, blisters and chafe that going so far on crutches gave me, I found enormous peace in the endeavour. I knew where I was going, I knew why I was going, and the rhythm I made with my step and sticks put me into something of a meditative state. Pain aside, the sessions themselves were quite pleasant. I was praised for trying as hard as I could and I saw steady, tangible results for my efforts, and that was vastly better than anything I had experienced in school.

Since the return trip wasn't time-sensitive, I didn't have to walk home. All I had to do was make my way to the nearest bus stop and wait for the next bus home. I didn't have to worry about the timetable, just the number of the bus I needed to catch. Being that I was relying on a public transport system that was not servicing New York or London, I sometimes had to wait up to an hour at the bus stop but I didn't see this as a waste of my time, nor did I find it boring, because I was out in the world, doing a thing I almost knew how to do, and—old people and pregnant ladies depending—I could just sit still and watch the world around me while I waited for my own life to begin.

I didn't have the first idea about what I wanted to do. All I knew was that I wouldn't know what to do about it even if I did have a clue. It was the question that everyone would ask me: *What are you going to do next? What do you want to do with your life? What is your plan?* Sometimes the question was taken out of the equation and I was battered with demands: *Buck up. Look lively. You need to be a go-getter. Don't let life pass you by.* Little did I know that letting life pass me by was the very thing I was suited to doing in 1996.

My sister's boyfriend at the time was apparently so appalled by my inability to go-get that he lent me his entire Tony Robbins cassette collection, clearly hoping that I could be persuaded to awaken some kind of giant that was apparently hiding somewhere inside of my person. I was immediately sceptical. Jessica's boyfriend was all the things in life I was not: he was a grown-up man with a private school education, a car and a driver's licence and a job as an executive in a large international corporation, and he was straight and in a relationship. I couldn't begin to imagine what kind of life advice could possibly apply to both him and me, apart from "Listen to Jessica." But I swept my doubts aside and accepted his tapes graciously and made my way down to my room to get started on finding out what I wanted and how to get it, or, at the very least, to find out how to want what the world wanted me to want.

If you've gleaned anything about me at all through reading this memoir, it should be that I am not a particularly lighthearted creature. Which should make my response to Tony Robbins, the king chin of motivational thinking, all the more incredible: I laughed from beginning to end. And then I listened again and laughed even more. And then I memorised it. It was the imagery it triggered in my head that made it so funny to me. I imagined how all the people who had listened to his tapes might have imagined themselves piloting jet helicopters, just like him, and then speaking to stadiums full of people who used to be just like them ten years earlier. Then, not being able to stop myself, I took it to its logical conclusion: emptying out the stadiums because everybody was either a motivational speaker or lying dead in their jet helicopters after the inevitable mass crash that happened after they had all foolishly filled the sky beyond its limits, crashing into each other, spinning out of control and then tumbling down in a smoky spiral before landing into the giant midden of twisted metal corpses that looked like a pile of spider crabs during metamorphosis.

This is not to say I didn't try to take the whole thing seriously. The issue was that I couldn't even manage to do the first thing Tony asked of me: imagine my future. Anytime I tried this seemingly simple task, all I could conjure was a dark void. It wasn't necessarily bad, it was just empty. I loved thinking about history, but experience had taught me that even with hindsight, the past is impossible to untangle with any kind of clarity, so it didn't make any sense to presume I could imagine any kind of reliable future. I did try, though. But as hard as I tried, I couldn't fill it with anything. Not a hope, not a dream, not even a jet helicopter. It's little wonder my mind would distract itself with literally translating everything Tony Robbins said into catastrophic ridiculousness.

My enthusiastic mockery of Tony Robbins was not my only hobby that year; I also continued my investigations into "figural" depictions in Western art. The first thing I did was create my own timeline from antiquity to the present. It was a long and laborious process, which felt to me like independent research but was essentially me plagiarising E. H. Gombrich's, *The Story of Art* and turning it into an illustrated poster. If anyone had seen my timeline, filled with my minuscule handwriting, visual shorthand and personal hieroglyphics, I doubt they would have seen the history of art before they saw the mad scrawlings of a mass murderer. But it was my first real attempt to externally manifest something that I could see inside my head. And as such, it was doomed for failure.

At the beginning of 1996 we had moved out of the rental home and into a new house, which Mum and Dad still live in to this day. This might have been another unbearable disruption for me had it not meant the return of Ronnie Barker into my life. I'd missed the weight of him on my feet at night, and I was thankful for his extra warmth in my new bedroom, an uninsulated little nook under the new house. With its own small bathroom, my little room gave me a sense of independence that I really had no right to feel, but I did anyway, because when I was alone in my room, I did not feel lonely.

The peace and solitude I carved out under the house was occasionally shattered when Mum would stomp on the kitchen floor above my room. There was a distinct language to it. Sometimes it would be a few playful stomps in the morning because she thought it was time I was awake, or she wanted to have a cuppa and a chat. Other times it was accompanied by yelling, which meant she could be angry at the world, Dad or myself. When it was all three at once, there was no ignoring the lead foot tap-and-thump dance as it happened above me, so I would tear myself away from my thinking and do whatever I needed to placate the storm.

One day, after a particularly intense stomp session, I poked my head in through the back door, ready for some kind of rage display, and was surprised to find my mum standing in front of the television in a state of open-mouthed shock. When she saw me, she beckoned me over and pulled me into her arms. "Have you seen this?" she said, pointing to the television. I was about to say that unless she had swapped the TV with an exact replica since yesterday then, yes, I had seen "this" when my eye and mind finally caught the drift of the breaking news coverage of what would become known as the Port Arthur Massacre.

If you are curious about the specifics of this event, you should look it up. I don't really want to porn it out for you here. I honestly find it quite painful to think about. In 1996,however, I thought about it a lot, and my thinking was as painless as it was obsessive. I thought about the young, golden-haired gunman, Martin Bryant, and the twenty-three people wounded as much as I did the thirty-five people who were killed. I mapped the two-day sequence of the horrific events over and over again in my head, and I learnt everything there was to know about Port Arthur, from its establishment as a penal colony to the strange and morbid tourist attraction it had become. Even if I hadn't been so eager to absorb all there was to know about the massacre, it would have been impossible to avoid it entirely. For almost a year, it completely saturated all the television and radio news broadcasts, knocking the gay rights debate completely out of the public's consciousness.

It was a period of collective national grieving. I didn't understand it, and this fact made me worry that there might be something wrong with me. The news was always filled with people dying horribly for no reason, and yet nobody in my world seemed to care enough to talk about any of those; I couldn't understand why this was any different. Of course, I could understand why people who had a direct connection with one of the slain might be grief-stricken, and I was sad for them, but everybody in the whole world seemed to be struck as if they'd had the gun pointed at them. Everybody, that is, except for me. I was watching the news with Mum and Dad and I must have made my lack of understanding known somehow, because Mum turned to me and said, "I thought you were kind but you're not. Imagine if you'd lost me and your father like that?" To which I answered, very matter-of-fact, "But I didn't." Mum shook her head in disbelief and turned back to the news. I got up and went to my room and turned back to my thinking.

In less than two weeks after the massacre, the Australian Government changed the nation's gun laws, placing strict control over the sale of semiautomatic and fully automatic firearms. A fact that should make any sane American insanely jealous.[⊗] The National Firearms Agreement included an amnesty period and a gun buyback program which ran from October 1996 through September 1997 and retrieved 650,000 guns. I became fascinated by the images of guns being destroyed by the truckload playing out on the news during that time. The sight reminded me of the imaginary metal jumble of the jet helicopters that I'd created when listening to that one-man band of chin-heavy motivation, Tony Robbins.

I thought about how I'd laughed at the image of all those poor imaginary people crashing their helicopters, and as my eyes scanned the piles of mangled guns, I began to join them up, making them into stick figures, then spindly robots. It wasn't long before I could see the horror of thirty-five dead bodies lying on top of twenty-three very frightened, badly wounded people in that pile of guns. My mind

---

[⊗] And as somebody who has had to heal themselves from the collateral damage of the toxic Tasmanian gay law reform debate that was unnecessarily exacerbated and prolonged by divisive political game-playing at the federal level, I too am jealous at how fast my government is able to change things when they want to.

turned the dead and wounded into people I knew, their flesh twisted and mangled, no longer filled with life, and therefore no longer part of mine. I had finally learnt how to do something that comes naturally to everybody else: only care about people who look like you. I was sickened. It was a horror show in my head that I didn't know how to think away. So, I did my best to not think at all. I have never been able to stomach any on-screen violence ever since, because I have never been able to turn off the idea that everybody feels pain, just like me, no matter what they look like.

Mum began to pick more and more fights with me. They upset me but I did not like arguing, preferring to hide until the rough stuff was over. But she seemed more and more determined that I engage head-on with her. Her complaints about me were no different than they had ever been—I was lazy, I needed to get a life, I needed to make friends, I needed to talk more, I needed to tidy up after myself—the difference was the rising levels of frustration that all of my shortcomings were triggering. It all came to a head one day when I made the mistake of coming upstairs as Mum was aggressively vacuuming the same patch of carpet over and over, while apparently stewing over my failure to be someone better. I tried my best to go unseen as I travelled across the room, but I failed.

I was barely in the room when Mum, without looking up, asked me if I had brought up all the dirty cups from my bedroom. I hadn't, I said. And that was all she needed to round in on me with her very long list of grievances. She would ask questions, but before I could answer she would answer for me: "Of course not," she would spit, still rubbing the same patch of carpet raw with the back-and-forth of the vacuum. The soundscape got painful very quickly, and together with the rapid rising of my own shame I was overwhelmed before I could remove myself. I kicked the vacuum cleaner and then turned to my stunned mother, fists clenched, and screamed with the loudest sound that had ever emerged from my body, "STOP IT. JUST STOP IT. SHUT UP." Over and over again until my voice finally failed me. Then I stormed out the back door. Apparently finding my voice again, I screamed to the general neighbourhood, "MY MOTHER IS A BITCH. SHE IS A TOTAL FUCKING BITCH I HATE HER!"

I was suddenly calm. Exhausted. But calm. Then I was suddenly very frightened. What had I done? I looked back up toward the house and saw Mum come out onto the veranda, grinning from ear to ear. She started to applaud and then she cheered. "Good one, girl! I just wanted you to feel something." I stood there, dumbfounded. My mum wasn't a bitch, she was a total fruit-and-nut bar. I was drained. I couldn't think of anything to say so I just waved, slapped my leg for Ronnie to follow, went back to my room and shut the door behind me. I was no longer upset; if anything, I was relieved to know that I was capable of feeling.

STOP! ELECTION TIME!

As gay law reform inched ever closer in Tasmania, larger forces were assembling through national conservative coalitions that were adopting a U.S. faith-based style of campaign that attempted to galvanize a moral panic about the safety of children and the degradation of the so-called "normal" family. It wasn't enough to meaningfully slow the momentum of the decriminalisation movement, but it did provide an alarming glimpse of the tone to come decades later in the marriage equality debate.

Before the upcoming election of 1996, the Tasmanian premier Ray Groom vowed that he would not govern without his party holding the majority in Parliament. When the progressive Greens party won enough seats that Groom's party was left unable to govern outright, Groom stepped down in what he described as an act of principle, but what I would call an embarrassing display of political petulance. His successor, Tony Rundle, basically said to Greens leader Christine Milne (a long-time gay law reform campaigner), "Let's get this done with as little embarrassment for my boys as possible." Nice.

1997

In 1997 Princess Diana died and Elton John had the number one hit, "Candle in the Wind," while Hanson introduced us to their lyric brilliance with "MMMBop." 1997was also the last year in which another Hanson, the right-wing politician Pauline, was irrelevant to anybody else but her. MMM nope. I miss those days. Britain returned Hong Kong to China, kind of, and the Australian prime minister officially refused to say "sorry" to the Stolen Generation of Indigenous children at a reconciliation convention, kicking off the "history wars" that continue to plague Australia (and elsewhere) to this day. On the home front, I applied to the University of Tasmania in Hobart to study a bachelor of arts, because I was a bachelor who loved art. And on the thirtieth of April, 1997 Ellen DeGeneres came out as a lesbian on her imaginatively titled television show, *Ellen*. It was a very big deal in the world of television, and an even bigger deal in the world of lesbians. However, the shockwaves that it sent through both of those worlds did not reach as far as the north of Tasmania, and made not even a ripple in my life, such as it was. I couldn't even tell you whether *Ellen* was ever aired in Tasmania. I wouldn't have been able to watch it in any case, as Mum didn't like watching American comedies on TV. Sometimes she would blame the accent, other times it was the humour she took issue with, but the thing she hated the most was the canned laughter. "I don't need to be told when to laugh. I'm not a bloody idiot." Personally, as I was a bloody idiot in 1997 I might have appreciated the guidance of a laugh track in my life.

Mum's opinions about television programs were as strong as any other subject, and as such, there was a long list of prohibited content. In addition to American comedies, sex scenes were strictly off-limits. Mum had never allowed us to watch sex scenes on television. Whenever anything appeared on the TV that looked even remotely sex-adjacent, she would be out of her chair and twisting the channel over with the TV pliers quicker than you could say "fake ejaculation." Censorship-wise it was very effective—I was well into my teens before I saw a full boob on TV. But if her goal was to repress her children's curiosity about all things sex, then the pornos that could be found under various beds indicated it was not a great success.

I had watched my first whole sex scene on TV with Nan and Pop next door when I was fourteen. Cool story. I'd wandered over the road after dinner one night, which was a thing I did from time to time, especially during the summer holidays when people were visiting and my own house was full of mayhem. I was always welcomed with open arms, a cup of tea and a toffee, then I would settle into one of their oversized upholstered chairs in the good room and watch whatever they were watching.

This particular night it was *Matlock*—which I'd never seen but it didn't take me long to work out that it was basically *Murder, She Wrote* but with a man. I liked watching crime dramas on TV because, unlike real life, I knew I had the same information as anyone else, and I'd worked out that all the clues to solve the mystery were always there to be found if you looked hard enough, so I was in the habit of watching shows like *Matlock* with a hawk-like intensity.

So, there I sat between my Nan and Pop with a cup of tea on the arm of my chair, chewing a toffee, scanning for clues and making a serious effort to solve the mystery before Matlock did. It was all perfectly aboveboard until it cut from the courtroom to a hotel room, daytime no less, where the main suspect (he didn't do it) was having sex with a woman, who was not his wife—what a twist. He was sitting on a chair and she was straddling his lap, facing him, and jumping up and down and having a good old moan. It was not gratuitous sex by any stretch of the imagination, but, as I had no imagination to stretch, it took a few beats for me to even work out what exactly was happening. As soon as I did, my eyes widened to saucer size, as I took as much of it in as I could before it got turned off.

When it became clear that the scene was going to play out, I stole a quick glance at Pop and found him oblivious to it all, busily brushing biscuit crumbs off his shirt. When I turned to Nan, I was surprised to see that she was watching keenly and tapping her foot as she did. When the scene ended, Nan sighed and said, "Oh well then.

There you go." Pop looked up, confused: "What's that then?" to which Nan responded, "Yes."

By 1997 watching television at all became tenuous because, as my employment status had become negligible, Mum began hounding me to find more gainful employment, and if I wanted to watch TV I had to watch it with Mum, who would rarely wait till the ad break to interrupt a show with a news bulletin that I was lazy. Unfortunately, the hounding did not include any of the practical guidance that I so desperately needed. None of my siblings had any trouble getting jobs or opportunities, but I was missing the piece of my brain that made it possible to walk into a place of business and say, "Hey! Here is my résumé! Gimme a job!" I did walk around the city a few times with a stack of résumés in my bag, but that's as far as I got in the process. Not for a lack of trying, I walked around the literal job block for weeks but didn't make the slightest dent in my résumé stack.

It was during this time of underemployment that I sat down with Dad and filled out my application for a bachelor of arts at the University of Tasmania in Hobart. I swear it was just to get Mum off my back, and not because I knew what I wanted enough to have a vision. If I had, I wouldn't have applied, because I would've remembered that moving to a new city is the sort of thing that makes me want to die earlier. As I waited for my future distress to be determined by the powers that be, I still had to make some kind of effort to get myself gainfully employed.

Scanning the classified section of the local paper, I quickly became aware that there were not a lot of jobs for someone like me anyway. Most required preexisting skills, and those that didn't all insisted that applicants have qualities like "enthusiasm," a "big smile" or "confidence." None of which I'd been blessed with. I supposed I could lie, but I doubted that I could get away with it if I ever got to an interview. I narrowed my options down to two jobs that sat with my personality and skill set: trainee backhoe operator, and fruit picker. I then narrowed my options down even further to jobs that I understood the basic concept of, and applied to become a fruit picker. The wonderful thing about jobs that require a relaxed attitude toward personal safety while paying less than minimum wage is that they tend to bypass formal interview processes. And so, as Ellen came out of the closet, I was picking apples so slowly I couldn't earn a living wage.

It was backbreaking work and I did it six days a week, ten hours a day. I'd get up at 5:00 a.m., and make my way into the city to the backpackers' hostel, where I'd be picked up with the rest of the itinerants and driven to whichever orchard needed our picking services that day. It was monotonous work but I really loved it. I knew what I was supposed to do and I could do it without thinking or talking to anyone around me. The fresh air was heaven and my body appreciated being used excessively. I would get home dusty, calm and exhausted. And to top it all off, I was finally working hard enough by Mum's standards that she was happy for me to eat and sleep on her dime, so we could all pretend I was earning an adequate income.

There were two types of people who were working the orchards with me, the drifters and the travellers. The travellers were young and from all over the world. The drifters were older, lived locally, and all had their stories of struggle—single mums, ex-cons, chronically underemployed. It was a potluck as to which group I would be bussed off with any given morning.

The backpackers all had their stories ready; you could ask them direct questions and their limited English made it feel safe for me to do so. They all assumed I was one of them, because I was their age and I struggled to speak English. Nobody really believed I lived down the road or that this was anything other than an interim job. I was the only person who assumed I was going to be an itinerant farmworker forever, never venturing much further than a few miles from home.

My favourite person I met while picking apples was Mia, and just so you are aware, that is a gross understatement. In her presence it became clear to me why it was called a crush; I lost full use of my lungs. I don't know how other people process their feelings toward a crush, but I did the only thing I knew how to do when I don't understand something: I collected all of the data. Mia was about five foot four. She had a fluid way of moving, as if her joints were all freshly lubricated. Her laugh came deep from within her, and it would shake her whole body. When she spoke to people and they were within arm's reach, she would always make contact, usually with a light touch on the arm. Her skin was the most radiant and smooth I had ever known, her complexion was olive and tanned at that, and not the orange tan you get when you fake it, but the rich deep colour you can only get by being young in the sun. I was both of those things at the time, too, but as I was still diligently *slip, slop, slapping,* I was a mottled mess of piecemeal freckle and alabaster white skin. Mia had only a neat feathering of freckles across her nose and two dark moles on the back of her neck. She wore her curly hair short and pushed it back with a hair band—which was either green, blue or a paisley pattern and never the same one two days in a row. She wore a pair of khaki shorts, hiking boots and a shirt, worn unbuttoned, over a tank top. She didn't change her clothes as often as her headband, but I didn't mind, she smelt like Christmas to me.

When I was in her presence, I would gather every detail I could about Mia so that any time I wasn't, I could take out my mental list and go through each and every detail and build my picture of her inside my mind, making a note of what was missing so that I could collect it the next time we worked together. Had I known how to imagine anything more than just what I could observe, or had I known how to invent a sexualised fantasy of Mia, I am sure I would have. But I didn't understand that I could do that, and even if I had known I wouldn't have been able to, because I didn't have the mind language to be able to construct such a fantasy out of. Apparently, watching my first sex scene with Nan and Pop had been so traumatic that my mind had repressed my capacity to recall the *Matlock* interlude for my own reviewing pleasure.

It happened at the end of a long day, and the crew were all waiting for the bus to pick us up and take us back to town. I was sitting on an overturned tub under an old oak tree at the edge of the car park and, as was my habit, I was eating an apple. I saw her walking toward me from a long way off, but I had no reason to believe that I was her destination. We had only spoken a few times, and, given my monosyllabic contributions to our conversations, I doubted I had made a very positive impression. It was only as she sat down next to me that I could believe it, and as soon as I did, I began to flip hopelessly through all the possible small talk options I could think of. She nodded at the apple I was eating and held her own up for me to see. "You're the only other person who eats the apples. I don't understand why you wouldn't!" she said, biting into what was left of hers. I knew this was the moment I was supposed to talk, and so I did the only thing I knew how to do: I told the truth and then added a "joke." "I am not earning enough to not eat them. These apples taste like money to me." She smiled at that, and perhaps that's what pushed me to add another, unnecessary detail: "I am going to the toilet a lot." I stopped with my confession when I saw that she had stopped chewing and spun her head to look at me. I could tell she was searching my face for clues about how to pick up what I had just put down, and I don't know what my face did, but apparently it indicated that I had made a joke. She laughed and so I took her lead and joined in with a quiet chuckle. The bus had pulled up by then and we both stood up to make our way over. As I gathered my things Mia waited for me, taking another bite of her apple, and said, "I never know when you are joking or not," to which I responded with a shrug and the truth, "Neither do I." She laughed again and flung her arm around my waist, where it stayed as we walked over to the bus together.

The apple season ended, and with it the torture of my unrequited crush. I was both bereft and relieved. I knew Mum would not tolerate my being unemployed for any length of time, so I was uncharacteristically motivated to line something up as soon as possible. Much to my own surprise, I got the very first position I applied for. Sadly, the job ended before it even began. I should never have applied, given the job ad had asked specifically for an enthusiastic and confident self-starter with a passion for sales. I knew very well that I only possessed the very opposite of these qualities, but I sent in an application anyway, because I'm the special type of person who goes for jobs that are advertised on telegraph poles.

Anybody who knew me, and most people who didn't, felt uneasy about my selling knives. And rightly so. It was dangerous enough for someone as clumsy as me to be working with one blade, let alone a whole gaggle of sharp edges. I needed hindsight to tell me what my mum had known from the outset—I'd stumbled into a borderline pyramid scheme, nigh on cult. But at the time, I was determined to grab hold of an opportunity à la Tony Robbins.[*] After I received my induction pack, I set about completing the checklist with a level of determination I'd never shown before. I dipped into my savings and bought the basic knife kit, and made a promise to myself that I would soup it up to the supreme deluxe kit as soon as I was able to, because that's what a winner would do. Then I took the rest of my money into the city and went clothes shopping for the first time in my life.

I had often dreamed of the freedom of buying clothes for myself, but as soon as I stepped inside Myer, I realised my dreams hadn't been comprehensive or realistic projections of actual consumer environments. What began as exhilarated anticipation quickly descended into something dangerously close to panic territory, and I found it impossible to navigate myself out of the hall of mirrors and perfume napalm that is the horror show of every department store's first floor. I must have looked helpless, because nobody who worked there made any effort to help me beyond spraying the occasional waft of toxic mist in my wake.

By the time I managed to wind my way to an exit, I was in such an agitated state it took all of my strength to be able to portray a dignified presence as I stood in front of the doors, waiting for them to part. I don't know how long I'd been trapped inside or how long I had been waiting for the doors to open, but judging by how much I startled when an old man spoke to me, I must have left my earthly body for a considerable amount of time. Crashing back to myself, I looked up at the old man who was now holding my elbow, desperately trying to work out if he was friend or foe, but before I could discern either way he was pushing me gently toward the door, which was being held open by another old man. I couldn't seem to protest,

[*] Speaking of cults . . .

and as I had been trying to leave, I didn't resist being pushed out the door, but it wasn't until he had me in the car park and was crouching down in front of me, holding my hand and telling his friend that I must be "retarded," that I began to piece it together. I had wrongly assumed the door was automatic and he'd wrongly assumed that I'd wandered away from my caregiver. I let my hand slide out of his, smiled as best I could and walked away. It was the first time in my life that I grasped that other people did not witness me the same way that I experienced myself, and it truly frightened me.

If Tony Robbins taught me anything, I couldn't tell you what it was now, but in 1997 I believed he had taught me that it was a sign of strength of character to be able to push through pain to achieve a goal, walking on hot coals and all that shit. So, I returned to the store the next day and got me a corporate outfit. To my mind it was a step down from the outfit I'd worn to pick apples, but a step up from the white dress they'd forced onto me at the delicatessen. I would've worn a suit and men's shoes had the handbook not specified that women had to wear a skirt, and if the woman in the menswear department hadn't so ferociously ushered me toward the escalator up to women's wear.

I did the best I could with what little money I had, but the outfit was still as sad as it was uncomfortable. The A-line skirt looked wrong on me, but it felt worse, because I hate wearing not-pants; and the synthetic fabric gave me so much static electricity that I would get a shocking zap if I even so much as looked sideways at carpet. The white blouse showed the bloodstains too easily, and as slight as the heel was on my closed-toe sandal, the shift upward in my usual vantage point was enough to trigger a sense of vertigo on any occasion it became visually hectic underfoot.

I had completely drained my finances to get my sandaled foot in the knife sales door, but I was assured during my unpaid induction that my future was secure, because everybody on the face of the planet needed new knives. I was sceptical. I didn't think many people could afford to fill the knife-shaped hole in their lives with the ones I was being taught to sell. I'm sure the "petit carver" was worth every cent of the $300 asking price, but I just didn't move in the kind of circles that had that level of disposable income. Nevertheless, I applied myself to learning all about the life-saving benefits of owning knives with three rivets, a full tang and a handle that might've been a spaceship in a past life. After a week of sitting and sweating in my only corporate outfit, I was told I was ready and was sent out to practice my sales pitch on twenty of my closest friends.

I started with my parents, because I literally had no friends. Mum flatly refused to participate. "It's a load of shit," she said, without even humouring me, but Dad cheerfully agreed to hear me out. While I set up the presentation, I gave Dad a folder filled with pictures of the very same things I was arranging on the table, just with better lighting and garnish. He flicked through it and whistled appreciatively. My presentation kit, which was made up of five knives, a pair of scissors, a chopping board, a piece of leather, a tomato and a five-cent piece, cost me three hundred dollars and five cents, plus ongoing tomato costs. I had worked out that I needed to sell about five basic knife sets to recoup my costs. So I knew I had to put the hard sell on Dad, even though I knew he couldn't afford a single knife.

Dad seemed genuinely rapt by my monotonously mumbled presentation, and by the end it was clear he wanted the knives. He sat fondling the "petit chef," still stained with a mix of his tomato and my blood. He looked over at Mum. "They aren't bad you know, Kay. 'They cut tomatoes like butter,'" he said, repeating my jargon. To which Mum responded, without looking up from her ironing, "So do my teeth."

I made my first sale in my second presentation. Delphi Dodds was a jolly pensioner who I'd met while working at the supermarket checkout.⊗ It had only taken one brief encounter for Delphi to join

⊗ You may have clocked that, in our last episode of *Hannah Takes On Casual Employment*, I was recovering from knee surgery and on worker's comp. Well, after my knee healed and I went back to work, they told me I was no longer allowed in the deli department, and repositioned me on the checkouts. Fair call. Then, six months later, they told me I was too vague and no longer allowed in any department. Which, I think, is what you call getting fired. Probably also a fair call.

my ever-growing list of friends who were old people. After that she would always go through my checkout even if there was a long queue, and I always had a long queue on pension day, because: old people.

It had been a few months since I'd seen Delphi, but she didn't hesitate to have me over to her house to talk knives. Despite the vertigo her carpet induced, I was delighted by her cosy home, especially the teapot and selection of biscuits she greeted me with. But I could tell by the decrepit condition of her décor that Delphi was not in the market for the kind of knives I was trying to sell. I persevered anyway because I needed the practice and the cash, and I buried the instinctual horror I felt when talking about a forever guarantee to a pensioner. At the end of my presentation, as usual, I was to use the scissors to cut a five-cent piece in half. This was the real party piece. Even though I'd been told it was illegal to destroy currency, I hacked through the coin nonetheless, because I'd been told that if I was going to sell anything then I had to stick to the script exactly. It always took an ugly amount of effort for me to make the cut, but it must have looked good enough for Delphi. She simply had to have the scissors.

"Are you sure?" I said, completely forgetting my closing-the-deal spiel. "They're very expensive!" I stand by this now, too, twenty-five years later with a comfortable amount of money in the bank; $250 is too steep for scissors, even scissors that could cut through leather. But I couldn't seem to convince Delphi that it was an outrageous price. She was determined to own a pair of these scissors, and she got up excitedly and went to find her chequebook.

I knew that Delphi was not a wealthy woman. She was surviving on a pension, and when I served her at the supermarket she'd count every penny, and would often have to return a few items to be able to meet her weekly grocery budget. I had all the evidence I needed to know that she didn't have the budget for a $250 pair of scissors. But if I had any misgivings, they dissolved when she handed me a cheque for the whole amount written out in her spidery old-person scrawl. I convinced myself that she was just one of those wealthy tight arses who pinched every penny that she met, so I was able to leave her house on a high of success and static electricity.

My third victim was our family friend Marilyn, and she lusted after the "petit carver." I really wanted her to have it too. "I could only afford half of that," she said wistfully, turning the knife over in her hands. I liked Marilyn and so I decided to help her out at the expense of my commission. "I'll tell you what," I said. "I get a fifty percent discount on products. I will buy the knife and you can pay." She gratefully agreed and fronted the $150 I'd need to make the purchase on her behalf.

It was a delightful plan in theory, until I found out about the unfortunate details of my 50 percent discount. The detail being I did not technically get a discount. The deal was that if I were to buy a $300 knife, I would pay 100 percent of that and then get $150 worth of other products. I didn't need to do any math to know that I was operating at a loss, but I still felt obligated to follow through on my promise to Marilyn. This meant that I would need a loan, and as little as I understood about the lending practices of financial institutions, I knew enough to know that I had fuck-all chance of getting a loan, so I explained my situation to Dad and he was happy to help, on the condition that I kept Mum completely out of our deal loop. When Delphi phoned shortly thereafter to cancel her order, I knew I had to quit while I was behind. "My son said I can't afford the scissors," she said, her shame bleeding through the phone to merge with mine. I reassured her that it was OK. And, thus, the last thing I did in the knife business was to tear up the cheque from my only genuine sale.

It took me a week to pluck up my courage to tell Dad that I couldn't pay him back. If he was upset, he didn't show it. When I offered him the tiny chopping board and the solitary steak knife—which was the best that $150 could buy—he told me I should hang onto it, that it was the sort of stuff I'd need when I moved out of home. "You'll have to buy the matching knife on your own dime, though!" he joked. I didn't get it; why would I need to use two knives to eat steak? But I laughed anyway because he did. It wasn't until I put my knife kit under the house with all my useless golf trophies that I put the joke together—I would need two knives because eating steak is something you should do with another person—and now that I understood it, the joke was not nearly as funny as Dad had thought. And that is how I ended 1997 as an unemployed barely adult virgin with a fully stocked dowry and an A-line skirt, living in a tiny room underneath her parents' home. Yet despite being so perfect for marriage on paper, I wasn't very hopeful about my future, and even less hopeful that I'd ever be in a situation where I'd need a second steak knife, even if I could afford it.

STOP! GOOD NEWS TIME!

The pressure to repeal the laws criminalising homosexuality in Tasmania had grown locally, nationally and internationally. Support for reform amongst Tasmanians had increased from 33 percent in 1988 to almost 60 percent in 1997—the highest level of support for gay law reform in any Australian state.

Greens leader Christine Milne was put to the task of facilitating yet another parliamentary vote on the reforms. The bill stormed through the Lower House and quickly reached the still resistant Legislative Council. Rallies formed outside Parliament House in Hobart, where energized supporters outnumbered volatile opponents. By a margin of just one single vote, the bill was passed.

On the thirteenth of May, the Criminal Code Amendment Act (1997) became law, receiving royal assent, and came into effect the next day. The celebrations and relief were dotted across the island. Milne declared, "Tasmanians can now redefine who we are as Tasmanians, we can stand up nationally and globally and proudly be a tolerant and inclusive society."

As time moved on, the bigoted men in the Upper House moved further and further from representing the views of Tasmanians, many of whom were forever changed by the persistent hatred that spewed across the state. Tasmania would go on to have some of Australia's most progressive sexuality- and gender-based laws and protections, but in this moment in 1997 it was enough that being gay was no longer a criminal offence.

1998

1998 was a year full of controversy. I was accepted into the arts program at the University of Tasmania in Hobart, despite having provided no proof of potential in my application. Bill Clinton stumbled over what the meaning of the word "is" is, and Andrew Wakefield put forth a grossly manipulated and aggressively repugnant study falsely linking the MMR vaccine to autism—more on that later. *Titanic* won the Academy Award for Best Picture. I still haven't gotten around to seeing it. Soon, Leo, soon! 1998 wasn't all bad, though. *Teletubbies* premiered in Australia, of which I have seen every episode, because I am the King of the Felt World, and the year ended on a high when I was offered a place in the Art History and Curatorship program at the Australian National University, which meant that soon I would be moving to the mainland. *Toot-toot.* Fuck yeah!

Before I moved to Hobart, I honestly believed that the elderly were the only people who could possibly enjoy my company, and even then I worried it was only because they were lonely and I was better than a chair. But at university I discovered that I was likeable to people my own age. Not all of them by a long shot, but enough of a handful that by the end of the first term I had carved out something of a social life, intermittent as it was. I had by no means transformed into a social butterfly, but I did uncover my latent talent for drinking.

I had my first drink when I was twelve, just after I took up smoking, and two years before I saw my first sex scene, for context. I'd found an old bottle of Galliano in Pop's shed one afternoon, a tall, elegant bottle that had three inches of yellow liquid I liked the look of because I had not yet pissed in a cup. Galliano is not supposed to be thick like jelly, nor is it supposed to taste like the inside of a dead man's arse, but that's what I got. So, I didn't drink another drop of alcohol until my eighteenth birthday.

Despite my late start, by the time I got to university I could hold a decent amount of drink and I really went to work on nurturing my talent. I didn't drink heavily because it was fun. The upside was that alcohol worked like a buffer blanket over my senses, with the added bonus that I could delude myself that I was actively participating in life, because, unlike most hyper-social situations, I understood the central purpose and motivation—to drink and get drunk—and just knowing what I was supposed to do gave me the illusion I was having a good time, even though I knew I wasn't.

I never went looking for drunk adventures. The only time I drank was when I went out. And I only went out when I was invited, but not because I wanted to drink; I was just so chuffed to be included. Usually I would be asked to go see a band, sometimes a housemate would invite me to an event at the art school, and Hamish even asked me to one of his famous slab-a-thons. (Basically, you buy a slab of beer, go to his house and drink it. The first person to drink their slab wins! No prize, just the honour.) And then there was the Pale Ale Challenge.

Unlike the slab-a-thon, the Pale Ale Challenge was impossible to win, because it was essentially a ruse. Here's how it went—you pay a door charge and get the pale ale challenge T-shirt, which was cheap, white and always at least one size smaller than the one you asked for. You put the T-shirt on and go to the bar, you ask for a pale ale and, after you pay, the barkeep will press a happy-face stamp in the first of the twenty-five squares printed on the front of your T-shirt. If you can drink twenty pale ales, you get the last five pale ales for free! Which is great, because you absolutely will not want them.

Given that I haven't been able to look sideways at a pale ale since that fateful evening, it's fair to say that as a promotional strategy, the Pale Ale Challenge was not playing the long game. But in terms of giving one man with a stamp a chance to fondle the breasts of scores of young women every time they bought a beer, then the Pale Ale Challenge was nothing short of genius.

The evening of the Pale Ale Challenge began at a pub with a girl I had known from my golfing days and a group of her friends. I was, as always, doing the same things while drinking that I would do while sober: standing on the edges of other people's conversations, watching, letting people talk at me, agreeing with everything and understanding nothing. But if I got drunk enough, I could almost believe that I was experiencing the world the same way as the person next to me, and that is not something I'd ever felt when sober.

At about my fifteenth beer, a very drunk guy tapped me on the shoulder to ask me why I had my T-shirt on back-to-front. "Because, I don't want to be groped every time I buy a beer," I told him, and he nodded as if to say *Fair enough* before asking point-blank if he might be allowed to grope my breasts. I laughed in his face and meant every inch of the "No" I responded with, which he must have taken to mean "Yes" on some level, because he wouldn't let any more than five minutes go by without asking if he might be allowed to cop a feel. He was being cheeky about it, sure, and I didn't feel pressured or cornered by him, but he was very insistent on the matter and bless him and his determination because at two beers shy of my twentieth, I finally relented and as soon as I did one of his hands was enthusiastically grabbing and squeezing both breasts for five brief, but very frenzied, seconds.

While I can't say I enjoyed the grope very much, I did find it intriguing enough that when he asked if he could do it again, I moved my bra aside so he could make a better grab of it. It felt better each time he had at it, but not enough for me to say I was loving it. Still, there was apparently enough in it for me that by the time I was draining the first of my free beers, his hand was still in my bra enjoying the grope he'd started when my glass was still full.

Not long after that we started kissing, and not long after that I realised I hated pale ale and pushed my untouched twenty-fourth away in disgust. And that's when the guy, whose name I did not know, pulled his hand out of my bra for the first time in a long time, so he could punch the air and shout, "Tequila!" I was far too naive in 1998 to know that when someone calls for tequila shots, the evening is already over.

As I watched him thread his way through the crowd to the bar, I tried to decide if I found him attractive, and the most I could say was that I thought he was neat. I wasn't sure if that meant that I was attracted to him, but by the time he got back to the table it no longer mattered because I had decided that neat was good enough for me, and that I would have sex with him. Shortly after, I handed my soul to tequila and we headed back to his place.

Everything had felt fairly nonthreatening until he shut his bedroom door behind us, and we were suddenly totally alone in the middle of the night, just me, him and a six-foot red lava lamp pulsating its best impression of hell in the corner of a damp, windowless room. We kissed and partially disrobed incredibly clumsily, and then, with his shirt off, my neat little stranger became suddenly very assertive and he pushed me backward onto his bed. I can only assume it was his intention to climb on top of me, but I will never know because I flew right off the other side of the bed. It wasn't the force with which he pushed me that did it, but rather it was his black imitation-satin sheets and their complete and utter lack of traction. We laughed and tried again. He didn't push me the second time; I fell off the bed all on my own.

I don't know if it was because he was too drunk or if it was the gracelessness of my falling, or the way that every single hair on my head was standing on its end courtesy of the massive amount of static electricity that I generated with all the skidding. But I suppose it doesn't really matter why his dick couldn't erect itself, I'm just glad we got bored at the same time and called it a night.

It was so clear both of us had made many very bad choices in life. My worst was clearly the one I made when I agreed to go back to his place, and he'd clearly had his worst at Harris Scarfe on Boxing Day when he picked up a set of black satin sheets and said, "Fuck yeah. This is what I want." To this day, whenever I hear any mention of "hell," this is the scene that will always pop into my head: Me crawling around in the dark, drunk, naked and searching for my scattered clothes in a dank little windowless bedroom in a share house in I didn't know where. My hair rigid with static and my over-groped breasts redder than the giant hulking lava lamp that was slowly pumping its red glow around the room, while a neat little man sat sulking atop his black satin sheets.

As horrific as the whole sequence of events was, it's a memory that I cherish because it's an experience that so many young people endure. I think of it as something of a rite of passage, and I just don't have a lot of those. Of course, my time over, I would never, ever choose those sheets to almost passage that rite on, but I am glad for my neat little black satin man and I hope he also got something out of our encounter, other than the dirty white T-shirt with twenty-four stamps that I left scrunched up on his floor.

Back in the very relative comfort of my own home—or rather, a worn-down share house that was the closest thing I had to a home at the time—I had managed to become firm friends with one of my housemates, an exchange student from Salt Lake City, Utah. Although he wasn't a Mormon, he was still the singularly most exotic thing I'd ever encountered[*] and his name was Weston Noyes. Weston was not my usual demographic of friend, given that he was intolerably cool, self-assured and, most remarkably, a genuine young person.

One night Weston shared that he'd had an intense relationship with a gay man just before he'd left for Tasmania. It had never become physical, but their feelings for each other were so fierce that he'd begun to pray he was gay so that they could be closer in every way. "But it didn't work," he told me, somewhat sadly. "You just can't be what you're not." I'd never heard of somebody wanting to be gay before, and I couldn't even begin to get my head around it. Why on earth would you make that choice?

In exchange, I told Weston my almost sex story, but I took out the

[*] The fact that a straight, white, cis male from America was easily the most mysterious creature I'd ever met should be a real indication of just how small my world was at the time.

fact that I had decided to sleep with Black Satin Man because I was hoping to discover that I was straight. I didn't mention the whole "neat" thing either; instead I told Weston that he had a body hotter than a hot thing that is hotter than usual. That is roughly, if not a direct quote of, how I described Black Satin Man. I also left out all of the sadness from the ending and just finished it up by saying, "It was like trying to push a marshmallow into a coin slot." Full disclosure—that line is not my invention; I don't know who said it, but whoever it was, I am forever in their debt.

At some stage, Weston's dad came all the way from Salt Lake City to visit Weston. My dad never drove the two hours down from Launceston, which I think makes me the real winner. Part of the tour that Weston gave his dad was a trip to the cinema, which surprised me, as I assumed they had cinemas in America. I went along, marking the beginning of my career as a trusty third wheel, in all sorts of different kinds of relationships. The film that we, the odd trifecta, watched was *Boogie Nights*.

I was aware of both Weston and his dad stealing very regular glances in my direction, so I did my best to maintain my composure as my sex scene tally was rocketing up faster than you can say "erection," which is, remarkably, the only thing I didn't get to see in that film. I don't think I did a very good job, however, because ten minutes in I'd stopped blinking, and by the twenty-minute mark my embarrassment was so high I broke out in a fever sweat that didn't subside for days. After a character put a loaded gun in his mouth and pulled the trigger, Weston's dad leaned over and asked if I was OK. I nodded and did my best attempt at a carefree smile. When another character was in the midst of being raped, it was Weston's turn to check in to see if I was OK, but I waved his concern away with about as much nonchalance as a brick, I am sure. Apparently satisfied with my state of affairs, neither of them checked in again, so neither of them noticed that my eyes were closed when Dirk Diggler was being gay-bashed in a car park.

On the way home, Weston and his dad had an argument about the appropriateness of the film. His dad complained that he had felt very uncomfortable watching such a film in my company, describing me as a sweet, lovely and "far too innocent" young woman. Weston told him not to be so patronising and looked to me to back him up. I was in too much shock to tell the truth—that I agreed with Weston's dad but desperately wished I didn't—so, I did the only thing I knew how to do under duress: I shrugged and said something I had prepared earlier. "You know, I'd only seen three films at the cinema before this, *Milo and Otis*, *Crocodile Dundee Two* and *Bedknobs and Broomsticks*." They both exploded with laughter and I sat back in my seat, happy in the knowledge that despite my colossal naivete, I was now at least sophisticated enough to know how and when to wield a "knob" for comedic effect.

I did not expect that coming out of the closet was something I would have to do in 1998,if ever. So, it was as inconvenient as it was shocking when Weston took it upon himself to tell me that I was a lesbian. We were in Weston's room when he dropped my own bombshell on me. He was sitting cross-legged on the floor painting and talking about himself, while I was perched awkwardly on his bed thinking about myself. In that way, there was nothing at all unusual about the situation—that is, until Weston told me I was a lesbian.

As adamant and firm as I was in my denial, I couldn't seem to shake Weston's confidence. "Trust me! I would know," he insisted. "My mother is a lesbian." My confusion must have registered effectively on my face, because Weston went on to explain to me that she'd been married to his father first. "My dad is like Ross from *Friends*," he said. I stared at him blankly. He laughed and I got the reference about fifteen years later.[⊗]

I went back to the cinema to see *Boogie Nights* again on my own, twice. It wasn't the sex or the violence that drew me back. It was the unfolding rhythm of the story, the way the colours, the costumes, the sets and the music combined to create a whole kind of world I'd never known before, and yet I could totally immerse myself in it and

[⊗] I must tell Jennifer Aniston, next time I see her, that I very much enjoyed her work.

share it with the characters and feel the same things that they did. I didn't know anything of the life they lived, not the sex, not the violence, not the partying, not the drugs. But I understood something of the desperation at the heart of the characters, even if I didn't understand the decisions they made or the world they had to navigate. I thoroughly understood the way that life is like an undertow for people who aren't tethered to the world properly.

I especially identified with Scotty, the character played by Philip Seymour Hoffman. I knew he was a minor character but I didn't care. He was the only one I would watch in any of his scenes. I knew he was supposed to provide comic relief, and each time I saw the film the cinema would fill with laughter whenever Scotty had a moment. But not me. I couldn't laugh because I was too filled with sadness, desperation, loneliness and all the other feelings I'd failed to feel in the living of my own small, insignificant life. Each time Scotty gawked in awe at Mark Wahlberg's Dirk Diggler, I saw myself watching Mia, and how I had hoped she'd notice me, and how I prayed that I'd know what to say and do if ever she did. When Scotty failed miserably in his attempt to imitate the style of those he worshipped, I saw my own sad attempts to emulate Lilly, the first lesbian I didn't know I'd met. And the way Scotty's belly would spill out of his ill-fitting top, and how he was always squirming as if he was trying to slip his awkward body into something more comfortable, reminded me of how I'd kept trying to wear my brother's football shorts even after my hips had grown well beyond them. When Scotty hungrily took each crumb of attention that Dirk Diggler barely threw his way, I saw myself taking the briefest of moments I'd shared with Mia and turning them into something way more significant than they were, giving them a glow and a warmth that I fiercely pretended she shared. And when Scotty clumsily tried to kiss Dirk, I remembered how close I'd gotten to sharing my feelings with Mia, and how much I had burned with the excruciating prospect of coming out and being rejected in the very same moment. I never did say anything to Mia, but I nevertheless felt the punch of Scotty's humiliation when Dirk rejected him, and I sobbed for him and I sobbed for myself.

I had felt deeply uncomfortable about the whole Weston scenario, and at first I tried to burrow my way backward into my inner closet. But when the chat dust eventually settled in my head, I found that instead of praying to be straight, I was now thinking about coming out. As critical and marvellous as this shift in my thinking was, it brought with it a whole world of dreaded questions I only had bad answers for. *Who can I tell safely?* No one. *Will my family reject me?* Yes. *How does one be lesbian?* You are disgusting. *How does one meet a lesbian?* Everyone will reject you. *How do I get out of this mess?* Kill yourself. Do it.

I knew Weston was right, of course. I had accepted my sexuality to a point, but I was still incapable of thinking that there might be anything at all good about it. I'm not talking about big concepts like "pride," either, just base level neutrality. I didn't even have that. I couldn't be sure I would be safe if I acknowledged it out loud. Homosexuality might have been legalised the year before but it was clear, even to me, that changing laws does not magically change minds.

It was all a shame, really, because what Weston had gifted me in that moment was the chance to come out, in a safe place, to the first adult friend I'd made under the age of seventy, and I didn't take it.

Weston finished up his exchange program at the end of the second term and returned to Utah shortly after that. I was bereft. He was the only person whose life in Hobart I had attached my own to in any meaningful way, his rhythms of living were the only ones I had bothered to learn to read, and when he left, I experienced pain in my heart. One thing made it OK, and that was that Weston was also sad. Looking back, this is so clearly the kind of wonderful rite of passage that I had always wanted, but I didn't recognise it at the time because I didn't think being normal could hurt so much.

After he'd left for the airport, I shut myself in my room, shut the curtains and lay on my bed in the dark and let all the feelings happen inside me. A few hours later, when my thoughts had begun to tip into the edges of dreaming, I was yanked out of myself by a knock at the door. It was Weston. He had missed his flight and he was back for another few nights. "OK," I said, and then I shut the door in his face. As far as I was concerned, I had already said goodbye, processed a good chunk of feelings about it, and as such, I had moved on. So, I left him to his own devices and went back to my own thoughts. Had I known almost exactly twenty years would pass before we would see each other again, I still don't think I would have done it any differently.

After Weston left, I made the decision that I would apply for a transfer and finish my degree at whichever mainland university would have me.

Just as with every terrifying new step I took in life, Hamish was there for me. I don't remember ever asking him for help. He just always took the initiative. It was he who invited me to join his cricket games when I was struggling to fit in at school. At high school he introduced me to all his friends, who were all only ever lovely to me. It was Hamish who got me the job at the supermarket, and he went out of his way to make me feel like I did it on my own steam. And he got me the job he knew I would need to make ends meet to get myself through university.

When I moved to Hobart, I did not reach out to him at all. It was Hamish who had me over for dinner and invited me to a slab-a-thon here and there. Hamish has always known how and when to help me without ever getting between me and all the mistakes I needed to make on my own.

Hamish spent a weekend helping me put together a bunch of applications for universities on the mainland, because we both knew I wouldn't do it on my own. I had decided I wanted to study art history, which I knew was not a course that would lead to gainful employment, but as it was the closest thing to an ambition I'd ever had in my whole life, it felt like the right thing to do. There weren't that many art history courses that I could apply to, so we had it all wrapped up by around lunchtime on the Sunday. We shared a couple of beers and laughed so much I almost came out of the closet.

He probably would have been the best person for it; we've always had a genuine connection that we've never needed to question. But I didn't. I don't know why. My best guess is I hated myself so much that I didn't think I deserved any kind of help or kindness.

I found out that I had been accepted into the Art History and Curatorship program at the Australian National University in Canberra two days before my final exam. I rang Hamish to tell him the news. It was a happy moment and it capped off a very big year in my life—I moved out of home, I scraped my way to a passing grade in my first year of university, I'd made friends, I grew up a bit, and despite my best effort, I did not lose my virginity on black satin sheets. It might have been the best year of my life if I hadn't been some level of suicidal the whole time.

By the end of the year, I wasn't able to leave my room unless I had to work or study. Everything else was scrapped, and I would lock myself in and worry about all of the things in the history of the world ever. It was not new for me to struggle in the world, but I had always found refuge in my own company. Even after the worst, most stressful days of my life had crushed my spirit to a pulp, if I spent a few hours on my own, in a dark quiet place, thinking about anything my brain took a fancy to, then I could bounce back as good as gold and bring some joy back into my thinking. But I had lost that life raft at some point in 1998. I couldn't think about anything anymore; all I did was lie on my bed and drown myself in the dark thoughts that would spew into my mind uninvited.

The slice of light that came with a chance to make a fresh start on the mainland was enough to drag the worst of my thoughts out of my regular thinking cycle. I found myself celebrating the end of exams with everyone else around me, and that helped me feel a little bit better again. I was having a drink with a friend one afternoon; we had planned to watch a film but the beer was too nice to leave. At some point, I was looking at my friend as she was talking and I realised I was seeing her differently. The late afternoon light was golden and the bar was quiet and I had started to study her more than I was listening. It was the line of her jaw that did it, and as soon as the idea hit me, I blurted it out before the cavalcade of second-guessing marched in to take my courage away: "I reckon I'm bisexual, a bit, yeah, maybe."

I wished I had had the guts to tell her I was gay, or at least had said "bisexual"⊗ more resolutely, but even so it was a huge and wonderful moment. She smiled and said it was great and then told me her cousin was a lesbian, which even I knew was only ever a thing that a straight person would say. I had told her because I'd wanted to kiss her. I had put the ball in her court and she caught it beautifully, held it with care but did not return it. I was not going to chase a kiss from her. I was not at a point where I could risk being told I was as disgusting as I thought. But it wasn't exactly a rejection, and I felt really great about everything for one hot minute. I had more life inside me than I'd had for years.

I rarely ever want to change things in my past. I figure I'm all right enough now and what's done is done. But if I could change one thing, it would be that night. Because it was hands down the highlight of my life up until then. I had poked my head out of the closet and nothing bad had happened, and everything just felt really good. But whenever I bring my memory of that night into my mind, I don't feel anything close to a good feeling; all I feel is badness. I don't even have the words to describe it, I just fill up with badness and I feel so much pain, I feel like I'm keeling into fear itself.

I got a little lost trying to get home. I was so lost in my thoughts that I forgot to get off the bus and was ten minutes up the road before I noticed. I figured I'd just get out at the next stop, cross the road, and catch the bus going back the other way. But I hadn't checked this bus's route when I got on, and by the time I realised it was going the wrong way, I was twice as far away from home than when I had started.

It was not a great neighbourhood, and I found myself waiting for my next bus near a small group of kids who were heading into town for a night out. They were really drunk. There were three boys and

⊗ Bisexuals are the best people. I see you.

two girls. They might have been a bit older than me but I doubted they were students, they were a bit rougher, and kind of reminded me of boys I knew in Smithton, restless types, always looking for either trouble or fun, mostly sweet but the rage was skimming under the surface, ready to burst. They were having a good time amongst themselves until one of the girls broke from the group and came over to me and said hello.

I don't know what I said but she laughed, she had the kind of deep infectious rolling laugh you always want to hear again, and I got two more big laughs before it all went to shit. I don't know what we were talking about, I wouldn't have thought I was flirting with her but maybe I was, maybe I had found a bit of pluck when I edged out of the closet, who knows? But it didn't matter what I thought, because her boyfriend had made his mind up that I *was* flirting and he charged over and shoved me hard in the chest. I staggered back and he lunged after me and shoved me harder again. "Keep away from my fucking girlfriend, you fucking faggot!" I didn't attempt to fight back, I just raised my hands in surrender, the last thing I wanted to do was give him an excuse to really hit me. That's when his girlfriend screamed at him, "It's a girl!" and laughed her lovely laugh and then it was all over as quickly as it had begun. His "sorrys" came tumbling out thick and fast, and then he offered what remains one of the funniest things I've ever heard, despite the trauma that surrounds it. *"I thought you were a fucking poof!"* he said. What a glorious moment of absurdity! He honestly thought I was a gay man making a pass at his girlfriend. To this day, the stupidity of it tickles me.

He continued to beg for my forgiveness as he adorably tried to straighten out my shirt where he had scrunched it. "I'm so sorry. I don't hit girls!" He kept saying it over and over, groping my breast more than fixing my shirt, but I wasn't inclined to believe him. Clearly this kind of thing had played out in their relationship before, she was his property, and violence was an acceptable defence of his ownership. My hunch turned out to be correct, and not only was this man capable of hitting a woman, he was the type of man who could justify his actions as he did it.

They'd only moved a few metres away before he spun back around. His head was cocked but his eyes were so still as they drilled right through me. I could tell the penny had dropped, but this time when he moved toward me his girlfriend just stepped out of his way. I don't think I'll ever forget how time seemed to fold in on itself, speeding up and slowing down all in that one sickening moment. He saw me for exactly what I was, and that filled him with burning hot hatred. I could see it so clearly in his eyes, how that unfocused and almost comical drunken rage from moments before had suddenly crystallised into fury so hot it pinned itself to me, and in turn, pinned me down into shame.

My shame was as hot as his anger, and I did nothing to stop the punch that came down on my throat, and I barely did anything to regain the breath that the punch had taken away. I simply buckled to the ground and absorbed the three fully loaded kicks that he landed before the bus came. Even after he'd stopped, I didn't try and move to help myself. I lay as still as I could. I didn't even flinch when he spat on me and called me a lady faggot as he left. I just stayed perfectly still until he, his girlfriend and the whole goddamned world got on that bus and left.

INTERMISSION

There were barely seven years that separated my leaving Tasmania and the beginning of my arrival at stand-up, but they did not feel like short years when I was in the middle of living them. Far from thriving, I lurched from one struggle to the next, and even with the safety of hindsight, I still can't find a clear sight line through the murk of memory that I call my Wilderness Years.

These years were the most precarious of my life, and I need not have survived them. I want to be sure that you understand that.

I want to make sure you are not reading my story like it's some kind of rags-to-riches inspiration porn. It's not. I want the world to stop demanding gratuitous details in exchange for empathy. Entertainment in exchange for understanding. But I am not in charge of the world. I am not even in charge of my own story, because, as I am so fond of saying, there is no such thing as a straight line through trauma.

So, let me repeat my earlier caution: Don't try and play "truth detective" with my story. But if you can't help yourself, if hunting for context alibis is your reading jam, I wish you luck and I look forward to not listening to your true-crime podcast. This is not to say I have not tried to give you my best estimation of this time, but if you begin to feel confused about time and place . . . Good. I wish you all the comfort and safety these years did not show me.

THE WILDERNESS YEARS

CINDERELLA PHOENIX

The sound of the audience hit me like a brick wall, so dense with intensity I lost my ability to speak. This was not a new kind of tribulation for me, pre-show nerves had always toggled with my mute button, but this time was different because it wasn't the fear of public speaking that took my words away, it was the sound of the crowd that did it. I'd known what to expect in theory, but theory can't prepare the body for the sensory-overwhelming reality of fifteen hundred people clapping and cheering all at once. I was somewhere between my first and second step onto the stage when the surge of it hit me, and when it did, I felt the link between my brain and mouth detach with such a snap it felt complete and final.

Social duress had been scrambling my brain for as long as I can remember, so by my late twenties I had quite the bag of tricks at my disposal that could get my mouth into gear before anyone had time to notice. The key is preparation. If I can get myself well enough acquainted with the first thing that I want to say, then I can kick myself into chatterbox gear with barely a sputter. It isn't enough to simply prepare "what" to say, I need to develop complete muscle memory around the whole process of a phrase. This means repeating it so many times that it loses all meaning and becomes a word bicycle that my mouth will never forget how to ride. The peloton of pre-prepared statements I've accrued over time has meant that I don't need to train as much as I used to when I was younger and life was just an interminable clusterfuck of the unfamiliar. I have no doubt that this lifelong habit of speech prepping was what gave people the impression I was something of a natural performer.

People had begun telling me I had a "talent" for comedy from the moment I left the stage after my very first gig. The most incredible thing about it was that I knew they were right. Not once during my entire twenty-seven years of life before my comedy inauguration had I ever entertained such confidence in my own abilities. I'd always understood myself to be average at absolute best. But I knew from the moment I raised my first laugh that I had stumbled upon a thing I could do better than most. It's not that I felt masterful—it was the effect the laughter had on me that did it. It felt very, very good. But I didn't interpret the laughter, I didn't drink it up as some kind of validation or approval. It was more about how it made me feel in my own skin. Never in my whole life had I ever felt such a deep and crystal-clear focus in the presence of others.

My first-ever gig was part of the national Raw Comedy competition put on by the Melbourne International Comedy Festival. Every year, heats are held all over Australia, from which the best emerging talent is siphoned into the state finals and the winner from each state then gets sent to represent at the televised national finals, broadcast from the festival itself in Melbourne. I can't claim that there was a strategy or much of an ambition that prompted me to give it a go. I was more than half joking when I'd mentioned to a friend that I thought I should enter. I'd been hearing a couple of comedy clips advertising the competition on the radio for a few weeks, and like most arseholes filled with beer and boredom, I thought it sounded like an easy thing to do, and I said as much to my friend.

We hadn't seen much of each other since I'd graduated, and were catching up on the intervening three years over a few drinks. His life was good. Mine was not. His life was following a recognisable trajectory. Mine was not. So instead, I focused on making him laugh by breaking my life into vignettes and sketching out stories for his amusement. When he asked what I was doing back in town, I told him I'd busted my wrist planting trees up north and was on my way to Sydney to see a specialist. I didn't mention that I was as poor as fuck and had no place to go; instead I told him about that one time I got run over by a drug dealer on a quad bike. Despite the darkness at their edges, the stories I told my friend were all very funny and I suppose that's why he encouraged me to enter the comedy competition.

When I'd left Tasmania, I had entertained a genuine hope that a degree in art history would lead to gainful employment in any gallery of my choosing. I was, of course, quite profoundly wrong. I'd taken five years to complete the three-year degree, and I was so exhausted after graduating, it was all I could do to pick up a few extra shifts at my casual job at a bookshop while I made a plan for the rest of my life. Sorely missing the structure of an institution to prop up my existence, and without a goal or a dream to propel me forward in life, I began to flounder very badly, making a sequence of terrible decisions as I did. Within just two years of graduating, I was an itinerant farmworker again, unhoused, and profoundly alone.

There was absolutely no reason for anybody to expect that my decision to try comedy would turn out any differently than any of the other countless pitiable decisions I'd made in life up until that point. At the time, I was aware that I was struggling, everything I attempted in life came unstuck, my own thinking included. But it's only now, when I look back, that I can see so clearly just how profoundly isolated and vulnerable I was. I did not pull myself out of this hole. I just got lucky. So many people work hard their whole entire lives and only ever go backward, through no fault of their own. People are trapped in cycles far worse than the one I was in, and it's just not their fault. So, I won't be claiming that it was some kind of superior grit of mine that got me through it. All I did was enter a comedy competition and had a bit of luck for once.

I was barely halfway to the microphone when, out of the corner of my eye, I caught the movement of a camera on a jib as it swooped down to track my progress across the stage. I had been told about the cameras during rehearsal earlier that day, but in the din of my fear I'd forgotten and so, as is my uncontrollable habit when surprised, I startled. And apparently, I startled visibly and humorously because in that moment the audience's welcoming applause turned immediately to laughter. And that was precisely the sound I needed to hear so I could return to my body and find my voice.

I've since been told that I'd won before I even reached the microphone, but as flattering as this story sounds, it is unlikely to be the truth and it certainly doesn't match my experience of the moment. In my version of events, I had no reason to be confident of winning, and I spent every second of the twenty minutes it took the judges to deliberate suspended helplessly in that excruciating limbo which opens up when you prepare for bad news and dare to hope in the same mind.

I wouldn't say I prayed as much as I pleaded. I was desperate to win, simply because I was desperate. I'd pinned all of my fledgling ambitions onto winning this particular token of external validation, not believing I had what it would take to make it in the world of comedy without it. I may very well have still "made it," but it's impossible to know how differently my life would've unfolded if I didn't win. But I did win, and this fact alone is enough to say that winning a national competition did give me my start in comedy. But a start is not the same as a beginning. The world can witness a start and so it becomes history, but all stories begin out of sight, with a thread only you can choose to pick up and retrace for the telling. But when it comes to this story, I've never really known where to begin.

To this day, whenever I'm asked how I arrived at comedy I find it impossible to answer with an effective story. The irony is that the truth of my life could be spun into PR gold, because everyone loves an underdog story. But at that time, I didn't think it was a good story. I thought it was shameful. Adding to that shame was my inability to adequately explain, even to myself, how I'd failed so badly at life, and that my success story was so thoroughly punctuated by failure it couldn't possibly ring true.

If pushed, I usually say that a friend entered me into the Raw

Comedy competition because I was making him laugh and he thought I needed to broaden my audience. Sometimes I will elaborate and say that at the time I was recovering from surgery and, unable to work, was looking for something to do. On rare occasions I'll go as far as to explain that I'd been injured while working on a farm and had undergone a partial wrist fusion. None of this is untrue, but it is a gross simplification. It does nothing to accommodate the reality of my situation, the drifting, the isolation, the houselessness, the rape and the abortion. But what can I say? There is just never a straight line to be found through a life punctuated by trauma.

A MASTER CLASS FROM MUM

I always knew that it was going to be an ordeal performing comedy in front of Mum for the first time, but it wasn't until she arrived at the venue that I understood the scale of it. I'd been performing for less than a year, and while I felt like that made me something of a professional, I knew I did not have anywhere near enough experience to be able to handle Mum in full flight.

The Hobart Comedy Festival was a small but well-supported event, and that evening the room was full and the crowd was especially excitable. I was only doing a ten-minute spot as part of a lineup of about six others. I had hoped that Mum might get overwhelmed by the good-natured hubbub of the evening, and so blink and miss me. My other hope for a good outcome was that Mum was bringing one of her oldest friends along as her plus-one. I was already very fond of Marilyn, but on this particular evening I was so grateful for her calming presence, I would've given her both of my kidneys and a slice of liver, and I would have carved said liver slice with the "petit carver" knife neither of us could afford some years earlier. But all of my hope of it being a smooth ordeal dissipated in a puff of dread as soon as I met them at the entrance, and Mum, skipping hello, launched straight into complaining about how much she'd had to pay for wine. There was no doubt in my mind that harvesting my own organs with even a blunt spoon would've made for a better ordeal than the one I was about to endure.

She made a good point, and I essentially agreed—the drinks were overpriced, but dismissing my plea to lower her voice anyway, Mum turned to the people behind her and informed them at a shout that she could've bought an entire cask of wine for the price she'd just paid for the two glasses she'd had downstairs. She was hamming it up, she wasn't out of control, and everyone around her was very much enjoying her show. But even so, I still steered her directly to her seat, without passing "Go" and by that I mean, the bar. As soon as I had settled Mum into her seat, I fetched her the drink she requested and went and stood up at the back of the room with the other comedians to watch my own hell unfold. I knew that Mum was more nervous than I was because gulping wine is how she copes. But from my vantage point up the back, I could see that she was now officially coping quite well. She was in very good form, in fact, and I was dismayed to see the people around her clearly enjoying the preshow entertainment she was providing. This was bad, because I knew that the more laughs Mum got, the bolder she would become; and the bolder Mum gets, the less aware of context she becomes.

The first comic on stage was Josh Earl, who, like me, was from the North West Coast of Tasmania, but unlike me, it wasn't obvious at a glance. That night he played guitar and sang songs about his family and his job as a librarian. I liked Josh. I still like Josh. But I knew Mum was not going to be terribly impressed, because she's always hated when people play music at her. Worryingly for Josh, he also ticked off another two of Mum's pet peeves—being "shouty" and short. I looked over and saw Mum shift in her seat and then lean over to say something to Marilyn, who laughed and shushed her at the same time. Then I watched with horror as Mum straightened, leant back in her chair and observed far too loudly, "He'd be taller if he sat down, you know."

There was a ripple of laughter around Mum, and although I couldn't tell if Josh had heard what she'd said, I could tell he'd registered the disruption. Sensibly, he chose to ignore it and continue with his set. At the back of the room, however, the other comedians were suddenly paying very close attention to the situation. Their interest had been piqued because comedians love nothing more than to witness their peers struggling on stage. I didn't know it back then—I was too new to the world of stand-up—but comedians fucking love a train wreck.

Josh's first song, which was about being a librarian, began with him "shushing" in the manner of a librarian, which extracted a good-natured giggle ripple from the audience. But Mum bristled—she's never taken well to being told to be quiet, so when Josh repeated his shushing, I was not at all surprised to hear Mum shout out a defiant "Don't you shush me!"

I could only watch in horror as Mum did what she does best and began to own the room. I have only ever been able to own a room if I have a microphone and I stand in front of a seated audience who are expecting me to say something. I can't own any other kind of room. But Mum has owned every single room she's ever entered, and I don't know why I expected this room to be any different.

Halfway through Josh's set I was already filled with my richest flavour of dread, and by the time he walked off I was well and truly overflowing. I won't lie, there was a little bit of pride mingling with my bad feelings. The room was electric and the comedians at the back were having the time of their life, and my mum had done that. She was the one who piqued their interest where none of their peers could. They were all on their toes and craning to see what the loose unit that was my mother was going to do next.

The next comic on stage was a nerdy man with very straight hair that reached down well below his waist, and I guessed, correctly, that Mum would have something to say about this.

"GAWD! Looks like Rapunzel's had a tough old life."

"Rapunzel" was Mick Lowenstein, a lovely, gentle guy who liked to build an imaginary, slightly surreal world on stage. I could see that Mum was having trouble following his stream-of-consciousness stylings, but I was relieved to see that her confusion had something of a silencing effect on her. But I knew it was only a matter of time before she would strike again. So, while the crowd settled back into the act, forgetting all about the loose unit in their midst, I remained on high alert.

Mum's involvement wasn't mean-spirited or calculated, she's just someone who gets caught up in the moment; and when the moment takes Mum, she'll heckle anyone and anything. I once heard her say, "That colour makes you look fat" to an actual house. The inevitable heckle coming for Mick struck him dumb shortly after he began mime-kayaking and doing a bit about Starbucks. For some context here, Starbucks had not yet infiltrated Tasmania, which was a point of pride for Tasmanians, so when coffee's biggest franchise kraken tried to get a tentacle in the door, it was met with furious resistance. So, Mick only had to bring the subject up and the chord was struck; the vibe of the room went from jolly to frosty hostility in a flip of an instant as murmurs of disapproval filled the space. As a Tasmanian, Mick should have expected this response, but clearly it was not what he had in mind, because he was thrown thoroughly off his kilter. And that is when my mum raised her now familiar voice above the furious fray and took the reins of the room right out of Mick's flailing grasp, asking, "What's Starbucks?"

Time stood still for the briefest of moments and then Mick, pulling his wits together slowly, restarted his mime-paddling and tried to pick up his bit at the point of interruption. He was obviously operating under two very foolish assumptions: one, that Mum had been joking, and two, that Mum can be ignored. I can understand why he would think it was a joke—surely everybody knew what Starbucks was? It was the talk of the town. But I knew for sure that Mum had asked the question because she genuinely wanted to know what the hell this Starbucks was. Needless to say, she didn't take too well to being ignored.

"No!" she demanded, "You need to tell me what it is!"

This time she managed to force Mick into addressing the situation, and he ceased his pretend paddling as he racked his brain for the best way to explain what he had thought was safely common knowledge. His whimsical stage persona had by then melted away, and his face was awash with fear and amused incredulity. At the sight of his faltering, the comedians at the back of the room were falling over themselves with pure hyena glee.

"It's like a McDonald's for coffee," he offered with hesitation.

"Oh," said Mum.

With great caution Mick started his bit up again, but he'd barely got the tip of his imaginary paddle back into the imaginary water when Mum struck again: "Oh, I thought it was a movie!"

Her timing was impeccable. The room exploded with laughter and all Mick could do was wait until the storm passed. After a time, he made his attempt to salvage his set, but it was clear that he was struggling to find his rhythm again. The room was not against him, but they were really, really distracted. Everyone wanted more from the loose unit. Eventually their attention did return to Mick and his invisible canoe, but of course, just as he hit his stride, Mum went in for the kill:

"Sorry! I was thinking of *Star Wars!*"

Mick stopped mime-paddling for the last time and, with as much grace as possible, he just left the stage.

I can confidently say that I have never again been witness to such perfect comedic timing, but as it was happening I wasn't marvelling at the comic genius of my mum, because I was the next act on stage and I was gripped by an all-consuming terror. I had just one small comfort to cling to, and that was that nobody knew the loose unit was my mum. Of course, that comfort was taken away from me as soon as my name was announced and Mum jumped to her feet and shouted, "That's my daughter!" The room was electric.

I was supposed to do a ten-minute spot, which meant stretching the five minutes of material I had well beyond its limits. This was even more problematic, because most of my material was about my mum and I knew she wasn't going to be silent on that subject. I was petrified. I'd never been heckled in my very short career.

I started with the carefully crafted jokes I'd written to confirm all the suspicions an audience would have about me. All those jokes can be boiled into one sentence: *I am a fat, awkward lesbian from Tasma-*

nia. These jokes got good laughs because Tasmanians like to hear about Tasmania, I looked very much the classic larger lesbian type, and the issue of my awkwardness had been confirmed just after the loose unit had claimed me as her spawn. The laughs were especially loud at the back of the room as my peers cheered for another train wreck.

"I'm the youngest of five children," I said, diving in, "which is weird, because my mum doesn't like sex."

I got good laughs from this.

"She doesn't like the word," I continued, "she doesn't like the act, and I'm pretty sure she's not too impressed with the results."

The crowd was delighted. I was delighted. Mum was not delighted. She stood up, turned around and shouted at the audience, "Don't encourage her! She's a dickhead!"

I then moved on to my material about my childhood dress code. "Most mothers like to dress their little girls up as princesses, but my mum preferred to fashion me into soft furnishings." Mum didn't rise to this first barb, but she called me out on the lie at the heart of my complaint about a particularly offensive tracksuit she had once made me. "I made that for your sister! And I don't sound like that!" But the audience, who had heard more than enough to know I was doing a very good impersonation, started howling.

Emboldened, I went off-script for the first time ever and countered Mum in her own voice: "Yes you do!" My little risk paid off. Mum walked straight into my trap, shouting back in the very same tone of voice I had taunted her with, "No I don't!"

The call and response went on for a few rounds and it gave me a sense of control, a bravery that I'd never ever felt on stage before. Sadly, for me, I did not know that bravery is the feeling where good judgment goes to die. I started in on a story that I had not, in any way, prepared for the stage. As soon as I started it, I knew I had made a huge mistake, because, unlike Mum, I do not flourish off-script.

The story was a family classic, so I knew my material incredibly well, and I was confident the tagline at the story's end was deeply hilarious. But the fundamental problem I had was that before I could get to this comedy gold, I had to navigate a very long and very joke-bereft setup. I was only a few sentences in when it became abundantly clear to both me and the audience that I am not a naturally charming raconteur. Sadly, there was nothing to be done; I had no choice but to keep going, because that's how train wrecks work.

The fact that the story was about Mum was enough to keep the audience on my side for longer than they ordinarily would have been. I knew I didn't deserve their patience as I blandly described the day Mum had come home from indoor bowls complaining of chest pain. "I think I've broken a rib." My impersonation of her dramatic self-diagnosis raised a bit of a laugh, but it died away as I took too long to get to the next relevant detail, which was the perfectly round bruise the size of a twenty-cent piece that Mum had shown us as irrefutable evidence of a cracked rib. "See, that's where my finger poked."

The improbability of a rib coming off second best in a clash with a lone finger was never not hilarious to us as a family, but courtesy of my clumsy retelling that night it was barely met with a few chuckles.

Somehow, I'd managed to lose the easiest of crowds. When I'd started my set, they were so well primed that I got an applause break for a well-timed look of confusion, but with metaphorical crickets having replaced their ready laughs, their collective fear was palpable and I felt my face fill with the heat of humiliation.

I knew I was making very basic mistakes. I knew that just because you can remember a detail of a story it doesn't mean that it should be part of the retelling; I knew that you should only choose the most relevant parts, because if you don't cull extraneous information then you won't be telling a story, you'll just be reciting a list of things you've remembered on your way to becoming a very dull person.

I didn't know this from personal experience of trial and error, I had learnt it by watching how other people tell stories; and the most valuable lessons always came from the most inept storytellers. I could write a textbook on how not to tell a story, and yet there I was being a textbook very dull person live on stage, verbalising my memory as simply and blandly as it was appearing in my mind's eye.

I wasted so much valuable time and audience goodwill recounting how Mum didn't go to the doctor or get an X-ray, and then I stumbled through a blow-by-blow account of how many people had asked her how she'd injured herself. All these details were true to the story, but unnecessary to the telling, and, as I was learning very quickly, quite lethal to the comedy of it. By the time I got to the punch line the audience so desperately needed, I was convinced it wasn't going to be enough to undo the damage.

"This is how Mum chose to describe the incident to anybody who asked . . ." I said, rather meekly, before changing my voice into my mum's: "Well. I fingered myself and I cracked a rib!'"

Despite my poor set, the room once again filled with laughter. And as I readied myself to deliver the killer ending to the story, the laughter began to morph into applause so I decided, somewhat reluctantly, to quit while I was ahead. But just as I was about to say good night, a very indignant Mum, who had never fully grasped the euphemism that made this story so funny, shouted over the tail end of the applause, "Well! I did!" I couldn't believe my luck. I suddenly had a way of getting to the closing punch line, the only thing I had to do was set Mum up to deliver it.

"But *how* did you break your rib, Mum?" I asked.

"I FINGERED MYSELF!!!!"

I felt a massive surge of relief wash over me as I left the stage, because not only had I survived my own poor judgment and narrowly avoided a disaster of my own making, but I also knew that I had my mum's full support.

NEW GAY COMIC 101

Dad saw me perform comedy for the first time two years later, in 2008, when he and Mum flew over from Tasmania to see my first solo stand-up show during the Melbourne International Comedy

Festival. Although he remained totally quiet throughout my performance and kept his post-show praise to a low-key minimum, it was
obvious that Dad was already my number one fan, a position he
maintains to this very day. Unlike most fans, however, Dad doesn't
gush about it, he archives it. There has not been a single word written about me that Dad hasn't read, cut and then pasted into what is,
at last count, three spiral-bound volumes of other people's gush. Unfortunately, his commitment to the task has meant he has collected
not just all the good stuff but also all the bad, and even some of the
ugly.

Like nearly all debut efforts, my first festival show was everything
I'd ever said that was remotely funny all bundled up into a vaguely
coherent hour-long cry for help. Now, after having written and performed nearly a dozen solo stand-up shows since this first one, I can
hardly believe how utterly impossible I found the prospect of having
to produce sixty whole minutes of comedy at once. Needless to say,
my fear and desperation led me to make many, many rookie errors.

The absurd title was the first poor decision I made. Everyone
who'd never heard the turn of phrase KISS ME QUICK I'M FULL
OF JUBES was understandably thrown. Clearly, I didn't think that I
was ever going to have an international audience, Jubes being a very
Australian thing. If I had been aiming for some kind of success in
America, I might have called the show *Kiss Me Quick I'm Full of
Gummies,* which is a good but distracting pun.

Sadly, the only people who had ever heard the phrase were my
own family, so I had no other choice but to begin the show by explaining that KISS ME QUICK I'M FULL OF JUBES was the special
code my mum used to describe a gay man of the especially effemi-
nate variety. My mistake was not the amount of time the explanation
necessitated—I was grateful for the amount of show it took up, to be
honest—the error was that I didn't understand the complexity of
what the title represented to me.

Essentially, I chose the name because I thought it would be a
quick, fun way to get to the character of Mum and her sense of humour. But I'd forgotten that it'd been a very painful expression for

me to hear for a very long time. I'd always known that Mum was just being playful whenever she'd describe somebody as being "a little bit kiss me quick I'm full of Jubes." But it wasn't until I started to shape my coming-out story into this show that I rediscovered the raw nerve it struck during the ten or so years I had been in the closet. It doesn't matter whether the compulsion to point out difference is malicious or good-natured, it will always hurt to be reminded that you don't belong to the only world you've ever known.

By the time I started to come out to my family, I'd spent so long in the closet that I wasn't entirely convinced I needed to go through with it at all. I felt like I had already drifted too far away from them, and I didn't expect that I could ever find my way back into the fold.

It took me the best part of two years to come out, because I decided to do it one person at a time. I didn't have a specific order in mind, so it was a fairly random process except for Mum. There was never any doubt that I would leave coming out to her until last, and that I was really only practicing on the rest of the family. I guess it could be said that I came out to my family the same way my dad taught me to peel carrots, fat end first.

The one thing all three of my brothers wanted to know when I came out to them was whether I'd told Mum yet—the echo of our childhood pact of keeping bad news amongst ourselves. I was in full agreement, and I might never have come out to Mum if it hadn't been for my sister, Jessica, who told me that it wouldn't feel like the right decision, because it wasn't actually a decision at all and, as she rightly pointed out, not telling Mum would just extend the dread and delay my life.

Jessica has always possessed a more thorough understanding of family than I have. I took it for granted that we would always be a unit, but she knew that our family was a bundle of relationships that all needed to be nourished individually in order to keep us together. And if she hadn't taken such particular care to nourish her relationship with me throughout those most difficult years, I doubt I would have emerged as the close-to-whole person that I have.

The real push to tell Mum was a healthy one. I had a girlfriend, Amy, she was a bubble of loveliness, we were a nice couple and I wanted us to be a part of my family. Amy had come out to her family, and they were all very golden with the whole thing, and I remain good friends with her mum to this day. It became easier than ever to entertain the possibility of a good time coming out, and I began to fantasise about the immense relief I would feel.

I ended up telling Mum over the phone. I hadn't intended to come out when I made the call; I was just inspired to share because we were having such a lovely conversation. I guess I'd hoped that the warmth between us would soften the impact of my news, but I was wrong and our chat soured in an instant. I'd barely finished delivering my dreaded news when she cut me off. "I don't want to know that. Why would you tell me that? It's none of my business," she said, her voice building with toxic venom. "It's not interesting to me. Why would you tell me something so horrible? I mean, what if I was to tell you . . . I was a murderer?!"

The call had not gone as well as I had hoped, but neither had it gone quite as badly as I'd always feared. Mum's ability to accept my sexuality waxed and waned. Sometimes she was fine, but often she struggled badly.

"I just didn't see it coming," she would complain to my sister, who, after months and months of counselling Mum over the phone, would sigh, "Come on, MUM! It just shouldn't have been that surprising. I mean, look at her. She looks like a lesbian. It's not rocket science!"

"Well!" Mum would say, getting defensive, "I'm not an astronaut."

How could she understand my world? We weren't even on the same planet.

About six months after I came out to Mum, one of my brothers got married and I took Amy along as my partner. It was a mistake. My family were not so ready to come out of their closet, and after the ceremony, I was told that Amy was not welcome to come to the reception after all. I was given a lot of different reasons; pretty much all of them boiled down to the same idea: I was being unfair. *Fair enough*, I remember thinking. As I watched Amy walk back toward the parking lot, I realised that I felt more alone out of the closet than I did in it. I felt as if I had made a monumental mistake by coming out, and I wished with all my heart that I could take it back.

THE BELL CURVE JAR

Earning My Keep

By the time I started stand-up comedy, the only jobs I'd ever had were entry-level hourly positions, and none had required any kind of skill I could brag about later. I couldn't read an Excel spreadsheet, let alone use the software, but I was very gifted at mopping around boxes. Comedy was about the only workplace that didn't demand any explanation for all the glaring gaps in my employment history. All I had to do was find my way onto the stage and convince each audience I met that I deserved my chance to learn on the job.

I had continued to drift about the place after I'd won the Raw Comedy competition, but eventually I settled in Adelaide, partly because I'd performed at the Fringe Festival and forgot to leave, and partly because Jessica lived there and offered me a place to stay. In 2009 I made the move to Melbourne to be closer to what I had decided was the best comedy scene for me. To help me find my feet, Hamish had offered me a room in the flat above the fruit and vegetable shop he and a friend had just opened. I was no longer unhoused, but, on the same hand, you couldn't accuse me of having pulled myself together.

My career had taken off quite nicely, but like all careers in the arts, livable income is not something you can expect in the first few years—if ever. Hamish came to my rescue again and gave me a casual job working the tills. It was a proud moment for me, to realise I had upskilled precisely zero percent in the previous decade. But I was happy to show off how good I was at mopping around boxes, and Hamish was happy to have an elderly-person whisperer on staff. I'm not sure anyone else would have kept a job open for all the touring time I had to take off when I was building my career. And without that place to live and work that Hamish had given me, I don't think I would have been able to be a working comedian at all.

In the beginning, the living arrangement above the shop was a situation worthy of a sitcom: two couples trying to navigate relationships and a new business, living together in a small flat with me, the single, hapless, sister-drifter who was trying to carve out a career in comedy. Eventually they all moved out, bought houses, got married and started their families. But I stayed behind, because while they were all ticking off life's boxes in the right order, I was only ever failing and flailing in all things that life demanded of me off stage. Unbeknownst to me at the time, there was a name for the root cause of my life-skill shortage, but I was too busy mopping around boxes and not paying bills to take time out to learn about "executive function" and how I didn't have any. Don't panic if you don't know what executive function is, you will learn all about it when I do.

External Scaffolding

We were having a coffee on Smith Street in Collingwood, sizing each other up, as it were. I can't imagine what Kevin thought of me, but I was very impressed by how much he reminded me of a wombat. When he asked me what I wanted out of comedy, I had to work hard to disguise the fact that I had never given it much thought. I was still living life like I was a pinball—just getting slapped about the place, hoping I didn't fall into a forever hole. But I knew enough to know that Kevin needed more than a stunning ability to surrender autonomy to convince him to become my manager, so I told him that I was mostly keen to build up my live audience. Then he asked me if I wanted to work in television. I most likely scoffed, before I answered with the first thing to come to mind: "Well, yes, if it helps get more people to buy tickets to see me live."

It turns out these were very good answers, because while Kevin has a great strike record at getting his talent onto the small screen, his real driving passion has only ever been live stand-up comedy. I knew he had all the big names on his books, so it never occurred to me that Kevin was making a shrewd decision to bring me into his stable. If anything, it made me question his scruples, but I kept that to myself.

I can take absolutely no credit for getting myself noticed by the most influential comedy manager in Australia. All I did was stumble into the talent-nurturing tentacles put out by the Melbourne International Comedy Festival. The comedy competition that gave me my start in 2006—Raw Comedy—was an MICF initiative. The following year, I was scooped up into the festival's new talent showcase, The Comedy Zone, with three other comedy novices, two of whom, Michael Williams and Celia Pacquola, were also Raw Comedy alums from the year before. We were each given fifteen minutes of stage time in front of a reliably full audience, when most other fledglings were busting a gut and losing a dime just to get a handful of bums on seats.

I was also given a nicely paid spot on the Roadshow tour, yet another MICF initiative, whereby five comics who had played the festival got thrown into a minivan and dragged all over Australia to perform in all the regional theatres who would have them. This was an incredible opportunity for a newbie. Not only did I get to perform alongside some of Australia's top-shelf comics as well as some amazing international talent, but I also got to perform in front of audiences who, unlike their city cousins, were just excited that anybody even bothered to come to town. They are the best kind of audience people.

When I began putting on my own solo shows, I was offered festival-run venues, which were highly sought-after bits of stage real estate. My first show had been in a 60-seat nook at the Melbourne

Town Hall that I could barely give tickets away to; but in my second year, I was upgraded to a literal cloakroom with 90seats that I all but sold out. With each successive year, I continued to chip away at it, incrementally stacking my success, going from 90seats, to 150, 200, then 400.

Again, I feel compelled to acknowledge how little of my success can be attributed to me. Of course, I was there, and I worked hard and had a bit of a knack, but none of it would've mattered had it not been for the festival infrastructure and some seriously skilled people propping me up along the way. When Kevin signed me back in 2009 I knew enough to be chuffed to have him as my manager. But really, I didn't have a fucking clue as to the gold mine of good luck I had been struck with. The thing about wombats is that they might look cute and cuddly, but they have this really hard butt-plate which they will use to crush the skull of any dingo stupid enough to put their faces into the wombat's territory. That's Kevin. And that's who offered to keep an eye on my career trajectory for me. With Kevin came my agent, Erin, and they are the longest relationship I've ever had outside my family.

Part of the handshake was that they would produce my live shows, so that meant I got a whole other team, publicists and producers and other administrative legends. This was a totally alien circumstance for me. I'd never known what it felt like to have this kind of support, to have other people invest in me, to take all the extraneous burdens away to make sure that I had the best chance to do the thing that I did best. It was as much a repayment of this debt as it was a love of my craft of comedy that drove me to work as hard as I could to keep getting better at what I did best. I knew I had to do whatever I could to make sure their investment in me was worth continuing.

Festival Baby

Every year, I would write a completely new hour of comedy and then perform it on the festival circuit. Regular stops included the Adelaide and Perth Fringe Festivals and the Brisbane and Sydney Comedy Festivals. But it was the Melbourne International Comedy Festival and the Edinburgh Fringe that were the most important fixtures on my working calendar. Melbourne was where I made money and built my confidence, and Edinburgh was where I lost everything and then some.

My reasoning for doing the Edinburgh Fringe was that it seemed like a logical extension of what I was doing back home, and my best bet to advance to the next career level—whatever that might be. Perhaps a coveted spot on a panel show? A Radio 4 series? Gum disease? I did dabble in the U.K. circuit for a little bit, but between the relentless late-night travel and the consistently inebriated audiences, I found it to be a fairly shitty existence all in all. I wasn't swayed by the romance of such a lifestyle, either. Because despite what all the films try and make you believe, being stranded on a train platform in the middle of the night is not actually romantic. I am a creature of logic, and festivals clearly offered a far superior career experience than anything the toxic cliques of the open-mic circuit or the male-dominated club racquet could ever offer me. I got access to some serious stage time, a chance to build my own audience and earn a livable wage, all without having to beg my way into a career one five-minute set at a time.

The Boys' Club

"I don't usually find women funny . . . but you made me really laugh!"

Every single female comic I know has had some version of this dead-end logic thrown at them, time and time again. *Women are not funny, but you are an exception! You made me laugh, you must be a freak.* I don't think there is much point in complaining about the fact that humans really do judge books by their covers; what I find so shitty is the way people will always blame a book for being an exception to a rule before they ever stop and think: *Hey, maybe my gross generalisation might be wrong!*

When I was starting out in comedy, the art form was not particularly burdened with a diverse population of performers. So, it was incredibly rare that I got to be on the same bill as another woman. I'm pleased this is changing, and I hope the industry continues to attract and nurture performers who are all kinds of "not normal." But when I began, if you were asked to picture a comedian in your mind's eye, most people would just grab their idea of a doctor and swap out his lab coat for a pair of jeans and a T-shirt. I certainly was not immune. I had the "all doctors and comedians are white men" as my default too, despite the fact that I was a female comedian myself with a lady doctor from Mumbai.

There was a lot of chat about humour and gender during the early years of my career, and the comedy industry was thick with the opinion that women were not biologically disposed to express the funny as well as men. It was Christopher Hitchens's pompous piece in *Vanity Fair* which first kicked this all off, but it trickled down thick and fast to where I was at the bottom of the comedy pile. For the most part, the comedians who most passionately supported Hitchens's argument all looked exactly like everyone thought a comedian should. As did their patron saint, Hitchens.

I won't bore us all here detailing the offensive pseudo-scientific reasoning that supported the "women are biologically built to laugh at men" fantasy, but I will paraphrase badly: Cave men killed big animals and this made women horny, because protein,[⊛] so the women would laugh at the men, which is how the menfolk knew that the women were ready to fuck.

Naturally I have embellished my paraphrasing, but I think it's only appropriate to distort the ideas of the men who distorted the ideas of other men who distorted the perception of half the human race to the point of erasure. The whole theory of natural-born male comic superiority depends on the premise that the comedy stage is

⊛ I do not have an intuitive understanding of either sarcasm or facial expressions, but go back and read the word "protein" and then roll your eyes. Like, really roll your eyes. So much so, that your eyeballs flip back into your head to look at your own brain, and then your brain should tell you, "Hey! Hey, hey! This is sarcasm."

an egalitarian platform, which is less a theory and more of an uncooked dick-drip marinating in bias blindness. But I never got terribly incensed about it, as I'd heard it all before. You can't study modern art and fail to notice that dick-swinging and pseudo-scientific justification of misogyny and racism is built into the bedrock of artistic "greatness" in the twentieth century.

What is most interesting to me, however—and I don't know if biology has anything to do with this, as it is a wholly anecdotal observation on my part—but women are a lot better than men at registering when someone has stopped listening, and they're also far superior at modifying their communication tactics accordingly. Which is, I would think, the kind of skill set that would go quite some way toward making someone "naturally" better at comedy.

Big Break

I had my fair share of terrible gigs when I was starting out, but I was consistently good enough that I was able to skip up through the ranks of the circuit. By 2010, I was earning enough so that I didn't need to supplement my income with shifts in Hamish's shop anymore. But it was only once I landed a job on Adam Hills's television show, *In Gordon St. Tonight,* that I began to feel that I was solvent. I'd first met Adam during the Hobart Comedy Festival, when I was a rank amateur and he was one of the best-known comedians in Australia. He was intrigued enough by my strange stylings that he offered to produce my first solo show, back in 2008. You can put that on the already long list of random acts of generosity that helped keep me afloat.

When Adam was developing his own weekly interview/variety show for the Australian Broadcasting Corporation, I tried out for the role of his trusty sidekick. I don't remember much about the audition other than that it was very chaotic, there was cake and I insulted Adam throughout the entire process. That wasn't my intention going in, it was just what happened under the stress of the moment. Adam and I do not have what you could describe as a similar approach to comedy. His earnest and relentlessly upbeat style tends to be heavy with audience interaction and grounded in something of an improv theatre style, which was in stark contrast to my own somber stage presence, which comes from more of a "don't fucking talk to me, here's something I prepared earlier" school of comedy. Nevertheless, we had this strange chemistry between us. I can't explain it, because I don't do chemistry, not with other people, anyway.

Our unlikely rapport aside, it was still quite the surprise that I landed the role, and no one was more shocked than me. I'd run the analytics; women who looked like me, and who were also queer and determinedly not effervescent, just did not get prime-time television gigs. Furthermore, it was quite rare for an actual female comedian to get the role of "the woman" on any kind of humorous show of any genre. A couple of producers sat me down before the first show aired and told me to expect some vicious kickback to my visible existence. It happens to all women, they assured me. But they needn't have bothered with their warning, I'd been fielding open hostility for most of my life.

Shame on Shame

I could fill the pages of fifty books with stories about my body and its shaming, although I don't think such a series would be fun for me to write or for you to read. You would think that my self-esteem would have improved as my success and confidence grew on stage, but being so open to public scrutiny and cruelty only made things worse. The whispers I had long held in my head about how fat and ugly I must be were externally corroborated by social media in the most horrific manner.

I got told I was a lesbian only because I was so fat and ugly that no man would want to touch me. I got told to kill myself because I was too fat and ugly to be alive. I got told that I was not funny because I was too fat and ugly. I got told that I was so fat and ugly that I wouldn't even get raped in a men's prison. As you would expect, I sometimes struggled to feel good about my success.

I am not comfortable with public recognition because they, the public, know me as a comedian, but I know that in most situations I am likely to be about as funny as a plank of wood. So when I heard an excited voice behind me at the train station ask if I was "that" comedian, I turned around very much hoping that I was not "that" comedian. Sadly, I was.

My fan was a teenage boy who clapped his hands in delight when I said hello. "My dad and I love you!" He grinned, and this took me very much by surprise. Dads and their young sons have never been my demographic. I could only assume that it was my prime-time gig that had broadened my fanbase. "Oh wow," was all I could think to say, but he was a fan, so of course he laughed.

As you would expect of an exchange between a teenage boy and someone like me, our meeting was brief and awkward, but just as I thought our exchange was over, he blurted out, "I hope you don't mind me saying, but I recognised you from your massive hips."

"Oh wow!" was all I could say before he continued. "This is really great because you've settled an argument between me and Dad because he reckons that your hips couldn't possibly be real, he reckons you must stuff padding or something down your pants! But I can see they're totally real and I am totally right!" There was nothing at all I could say to that except "Oh wow" again. I only managed to say that after he'd left, but I'm sure he would've laughed.

I wish I could tell you that this is the only time I have been presented with a stuffed-pants theory. So many people have queried the authenticity of my hips, and sometimes I wonder what they think about me after I tell them they are all natural. Do they think less or more of me? But mostly, it devastates me to think that my dimensions are cartoonish enough that people think I would do it for a laugh. I didn't help the situation. Every time I walked on stage, I would make fun of how I looked. I was very good at it too. I am way better at fat jokes than anybody who thinks they're funny.

"I've always been very thick of the thigh. I once scalped a girl playing leapfrog."

See? Fat jokes were my bread and butter, which is a shame, because that kind of bread and butter is basically a shame sandwich, and shame is never part of a healthy, balanced diet.

Momentum

To this day, I don't know what my role on *In Gordon St. Tonight* was, exactly. All I ever seemed to do was stand to the side while Adam interviewed, toss in a few pithy asides and look generally confused. Which was playing very much to my natural skill set. I learnt a lot of things during my time on the show, such as I don't like wearing makeup, and also that makeup artists don't really give a shit if you hate wearing makeup. If you're a woman, you must submit to spending at least an hour in the chair.

"But why can't I just get makeup like Adam?" I asked during the second season, which solicited this incredibly nuanced two-word explanation: "Oh honey." I also learnt that I enjoy being part of a team, and that there are a lot of amazing people supporting jerks like me, making us look way better than we really are. I also learnt that I am not a good fit for live television, and my exhaustion compounded itself throughout, so by the end of the third season I was happy for it to be the end, even if I was going to miss being part of a team.

Adult Shopping

I had bought myself a chesterfield couch as a memento after my first season on Adam's show. But by the end of the third season, it had not yet arrived. I'd ordered it online, surprised that I could get it so cheap. The last I'd heard, it had been held up in Singapore, which was what gave me the sneaking suspicion that my bargain price three-seater was actually a drug mule and began to prepare myself that I would never receive the couch. On the same day as purchasing my elusive sofa, I had also bought a filing cabinet and a desk. They were both very practical pieces that I absolutely needed, but it was a regrettable impulse purchase nonetheless, because I had no way of getting such large items back to the flat. My bike was sporting some flash panniers by then, but not even they were equal to the task.

In the fifteen adult years that a bicycle was my primary mode of transport, I was hit by a total of five cars. Fortunately, only three of them were moving, and of those, only one of them was travelling at speed on contact. I sustained various injuries ranging from a broken ankle to a bruised liver. But my worst injury came from being doored by a parked car. The reconstruction of my clavicle took multiple surgeries over several years, and although I have recovered full range of movement, I am never not in pain.

You would think such a string of traumatic accidents would have motivated me to get off the bike and learn to drive. But when it came to teaching us kids how to drive, my parents had made their apathy quite clear well before it was my time to learn. Unfortunately, I discovered that people who were not my parents were just as reluctant to teach me to drive. So really, I didn't have much choice but to wait until I could afford to pay a professional. And since I couldn't read a bus timetable, genuinely loved cycling and was all too accustomed to a life without the ability to earn a living wage, I was in no hurry to gain the ability to arrive places a little less sweaty.

But as Hamish drove us back home in the shop van, my desk and cabinet safely stowed in the back, he suggested it was time for me to get my licence. I was about to protest when I remembered that I wasn't poor and without a home anymore. By the time the final season of Adam's show had wrapped, I had my full driver's licence, I owned a little car, I had a fancy chesterfield sitting in a shipping container in Singapore and I was feeling very fine about life, which was finally exhibiting some semblance of normality. I'd even had a relationship that had ended well. Not that I wasn't sad when Joanna and I broke up, but it felt like a normal kind of shitty, not the monumental dumping I usually got with a character assassination chaser. We are still friends. That's peak normal, no? It also helped that I could blame it all on the fact that it was a long-distance relationship— she is based in London—and paper over the fact that I had reached my mid-thirties and was still unable to successfully navigate an intimate relationship beyond the honeymoon phase.

To top off the big upswing of my life, I had also been asked to join the cast of one of my favourite televisions shows, Josh Thomas's *Please Like Me*. It was a career highlight for me, because not only was I going to be in it, but Josh had asked me to write for my own character. To be given the opportunity to be the actor who delivers your own material for a television show you love is pretty much the greatest kind of screen work for a stand-up comedian. I was as happy as a clam, even though my character was a fat depressed lesbian called Hannah.

In even more impressive news, and I don't want to get all smug and humblebrag on you, but I was also on the way to getting my taxes in order. I had gotten at least as far as putting all the receipts from the past seven years into garbage bags and shoving said bags into the unused fireplace in my bedroom. The filing cabinet still stood empty, but it was perilously close to being used. It felt good. But the most important object that I had accumulated on my way to Club Adulthood was my bedside table.

It wasn't a fine piece of furniture by any stretch; I actually picked it up in hard rubbish.⊗ It was what it represented that put it at the top of my most treasured possessions list. From the moment it found its place beside my bed, I couldn't believe I had waited so long to find one. I finally had somewhere safe to put my glasses, and to me, that meant I was more than not homeless, but I was safe, and I had not felt safe for a very long time.

A Peek at a Peak

I wrote *Happiness Is a Bedside Table* in 2012, partly as a celebration of my reaching practical adulthood: a driver's licence, a bedside table and something that might even look like happiness, if you were to

---

⊗ At best a side-step from shopping at the actual dump, but what can I say? Old habits die hard.

squint. It was also my best attempt to change the way I thought about my body. It was my most finely written work to date, and it was also my most successful. I sold out just about all of my shows, and I got more standing ovations than I could cope with.

Within the show was a story that remains one of my favourite pieces of stand-up that I have ever written. I won't regale you with the entire tale now, but suffice it to say that it described the excruciatingly embarrassing occasion when, at fifteen years old, I got stuck in a children's waterslide. When Mum saw this show, she told me how she'd remembered me telling that story exactly the same way when I was a teenager. And it was true, it was the same, save for the layers of jokes I had added for the professionally delivered version. I can still remember standing in front of the fireplace in our lounge room, reducing my small, familial audience to tears and fits of helpless laughter. I also remember telling it about ten times before then. I'd told it the same night that it happened. They say that comedy is trauma plus time. But I have never needed time. I have always written my stories for laughs at the same time as the humiliation is tearing my self-esteem to shreds. This is my gift.

But unlike the jokes I had written to diffuse what I assumed everybody was already thinking about my body, this story felt constructive. I felt it in the way that people responded to it. I could tell that nobody was laughing at me, they were laughing with me, connecting through their own version of adolescent body image trauma. I had a glimpse of what it felt like to be just like everybody else, instead of the fat ugly spectacle I always felt I had been.

Happiness Is a Bedside Table was the first show I ended on a high note, but the fun stopped, sadly, about six months later, when a woman came up to me after a show to tell me what was wrong with me. This messenger, who I am about to shoot, was a very thin, spindly woman who was inspired to diagnose me because apparently my body was screaming "Help me" even though my voice had very clearly been saying "I am fine" throughout the show.

I listened. Of course I did. I always listen, even though I always find it so painful to listen to thin people lecture me about fat. But I listened, because I have also been lectured by people who don't believe I qualify as "fat" and so they don't think I have any authority to talk about body image on stage. My body is just wrong, I have been told as much my entire life, so there is nothing else left to do but listen.

After informing me that I had a condition called lymphedema, she suggested that I get myself assessed before giving me a greasy smile of pity dripping in smug and dashing off to project her issues onto someone else. What did she think I was going to do? Wait until I had an appointment with a specialist to find out what the fuck she was talking about?

I was already misspelling it into a Google search before she had left my line of vision. And the very moment I pressed the tab for an image search, I lost every bit of confidence I had been slowly and painstakingly rebuilding since I was fifteen years old. As the screen of my phone filled up with images of women standing in the horrible glare of medical fluorescence wearing nothing but paper underwear and replicas of my own legs, I felt my whole life cave in.

I just stood there . . . horrified. Horrified at myself, because I was repulsed by these poor women and I knew that meant I was repulsed by me. Still. But really, I should have saved all my repulsion for that stupid fucking meddling woman, who had just watched me tell my favourite story and bring a whole crowd to tears of laughter—laughter that was not cruel but rather born of recognition of adolescent anguish. But all she could think about was what I might look like naked and how I needed to be fixed, by her. But like I said, I have a gift for turning humiliation into comedy without needing any of the time normal people need, and not five minutes later I had two of my fellow performers crying with laughter as I told them that I had a disease which meant my legs were not limbs, as I had always assumed, but were in fact two load-bearing vertical rivers of cottage cheese. What an embarrassment of riches my body is.

DOWN!

Fingers of My Thinking

The first time I took Valium was the first time that I experienced being unbothered by my own body. The thing is, until the calm of that little pill spread its lovely little tentacles all through me, I had absolutely no idea how uneasy in my own skin I'd always felt. I am not just talking about pain, either. It's more of an extreme and ever-present awareness of my body, as if I don't quite fit myself properly, as if my flesh is a pair of underpants that is forever sliding up the butt crack of my soul.

Despite the revelation, I didn't rush to take Valium again. I didn't want to become addicted or, worse, to have it lose its effectiveness, so I resolved only to dip into my stash in an emergency. In my life, not sleeping often constitutes an emergency situation. I don't sleep very well. I never have. My brain is too busy. Anxiety is sometimes the root cause of my wakefulness but it isn't the only culprit. Sometimes I don't sleep simply because I'm having too much fun solving problems. Not real problems, to be sure, just creative problems. I'd always done this. When I was a kid, I would lay awake at night imagining how I could pack my school bag more efficiently, or different ways I could rearrange my bedroom. As I got older, I moved on to the impossible knot that was the social politics of teenage girls. But that messed me up so thoroughly I became a helpless blob of flotsam in a spiral of my anxieties. Of course there was a time that thinking about art was a reliable buoy for my spirit, but my continued failure to formalize my thinking appropriately into a viable career had drowned all that.

It wasn't until I started doing stand-up comedy that the pleasure began to return to my thinking. Unlike social interactions, I knew where I stood in relation to an audience. I understood what was expected of me. And best of all, I found that jokes were a problem I could solve in a vacuum. I would get home from gigs and climb into bed, and even if my body was desperate for rest, my mind would not cave in until all the problems of my set had been solved.

It was never forced or desperate, in the way an anxiety spiral could be. I'd close my eyes and my mind would come alive and the fingers of my thinking would begin feeling their way over the cogs and mechanics of my sets. And whenever I hit a solution—a better punch line or funnier turn of phrase snapped into place—my thinking became nothing short of thrilling. As good as flying in your dreams.

My shows have always been their own beasts, and they were all great puzzles in their own way. But none of them had felt so difficult to pull together as my 2013 show, *The Exhibitionist*. It didn't matter how many sleepless nights I put into solving it, I just couldn't crack the nut of that show. It was working well enough, but I couldn't find the internal logic of it. It was a watch with a face, but no tick or tock to make it really work. But the problem was not the show. It was me.

Whiskey and Valium

I was dragged from the deepest of sleeps by a terrible crunching sound, a screech of metal on metal, and I felt a visceral ripple tear its way up my spine. I woke with a gasp and I pulled my phone out from under my pillow. I had only been asleep for twenty minutes. That seemed unfair. I had taken some Valium and a couple of fingers of whiskey; I should have been dead to the world. I understood the dangers of doubling up on depressants when I washed the Valium down with whiskey, that's why I put a good chunk of ice in the glass; it's called hydration.

When the noise ripped me from the depths of my artificially engineered slumber, a thick grogginess clung to me into the waking world. It was as sickly as it was discombobulating. How must Lazarus have felt? The sound happened again. It was an even higher pitch this time and I threw my hands over my ears, put my head between my knees, trying in vain to stop the sound from hitting my spine again. What the fuck was happening? I wasn't afraid, I was angry. That's what high-pitched sounds do to me; they tip me into a rage.

I'd barely recovered when I heard a voice. A man's voice. I couldn't tell if it came from the shop below or outside. I heard it again and my rage was replaced by calm. That was what adrenaline does to my body. It shifts my gears down to almost neutral. It makes me sleepy, and this is not good in an emergency. Humans are given two options when faced with mortal danger: fight or flight. I'll give you the third: narcolepsy. To the point where I think even if I was murdered, I would still technically die in my sleep.

I crept out of bed and went to the window. In the reflection of the news agency windows across the street I could see that the roller door of the shop below me was up about two feet. I looked at my phone; it was way too early for someone to be opening up. I looked back outside and that's when I saw a figure crouching and looking under the door. I quickly phoned Hamish. Much to my surprise, he answered almost immediately. "What's up, Gods?"

"There's someone breaking into the shop . . ."

I heard him scrambling out of bed. "Hang up. I'll call the police. I'll be right over."

I hung up and looked back out the window. There were now two men. This was not good. I lived alone, and the roller door was the only thing that separated me from the outside world. Once through, all they had to do was come upstairs and there I would be. And they would come upstairs, because that's where the safe was. My phone lit up. It was Hamish: "Hang tight. Police on their way." I wasn't sure how I was supposed to hang tight. I went into the office next door and plucked out an iron from Hamish's golf bag and made my way down the hallway and positioned myself at the top of the stairs.

I gripped the club low with both my hands, and raised it up behind my back and waited in the dark like I was in a league of my own. My brain, which has never liked to be as still as my body, began providing me with a loop of possible outcomes. It felt incredibly good to see with great detail all the violence I might be able to inflict. I visualised myself striking the first stranger who came up the stairs, again and again; I saw myself swinging down and hitting the bull's-eye, square onto his groin, with brutal efficiency. I wouldn't want to kill them. But I would if I had to. Not to save my brother's money. He had insurance. I just did not want to be raped. Not again.

I don't know how long I had been lying in wait at the top of the stairs, but when I first heard the police siren suddenly flare up, it felt like hours and seconds at the same time. As I raced back up to my room at the front of the flat, I could hear a lot of shouting; my bedroom was awash with the pulsating red and blue of flashing light. I was still trying to make sense of the chaos below when my phone lit up. Hamish: "Well done, Gods. The police nabbed them red-handed!"

Lucky for them, I thought. Otherwise I might have gelded them, smashed their faces in and terrorised them to something close to death. Hit with a sudden bone-deep fatigue, it was all I could do to climb back into my bed with the golf club next to me. The police lights were still flashing and excitable voices were still carrying up from the street below but none of it mattered. I was asleep before my head hit the pillow.

Self-Evidently

Mum was in the midst of her usual pre-Christmas haberdashery campaign when I'd arrived back home four months earlier. There was festive themed fabric debris strewn all over the dining room, nothing was finished, but Mum was in good spirits despite the looming deadline. I made myself a cup of tea and plonked myself down on one of the green chairs, expecting Mum to give me a bit of a show-and-tell of all her half-finished Christmas presents, but instead she just shoved a plastic bag into my hands.

"I just want to make sure you had all of these before I dropped dead."

I peered inside and saw a jumble of all the photographs my parents had ever collected of me. It was a striking gesture, really. "Here is all the proof I have of you. Take it. I don't want it." I could hardly blame her. I did not leave a charming photographic impression, a fact made even more tragic by the plastic bag presentation.

"I like the photo album, Mum. Really neat."

Our family didn't have a camera in my living memory, so my photographs were all either taken for school or by family friends. In most, I was usually arranged next to whoever was visiting at the time. I never looked particularly happy, sometimes I looked downright furious, especially if I was smiling. I tended to be looking somewhere off to the side. In some my stare would be tinged with uncertainty, in others I looked a little bit brittle, in others I seemed startled, but in most my face would indicate there was something of a vacancy within me. None of the photos seemed to match how I remembered myself as a kid. I looked so vacant and yet I only ever remember being filled to the brim with life and all the thoughts.

"You were always off with the fairies," Mum kept saying as we went through the bag together. I bristled. People have always said that about me, and it has always shit me when they did. Who are these fairies? I don't have time for fairies.

Mum hadn't given away all evidence of her offspring. She kept the framed family portrait that had always hung in her and Dad's bedroom. All five of us kids crammed together in front of a mottled brown background. I am sitting in the front, doing my absolute best attempt at a smile, looking straight ahead; my eyes are scrunched up into a squint, my cheeks are rosy red, and my mouth is stretched into a smile so big and wide that all my clenched little baby teeth are in full view. You've never seen a happier grimace. The only solo photo of me that survived Mum's culling was the one that had been living its dust life on the bureau in the lounge room. It was not recent; it'd been taken decades earlier at Ben's wedding. I knew it was me, but only in theory. If I am being honest, I would say I looked more like John Denver circa 1974.

As I was flicking through one of my school reports that Mum had thrown into my stash, a bunch of photographs fell to the floor, five baby photos. I picked them up and I studied them closely but I couldn't make much of my baby self from the photos. I was asleep in four of the five, and in three of them a good portion of my head had been cropped out. "Were you drunk when you took these?" I asked Mum, flipping her a photograph of a headless pair of chubby baby legs laid out in a cot. Mum looked over her glasses at me. "That might not be you, darling."

Your Face Is a Face

I knew that the glorious agony of adolescence which filled my plastic bag of photographs was exactly the stuff that comedy gold could be spun from and so, naturally, it became the seed for my sixth stand-up show, *The Exhibitionist*. But beyond this desire to mine my own personal tragedy, I was also struck by how much my bag of photographs felt like a relic from a long, long ago past. How marvellous that, as someone in my mid-thirties, I could be documented in a way that would be almost alien to people little more than a decade younger.

Even in the way back of 2013, smartphones and social media had already become so ubiquitous and pervasive, it was hard to believe that there was ever a time when most people on earth only knew the people they could touch. That mirrors and portraits were for a long time only for the incredibly wealthy; and until very, very recently, most people on earth never got a chance to look at their own image at all.

For me, stand-up comedy was always an act of self-portraiture. On stage I could control how the world saw me, what piece of myself to show. But I didn't always understand that my physicality also participated in how I painted my self-portrait on stage. When I first started, I believed, firmly, that only the words I spoke had the power to convey the meaning of me. I couldn't have been more wrong.

An audience will have already made up a million minds about a comedian before they even reach the microphone, because it doesn't matter how clever you are, your body will always be your context. Your words, your jokes, your material, are just the tools you use to spin it.

I made a decision very early, after watching one of my sets online, never to study my own performances. I was confused by what I saw. By *who* I saw. I spoke so slowly. My voice was so soft. Why did my eyes bulge? The next handful of performances I did afterward suffered because of that self-consciousness. My jokes didn't land because I was too busy pleading with myself to stop pushing my glasses up, or whatever was on my seemingly endless list of *don't do thats*. But when I didn't think about how I appeared, I was consistently funny.

Early in my career I had been invariably described as "deadpan." I couldn't disagree more. I wish I were deadpan. It's a very effective comic device. It is like the better-natured and kinder-hearted cousin of sarcasm. But deadpan delivery needs impassive expression, a stillness of face—a seriousness, if you will. My face is hardly ever impassive; it moves from one expression to another with barely a pause between. It can be so mobile it practically ripples. My guess (and I am correct) is that it was the monotony of my voice and how still I stood that tricked people into believing that I was a deadpan comic.

For the first few years I performed, I would stand motionless behind the microphone, my feet planted and my body rigid. Over the years, I learnt how to modulate my voice. It was something of an organic evolution, not a fix-me-up. I had spent hundreds of hours on stage experimenting with all the different ways to squeeze laughs out of a crowd. I had also watched just as many hours of other comics doing the same. I couldn't ignore it: the power of a joke is not in the writing; it is how you wrap your voice around it.

Once I learnt how to animate my voice and began moving around on stage more, I became a demonstrably better comedian. The correlation was undeniable. Laughs got longer and louder. I learnt how to roll one laugh into the next. I learnt how to build momentum over the course of an hour-long performance, by varying the rhythm and speed of my delivery. I learnt how to punctuate silence with a frown, impregnate a pause with a meaningful sigh, how to string a punch line out for miles by not saying a word. And that's how I learnt how to play the audience like a fiddle.

I was what is called a "low-status" comic. I wrote my jokes and performed them all as a signal to my audience that I was not better than they were. When this is done in service of a joke, it is called self-deprecation[⊛] but in the big wide world, it is called "I am not a threat! Please don't punch me!" I didn't decide to be this way on stage; this persona was just a natural extension of myself and who I needed to be in order to survive, both on and off stage. But as I became a more confident performer, my confidence began to bleed into my sense of self off stage, and yet I didn't feel there was room for me to close that loop and explore my personal growth on stage. Which is to say, position myself as having higher status than I began with. An audience is like a small town; try to become something other than what they understand you to be, and you run the risk of hostile resistance and outright rejection. And so it was, with each passing year, I felt myself losing something of my authenticity. And authenticity is the secret sauce of successful comedy.

There was an exception to this, however, and that was whenever I spoke about art on stage. On these occasions, I would suddenly become what is called a "high-status" comedian. I was so much more confident, and effortlessly so. I figured it was because I wasn't

⊛ Not to be confused with self-defecation or self-depreciation. Although . . .

trying to explain myself; I was simply sharing something I loved with my audience. But it was a little more complicated than that.

Since *The Exhibitionist* was a combination of both stand-up and art history nerdiness, I began to experience a clash between these two conflicting on-stage personas. I wanted to land in the space between these differing ideas of me. But I just couldn't seem to do it, and the struggle of trying was breaking me apart. What I didn't know was that it wasn't just the show and my performance of it that I was trying to click into place. It was the very idea of me. I lay awake at night, wrangling in vain, and if I got close I would either disappear into complete fiction or shatter into a million little pieces of truth.

Squalor on Down

I didn't end up solving my show before the end of my Melbourne season, but without a show to turn over at night my brain replaced it with a void around which my anxieties could go spiralling. I had two weeks before I had to go away again. I wanted to pick up all the life pieces I had dropped during the festival, but I couldn't get myself together. I was living in squalor. This was not how I wanted to live. I don't like filth at all. I crave order, because I live my best life in clean and uncluttered environments; but despite my instinct for neat, I had somehow managed to foster the methodology of a slothful teenage boy.

It began with just one small act of "I can't be bothered." I had finished my dinner, and acknowledged the fact that the dishes needed to be done, but then I would not do them. I did the same thing the very next night. And then the next. I had fooled myself that I would do all the dishes once the festival was over, but I never acted on these intentions. So even without the excuse of a show, I would still look at the pile of dishes, feel totally overwhelmed and sit on the couch and rock.

I had been living in the flat above my brother's fruit and vegetable shop for almost five years. It's not surprising that I didn't know that I was struggling at the time, because I had experienced far worse. I mean, when I started stand-up, I had been functionally unemployed and without a home, and both circumstances had felt permanent to me, so having a lot of unpaid parking fines and a habit of sleeping in my clothes seemed like small fries in comparison. Before comedy I lived day-by-day, I just struggled and lurched from failure to failure, and if I ever thought about my future, I would see nothing and dream of even less. But at least my life had been small back then. Comedy made my world very big. Too big. With comedy came chaos.

A full week after the festival, I bargained with myself that I needed to clean the kitchen before I was allowed to leave the house for fun. That was a dud bargain, given that I wasn't even leaving the house for necessities by then. I had long run out of traditional food vessels. I was forced to be creative. What most people would call toast I was calling an edible plate. I didn't get to the point of eating directly out of tins, I'm not an animal, but I did pour a tin of spaghetti directly onto the microwave plate, which I then ate cold. That might seem like a thing that would signal that life had devolved into a grim reality, but I was still able to turn a blind eye to the shame of my squalor. The thing that woke me up was when I began drinking my tea black.

I had always been very particular about the way I would take my tea. When I drank with Nan and Pop, it had always been made with tea leaves in a pot, and drunk from a fine china cup with a thin lip and never not a saucer. But once I was forced to fend for myself out in the big bad world, I found I could settle and enjoy tea from a bag made in a mug. The line I drew and could never cross was that it must be brewed strong and then balanced with a good splash of full cream milk.

My tea mug had been the only thing I had taken to rinsing during my marathon of sloth. That I could get my act together enough to drink my tea out of something clean was enough to fool me that nothing was wrong; but when I ran out of milk and began to drink my tea black, I knew I was in a very bad place. Buying milk had become impossible, and to put that in its brutal context, I was living above a shop that sold milk.

Relationship Status

It wasn't the first time I had become a shut-in after a festival. A few years earlier I'd spent about a month trapped in a very small flat in North London, after a month at the Edinburgh Fringe Festival had left me with nothing in the tank and venturing out into the world became impossible. When I was in the midst of my shop squalor, I failed to see the obvious connections between these two episodes. I put that down to the fact that it was a slow slide down in Melbourne, whereas in London it had begun with a sudden plot-losing episode at Angel Station.

It had been peak hour, and I got pulled into the station as part of a sea of people. I'd meant to top-up my Oyster card, but the cram of bodies felt too purposeful to break directions with safely. I had hoped there was enough on my card but that was dashed when the turnstile remained locked into place. Unable to go forward, I became the cause of an angry bottleneck, and everyone took turns sharing their frustration and anger with me as I tried to make my way upstream.

I was only a bit flustered at first, but when one man dropped his shoulder to make heavy contact with me as I passed, my embarrassment quickly turned to panic. He was very solidly built, and when my shoulder hit his I was spun off my axis. "Fucking tourist," he muttered, as if I had orchestrated the contact. But that wasn't what made me burst into tears, it was pain that did that.

The screech of a train straining against the tracks had made its way up from the depths of the station, tunneled into my ears and raced down my spine. I almost doubled over from the pain of it, and as I fought to regain my equilibrium, I discovered I was crying. I sorted out my ticket and made my way toward the platform. The rush had abated a little bit, but the escalator was still quite full. I moved to the side and watched the posters for West End shows flip past me. The escalators in the Angel tube station are amongst the longest of the Underground, and about halfway down the vertigo began. I shut my eyes and held on. Sounds became too much. My distress was already reaching crescendo when I tripped off the bottom. A kind man began helping me to my feet, but I couldn't hear what he was saying. He guided me to a wall, out of the thoroughfare, and then left. I slid down to the floor and stayed there until it subsided. I didn't know what it was at the time. But I knew when it had passed. And when it did, I went straight back to the flat and stayed put for weeks.

So that was what sparked my London month of agoraphobia, but there was also an easily identifiable root cause underlying it. I had stopped taking antidepressants. It wasn't a decision; I had just forgotten to pack my meds when I had headed over to the Edinburgh Fringe, and rather than jump through the many hoops I needed to get myself a script in the U.K., I decided that I may as well just stop taking them. There could never be a more perfect time to abruptly stop taking antidepressants without any medical supervision: I was overseas, thousands of miles away from my family, friends and support network, and I was about to do the Edinburgh Fringe Festival.

By contrast, my Melbourne squalor episode did not get sparked by a traumatic public meltdown, nor was it preceded by an abrupt cessation of a medication. So even as the flavour of my distress felt exactly the same on the inside, I was unable to remember that I had been through that same flavour of darkness before. Perhaps, if I had been able to connect the dots, I might have been able to see the bigger picture: I was having another major depressive episode. I might also have realised that there had been two very significant elements that united the two episodes. They both happened after particularly exhausting festivals, and both times I was in a relationship I didn't know was ending.

Furious Incompetence

I'd last seen Sam on the closing night of the festival. Since then, we'd only communicated through text, with the occasional call. She led a full and independent life, so it took another fortnight before I got us to the point of conflict. But she had insisted that we see each other before I left, and I knew I had to emerge from the black hole that my life had become, so I agreed to meet her at a café.

The first hint of trouble was how angry the café itself made me as soon as I walked in. It was a concrete cube, and instead of tables and chairs, it had milk crates with squares of synthetic turf for cushions. In 2014, making fun of hipsters had become something of a comedy hack subject, though to be fair, I'd been hostile to the "hipster aesthetic" long before it was cool, but I don't like to brag about it because that is such a hipster thing to say. I hated the way hipster businesses would steal survival strategies from the economically helpless and then charge a fortune for whatever service they were hocking—in this case it was serving food on chipped and mismatched plates, and hot beverages in mason jars. When I was a kid, we drank out of vegemite jars because I was one of five kids, and when glasses broke there was not enough money to buy more.

I hated Fletcher the moment I saw him dancing around behind the counter doing nothing but looking busy. He was wearing a too-small knitted jumper with Garfield on it; the stitch was coming loose on the shoulder. Fletcher is one of those people that are pretentious, but you have no idea why. Why are you so smug? Why do you get to make me feel bad about myself? You are a *barista*, not a *barrister*.

When I was between homes and drifting badly through life, I met my fair share of hippies with safety nets. Rich kids with a chip on their shoulder who were slumming it by choice, all pretending that their motivations were spiritual and not just bog-standard teenage rebellion taken to an extreme. I had hated them because, to me, they seemed incapable of seeing what a privilege it was to be able to reject what was expected. I had never felt as if I'd ever had a choice. My rejection was thrust upon me. But, as infuriating as I found the trappings of late '90s hippiedom, I would take their privilege-gaslighting over the ironic smarm of this particular type of hyper-aware mid-aughties hipster any day.

We reached the counter and Fletcher greeted us: "Hi. I'm Fletcher, what can I get you." He sounded both bored and impatient, and that only increased my ill will toward him, but my girlfriend, oblivious to my stewing mood, responded cheerfully: "Can I have a skinny latte, please?"

To which he responded, "We don't serve skim milk here."

Although I am a staunch supporter of using full cream milk in a hot beverage, I don't judge people who choose watered-down dairy, but the slimy ball of false nostalgia named Fletcher managed to say it in a way that made it sound as if she'd ordered a glass of Nazi with a side of blackface. Sam apologised in a faltering tone that made it clear she was accepting full responsibility for her ignorance, but I was not so ready to absorb Fletcher's lactose intolerance.

"Don't mind her," I said icily. "She's just woken up from a coma. She still thinks it's yesterday, when skim milk was OK."

I was well aware that I wasn't speaking to Fletcher with my best humanity in hand, but I was also aware that it had no effect on Fletcher whatsoever, because he had the personality of a Teflon skillet. It affected Sam, however. She did not like seeing that side of me. My mean streak. She didn't care a jot for my brooding, snappy, volatile side. "I hate this. I don't know who you are when you get all Dr. Jekyll."

"But he's the nice one." I didn't mean to make it worse, but I did.

"You're doing it again."

I wanted to know what I was doing again, but I was afraid to ask. I didn't want to make it even worse. I was trying my best to keep a lid on it. I always do. Sometimes I can. But never when I'm in a bad way. And I was in a bad way.

We each took a milk crate and tried to restore our peace, but it was hard to do because I was sitting on a milk crate in a concrete cube. By the time Fletcher bounced over with our drinks, we had managed to establish an uneasy peace. "Look," I said, trying my level best to be charming, "I'm paying five dollars for a cup of tea that I have to put my own tea bag in and then not drink it, because the cup is too hot to hold. It's too hot to hold because it is made of glass and it doesn't have a handle . . . You know why? Because it's a jar!" I had wanted it to come out as lighthearted observational comedy. It was hack material, but it wasn't a ticketed event, just a misguided attempt at being charming. But Sam was not at all charmed. My tone had been wrong or something. "What the hell is wrong with you?" she asked.

I started to ask her what she meant by that when Fletcher suddenly appeared again, this time with our breakfasts, and began rearranging our table with great theatric ceremony. Sam pointed at one of the chipped ramekins of mystery condiments Fletcher was arranging on the Ping-Pong paddle in the middle of the broken miniature wine barrel and asked, "What's this?"

"Crab apple preserve," he said, standing up smiling, nay, beaming, "Made in-house."

Oh my god, I thought. *Fletcher is . . . proud? Why?* After he left, Sam leant in conspiratorially: "See!"

I didn't see. I didn't have a clue as to what point she thought had just been illustrated. Sam clearly thought something positive had just occurred, but I was too furious to even begin to guess. "Crab apple preserve!" I said with great and genuine incredulity. "Why would anybody preserve crab apple!?"

"I can't believe you!" Sam sighed. Exasperated.

I didn't pause to engage with her train of thought, however, because mine had already left the station.

"If it only takes one apple to spoil the barrel—that apple would have to be the crab apple. It is so bitter it'll pucker the fuck out of your face before you've finished your first bite. Apples are usually so reliable. They won't blow your mind . . . but you can rely on them. Not the crab apple, though. Why would you preserve something so devious? I bet it was a crab apple that got Adam and Eve evicted, you know. I mean, it's stupid. It's a stupid apple."

When I eventually ran out of steam, Sam didn't pick up the conversation where I had left off. And we finished our catch-up in silence. The silence continued as we made our way back to her car, and it wasn't until she opened the driver's side door that she finally said something: "Hannah, you need to take your mental health seriously. I can't deal with all this."

As soon as she had said her piece, Sam climbed into her car and slammed the door. It was probably for the best, because if she had expected me to respond I would've sorely disappointed her. I couldn't think of a single thing to say, and I very much doubted there was anything I could have said anyway. It had hurt so much to hear it, I lost my ability to speak. So, it was all I could do to stand, wait and wave until her car had turned the corner out of sight.

Sock and Awe

I opened the curtain, because that's what healthy people do. But I wasn't healthy and the late afternoon light, soft and golden as it was, felt utterly revolting. I closed the curtain. Downstairs I could hear the shop going through the motions of closing time. It wouldn't be long before someone would be up to count the till, so I decided to wait in my room until everyone had gone. I wasn't in the mood for any kind of small talk.

I tried to make a mental list of everything I had to get done in less than half a day, but I was too anxious to imagine any kind of priority: a month's worth of washing up, six years of taxes in arrears. I needed a shower. I needed to pay all my parking fines. I needed to pack. I needed to pay rent. I needed to find out what airline I was flying. I needed to get my niece a birthday present for last month. I needed to book a taxi for the morning. I needed to buy my other niece a birthday present for last year. I needed to find the address of my hotel in Sydney. I needed to fix my relationship.

I looked around. The room was a very hectic mess. My desk was covered in undone paperwork, as was my chair, and my fireplace was still filled with god knows how many years of receipts. I hadn't done any washing for six weeks and dirty clothes were all over the floor, split into piles like little mixed salads of filth. My laptop and note-books had been my bedmates for a month, but it was becoming hard to see where I actually would fit amongst all the crap. No wonder I couldn't sleep. A pen had leaked all over the duvet. Red. Nice. I wondered whether I'd found the pen and sorted it, or if it was a disaster in progress. I leant against my filing cabinet. It was still empty.

I heard someone come up from the shop. I startled. I hate to be startled, which is unfortunate because I startle embarrassingly easily, and ever since the attempted break-in I'd become even more startle-prone than usual. It wasn't that I was worried about there being another break-in; the roller door had been replaced, a security system installed, and arrests made. I wasn't afraid at all. But my body was.

I heard the office door open and I felt a panic rising, my mind began racing, careening and circling around what felt like all the thoughts I'd ever had. In an effort to keep myself calm, I turned my attention to the office next door, and I began to match the sounds I heard with a scene in my mind's eye. I had listened to the closing process many, many times. I knew which chair they sat in by the squeak it made. I knew which coin denomination was being counted by the pitch of the sound it made as it was being dragged across the desk toward the waiting palm at the edge. I could tell when a count was almost done by the way the dragging suddenly sped up.

My eye caught the golf club under the bed. I picked it up. I turned it over in my hand and began thinking about the break-in. I turned the scene over in my mind. I remembered how I had planned an attack, how I had resolved to swing the club into the first dick that came up the stairs, and follow it up with a knee to the face then a rampage down the stairs. I was struck by how real it felt, even though I didn't go through with it. I was struck by how violent it was and by how comforting that violence felt. It wasn't a fantasy, I didn't want any of it to happen for real, but the violence of it made me feel safe, it made me believe I could be more than a helpless and passive victim. Not like last time.

Perhaps if I had killed them, then I could've gone to jail. I'd had intermittent fantasies about going to jail since I was a teenager. It was a thing I did whenever I was sliding into suicidal ideation. In my mind they were interchangeable ideas. I knew my idea of what it meant to be in prison was naive and one-dimensional. I knew it wasn't real; a place where every day was the same and all the decisions of my life were made by other people. There would be no taxes, no bills, no rent, it would be acceptable to hang posters on my wall as an adult, and for some reason that really appealed to me. I didn't want to go to jail, I just wanted to check out. I wanted to step off the spinning of the world. I didn't want to kill anybody—not myself, not potential rapists. I just wanted everything to stop.

The printer fired up next door. Startled out of my thinking, I was impressed with how far I had let my mind stray from the task I had given it. I heard the squeak of the chair. They were nearly done.

I waited until I heard the back gates smash together to be locked before I got up off the floor and winced at the pins and needles in my legs. It was so bad they felt less like limbs and more like Doric columns. How had I not noticed that? I hobbled down the hall, cursing the painful return of circulation to my legs and dreading the mess that was waiting for me in the living room. I was shocked by what I saw, and sickened by what I smelt. There were dirty dishes everywhere, all over the floor, atop piles of books, balanced on both arms of the couch. There was a wet scarf smooshed into one corner of the room. I'd used it to clean up the glass I had broken and all the milk that was in it. I had cut my toe and there was still the trail of blood I had left behind after I had finished "cleaning."

If I had been of healthy mind, and not responsible for all the mess, I would have been absolutely fascinated by the debris and all the questions that came begging with it. There was a shopping list written on a dirty chopping board, in pen. A teaspoon with an unidentifiable pool of congealed darkness in its scoop was perched inside a hat. There was an opened but uneaten tin of tuna sitting on the soil of a long-dead houseplant. It was all exactly as I'd left it, but it was somehow worse. As if leaving the flat had gifted me with fresh eyes and now I could see how horrifically I was living, and, by extension, how horrific a human I was. I felt defeated by the sight of it. *I'll pack first*, I thought.

I like packing suitcases. I find it soothing. Even when I am on tour, I will unpack, repack and sort my cases several times a day. I like seeing everything I need neatly Tetrissed into a small space. When I first started touring, I was always forgetting one thing or another. Wallet. Medication. Socks. Over the years, I'd developed a system that had all but solved this issue: I packed from bottom to top. Shoes, socks, trousers, underpants, bras, T-shirts, outer layers. Next, I would choose my hat for the trip. I hadn't yet mastered the packing of my non-clothing needs, I was still prone to forgetting my toiletries, my laptop and such, but it had been years since I had left home without any trousers.

I dragged my suitcase out from under the bed. It was still half full from my last trip, so I dumped it out on top of another pile of crap on the floor, and looked around for some socks. I started sifting through the mess on the floor, but I couldn't seem to find so much as a single pair. But instead of becoming frustrated, as I had by the sight of the living room, I became really, really invested in solving the sock problem. Like really, really into it.

I began by picking over each pile of mess, more methodically this time. Taking every sock I found, no matter how dirty, and throwing it onto my new pile. I called it my "sock stock pile" and felt pretty good about myself. Once I had completed two rounds of my mess and had found as many socks as I could, I cleared a space on the floor and laid them all in neat lines. Once I had my socks all laid down in their rows, I began the pairing. It was like a shit game of memory. *Where have I seen this sock before? Oh, over there, where I can still see it.* I focused on the task with all I had, and everything else disappeared. I was living my best life in a "sock void," because it was the closest thing to my version of prison that I could manifest.

My sock-matching reverie was broken when a string of texts from Sam lit up my phone. I opened them hoping for new information, but she just wanted to reiterate what she had already told me at the car. Three texts, same message, different nouns. *Mental health. Mood. Anger.* I sent one reply back, I don't remember what I wrote but I made it worse. The reply was one word: *Stop.* So, I did. I'd been trying so hard all my life to control my moods and I knew it was impossible. I didn't know how to tame them. I'd made so many efforts all throughout my adult life. More often than not, it led to misdiagnosis and inappropriate, sometimes dangerous, medication. Premenstrual dysphoric disorder, psychosis, borderline personality disorder, bipolar, irritable bowel syndrome, too much fat, etc., etc. The only diagnosis that had made sense to me was complex post-traumatic stress disorder. But nobody could seem to help me escape the grip of it. Sam wanted me to see a therapist, she wanted me to get help, but I couldn't face another dead end. It was over. I just wanted to be alone forever.

It was dark outside. I looked at the time; it was already half past ten. I'd lost hours to my sock-sorting mission. Hours. I hadn't noticed. I still had a kitchen full of rotting filth and a 6:00a.m. flight, and all I had to show for my effort was a lot of paired socks. I threw my phone onto the bed with all the other shit that should've been on my desk. I had found mates for all but three of my socks. On the face of it, I guess you could say that I'd done a pretty good job, but I couldn't draw such a conclusion at the time because I was not living anywhere near the face of it. All I could see was what I hadn't done. I looked at the three solo socks. I needed to find them their pairs. I didn't want to think about anything else. I didn't want to think about the end of my relationship, I didn't understand what had happened. I just wanted to think about my socks. I cast my eyes around the room. Where might I find my three rogue socks? Maybe they were in the living room? That was a very unhappy thought.

I'd had quite a few episodes like the one I had then. But I'd always understood them to be panic attacks. They certainly began with panic. My mind, racing with too many thoughts, would begin to spin out of my control. Then my ears would start ringing with all the sounds within earshot; the softest sounds would merge with the loudest so I couldn't understand what was close and what was far away. I'd become totally and utterly overwhelmed and began to pace, shaking my head and whatever else I could move to make myself feel better. I must've tripped on my floor mess or something, and after I cracked my head on the filing cabinet the last thing I remembered was the echo still reverberating around in the great big empty inside it.

But Seriously, Folks

I drove myself to hospital. It was a terrible decision but I still hadn't organised ambulance insurance. The emergency department was not busy, and I was seen to pretty quickly. I was asked all the questions, and my head was dressed with a couple of butterfly stitches. Once the wound was cleaned up, I underwent a few tests. The doctor wanted to find out why I passed out. I was secretly hoping it was a heart problem. But no . . . For the second time that day, I was told I had to pay attention to my mental health. It was not exactly a Sophie's choice for me; I *couldn't* take my mental health seriously. I had carved my on-stage persona around the fact that I was depressed.

"Get on top of it," said the doctor. "Take it seriously, please," she implored.

"I have a busy day ahead. I have a six a.m. flight to catch," I deadpanned. She didn't laugh. I smiled. She didn't. *Her loss,* I thought.

"What happened there?" she asked, pointing to another, old, scar on my forehead.

"I used to play hockey." It wasn't a lie as much as it was an unrelated fact. The truth was too messy for this moment. I was in no mood to remember the time I had been raped and how I'd tried to put up a fight.

I stopped at the supermarket on the way home and bought myself some socks, underpants and an apple. It was four in the morning and I was strangely calm. The fog and slog of my thinking had been removed, the compounding anxieties of the past few months had been exorcised. My pipes were clean. I packed my suitcase in record time, after which I went into the lounge and picked up all of my dirty dishes, took them into the kitchen and separated them into three piles. The least dirty pile I passed under the running tap for a cursory rinse. The medium dirty I stacked in the fridge. The worst of the worst were either homed in the freezer or went straight into a trash bag. Once that was done, I took the bag for a quick circuit of the flat and picked up every bit of actively rotting stuff I could find in under ten seconds. Then I washed my face, grabbed my suitcase and made my way down to catch my taxi, dropping the bag of rot into the skip on my way out. I can be very efficient under very particular circumstances.

Technically, I didn't miss my flight. Quite opposite, really. The issue was that I had booked a 6:00p.m. flight for the following day. I was very, very early. Prohibitively early. Unfazed, I made my way to the airline service counter to see if I couldn't wrangle myself an earlier flight. After I cheerily explained my predicament, the guy behind the counter accepted my challenge and got me a new ticket.

"What happened to your head?" he asked, handing me my paperwork.

"I sneezed and knocked myself out on a filing cabinet." He laughed again. I'd rehearsed this response in the taxi. I knew the question would be asked, and the only way I knew how to take my mental health seriously was to make a joke out of it.

Very Special Specials

I had not expected such a positive outcome when I first formed my very brief and very destructive friendship with cocaine during the Edinburgh Fringe later that year. I'm not really interested in sharing the adventures I had whilst under the influence.[⊗] That story has been told a million times. And in any case, I doubt you'd be very interested, because neither cocaine nor people under its influence are at all interesting. It doesn't matter how fast you talk; boring will always be boring.

But there is one very interesting thing I discovered whilst on this mini bender of mine: cocaine did not speed my brain up; it slowed it down. I got some shit done. And I got the shit done in a timely man-

---

[⊗] But I will say this—I'm glad I dabbled back in the day when it wasn't commonly mixed with opiates.

ner. And I had a really nice time in my head, because the whirlwind of my usual thinking slowed down enough so that I could pluck out suspended thoughts like I was the boss of my own brain. It felt exquisite.

Another lovely side effect of this gift of clarity of mind was that I was able to make better decisions, such as, for example, opting to seek professional help and not embarking on a Class A drug habit formed in a foreign country. And so, it was shortly after returning from the U.K. that I embarked on my first genuine attempt to take my mental health seriously. And not long after that, I was diagnosed with ADHD. It completely transformed my life.

Dusting Off

After my brief dalliance with cocaine, I was unfazed by the prospect of being medicated. But I had no idea how much better my life was about to become. I had been treading water my whole life, and twenty minutes after I took my first dose of prescribed Ritalin I realised I was in the shallows and that I could just stand up. I felt like I had the potential to control my life for the first time.

Not long after I began medicating, I found myself openly weeping in a restaurant when the waiter came over and began reciting the specials. I began to weep because I could hear what he was saying. Until that moment I'd had absolutely no idea that I'd never before heard the spoken-word special menu at a restaurant. I would just watch people's mouths move and believe that I'd heard them. Despite my tears, I was happy. I was so deliriously happy, in fact, that I ordered from the specials, even though they all sounded terrible. I didn't care. I would've ordered a plate of crab apple preserve.

I began to work very closely with a psychiatrist to try and get my life back on track. I'd always assumed I was disordered in my moods, and so I had always tackled problems from emotional angles. Now I was being taught the skill of looking to my environment for my solutions. I solved my sock problem, for example. I threw them all out and then I bought twenty pairs of the same sock. I don't even put them together anymore, I just put them in the sock box as forty singles. I reach in to get two socks, and it doesn't matter which I pick, they will always be a pair.

My psychiatrist also walked me through each step I needed to take to get my taxes sorted, and he helped me apply for an exemption for the fifty-odd parking fines I had accrued in my first two years of being a licenced driver. I began to feel optimistic about life. I stopped drinking. My moods calmed down. My relationship with Sam was strengthening, and I began to believe it was possible for me to finally get myself to at least the starting line of normal. I couldn't have been more wrong.

Too Soon

According to the expectations hardwired by decades and decades of relentless stereotyping, lesbians are supposed to move in together on their second date at the latest. Of all my exes before Sam, I had lived with exactly zero of them, because they had, correctly, assessed me as unsuitable for cohabitation. My preferred term is: unlivable-with-able. My decision to accept Sam's invitation to move in was in no small way influenced by my fear of having my lesbian status revoked.

It was a terrible mistake. It was too much change for me at once. I was navigating a brand-new diagnosis, and adapting to new treatment and medication, not to mention touring and writing on a television show. It was really very foolish of me to expect that a happily ever after would be possible under such circumstances. I fretted away many a night's sleep, terrified that I wouldn't be able to maintain my Jekyll while living with a significant other, and if I didn't have my own space where could I hide my Hyde?

When I moved in with Sam, it took very little time for my optimism to sour into failure and frustration. The medication had lifted the fog of my thinking but it couldn't change the way I was wired. Mistakes were still happening; I was still getting regularly overwhelmed, I was still letting everyone down. I was still that person.

My moods began to flare up, and it wasn't long before Sam and I were fraying at the edges again.

As much as I regret moving in with Sam, I don't regret the high hopes I held going into it. Optimism for my own future was not a privilege I had experienced very often in my life, so I don't want to be too harsh about that little glimmer of it, despite the disastrous end it led me to. But I do hold substantial regrets about my decision to use my next show as a celebration of my relationship "success" and an unveiling of my brand-new diagnosis. At the time, I was working under the assumption that I had a responsibility to keep my audiences up-to-date with the bits and bobs of my life, which I absolutely did not. The other dodgy foundation I was building was my conviction that my ADHD diagnosis had given me the final piece of my human puzzle. This was not just wrong, it was dangerous, because when I decided that I was "finished" I lost the ability to see that my life was unravelling, and unravelling very destructively.

I was finally in a healthy relationship, I told my audience. I credited my diagnosis and the medication for my leg up into proper adult status. I posited that by having a better understanding of myself, I was able to better understand my own needs in a relationship. I'd never spoken about my relationships on stage before; my sexuality had always been a theme in my comedy, but I'd only ever danced around the stereotypes. I never talked about actual matters of my heart. The show was a good one but when my life fell apart, the show could only crumble behind it.

I had never tried harder at anything in my whole life than my relationship with Sam, but it still ended with failure, and the turd cherry on top of that shit sundae was that I was dumped very unceremoniously halfway through the Melbourne Comedy Festival. All the while I was doing a show every night pretending to celebrate how I suddenly knew how to live life. I didn't have anything inside of me, I didn't know how to rewrite a show in the middle of breaking down. My agitation and distress became so acute that I had to be taken off Ritalin and put back onto antidepressants, and it got so bad in my head I developed a stutter. I got through it. Of course I did.

Hello. But I didn't emerge from the experience as a person who was wholly committed to the living of life.

Square One. But Different.

The reason I got Douglas was because Sam and I couldn't get legally married. Well, that was the joke reason; we never spoke about marriage. The real reason was that I couldn't think of a better gesture of commitment than a puppy. Obviously there are much better ones out there, I just couldn't think of one and I really wanted a dog. I'd been wanting to get a dog for a long time but my life had always been too unstable, and I had been too unable to look after myself alone. I loved Douglas the moment I met him, but Sam did not like him at all. It might seem monstrous to reject a cute puppy, but, to be fair, Douglas was a really intense little guy with unnervingly human eyes, and a habit of snacking on his own shit.

For some reason it felt extra harsh that Sam dumped Douglas when she dumped me. But Douglas turned out to be a pretty great dog, so it's tough to claim our double rejection as being legitimately traumatic. The breakup was, however, very difficult for me to process. I wanted to be in a partnership more than anything. I come from a family of marriers. It's all I knew, and I always did my best. And yet I just couldn't steer the Good Ship of Intimate Relations out of the shallows.

I was abruptly spat out of Sam's orbit when we broke up. All the people, all the conversations, all the plans, all the dinners, all the group chats. The entire social and physical landscape that had become my day-to-day reality suddenly evaporated from my life. Because Sam and I didn't merge our lives so much as I was absorbed into hers. And it was not a life I would ever design for myself. No outing was ever complete without a gaggle of friends, no gap in the diary was ever tolerated, and no plan was ever carried out as planned, because for Sam, the meaning of life is: surprise! We were not alike at all, but for some reason my rhythms were not factored into our shared time, and once we moved in together all I ever had was shared time. It wasn't that I didn't know how to advocate for quiet time. It was more that I wanted so badly to be the person who loved going out, hanging out with groups of friends, because that's what well-adjusted people all do. I'd seen it in films.

I was back living above the shop. Hamish didn't mind me staying, but he made it clear that I had to find somewhere else to live soon. Finding a place to rent when you have a dog is very difficult. After a handful of lease application rejections, I started to look for more creative solutions. That's when I found the ad for a shipping container on a vacant block. It was clean and tidy but it didn't have any running water or electricity. It didn't have a bed because it was a building site office, but some old bloke agreed to let me live there with Douglas for a year. Fortunately, my brother and his wife staged an intervention. They reminded me that I had a reliable enough income to be able to rent an actual house and not move into a crime scene, and then they helped me find a little rental down the road from them.

Bloomfield, as I came to call my little cottage, had a huge backyard. The entire space was enclosed by a high fence, which gave me an enormous sense of privacy, even though there were two apartment blocks stacked on top of me beyond the back alley. Just off the back steps there was a stretch of concrete and if you squinted you could call it a deck, though you would be lying. Beyond that was a grim expanse of patchy lawn, and right down the back was a dilapidated cubby house flanked by two trees, one was an apple tree and the other one was dead. I had always wanted a garden, but had believed that you had to own the soil before you could till it. As Nan had always said, it's not the garden that matters, it's the gardening. And a therapist once told me to get myself a plant as a way of curing my depression, after which I killed a succession of succulents.⊗ I made peace with the fact that I would eventually lose my garden and set about turning the back of Bloomfield into my own little oasis. I

⊗ It takes dedicated neglect to kill a cactus. They can survive a drought in the desert.

turned the patchy and scruffy lawn into a spongy carpet of loveliness. I put in a vegetable garden, and once I proved I could keep a succulent alive I graduated to dahlias, sweet peas and climbing roses.

I had found my home. A home in a way that I had not known since leaving Smithton. But better. For the first time in my life, I did not have to share a jot of my living space with another person, I could just close the door behind me and be in my own private little bubble of quiet, and it felt incredible. Bloomfield was my little safety patch, a shell against the world, and it was where I finally began to piece the puzzle of my life together. At first I was focusing on very, very small victories, like keeping plants alive and training Douglas not to eat his own shit. Eventually I began to tackle more significant problems, like why I was so fucking terrible at life.

Trigger Me Timbers

I began my first session by outlining the very long list of problems I was hoping the therapist could help me untangle. I was trying to give her a chronological overview but she kept interrupting me, asking me several questions about each point I brought up. She would hold her hand up and say things like "Let's just pause for a moment. What is it about _____ that makes you feel so _____?"

I began to feel frustrated. She said, "I sense some hostility."

I sat back in my chair and sighed. "I'm trying to give you the broad strokes of things, you know, the whole picture. The questions are throwing me a bit, I suppose."

There was a long pause. I waited for her to respond. As far as I was concerned, it was her turn. The silence went on for so long that I began to worry she had actually asked me a question and it was, in fact, my turn.

"Are you OK?" I prompted.

"Yes," she answered calmly. "Are you?"

"No. I'm not. Very much not. That is why I am here. It's kind of the point of this."

"There's that hostility again."

I apologised. I tried to reassure her that I didn't feel any hostility, I was just confused. This was met with another pregnant pause, so I decided to pick things up where I'd left off, and I began to list my relationship issues.

I told her how four of my girlfriends had told me they were afraid of me. Two of them told me I was a sociopath. I told her that I had worried almost daily for the past ten years that I was a sociopath. Then I told her that I had decided it would be for the best to assume that I was a sociopath, and just try my best not to be sociopathic. Fake it till you make it, I told her, and that's how I had been approaching all my interactions, by digging deep into the hat of good manners my parents had raised me with. I always asked after people, I told her, said my hellos and never not a thank you, but, I confided, I worried that I would lapse and hurt people accidentally. I hurt people accidentally all the time, I explained. She laughed. I had not expected that. She explained that if I were a sociopath, I wouldn't spend any time worrying about hurting people. Part of being a sociopath is having significantly low regard for other people. It made so much sense, I felt instantly embarrassed.

"Why am I so bad at relationships then?" I asked, without much hope that I would get a reasonable answer. The therapist, however, did seem to have an answer at hand and spent the remainder of our session edging around a story I'd heard before. She didn't have to use the official terminology, I knew which diagnosis she was forming around me, and my heart sank. At the end of the session, I thanked her, paid and never went back.

It's very easy to see why I would invite a diagnosis of borderline personality disorder. I tick off a lot of the things on its Greatest Hits list. Unstable relationships. Self-harm. Explosive anger. At a glance I fit the bill quite well, so much so that when I'd received the diagnosis the first time, I got on board with it. I studied the shit out of borderline. I learnt everything I could about the situation. It was during my last year at university, when I had some decent access to mental health services. I committed to the therapy. But I could never quite recognise the kinds of emotional landscapes that this disorder was supposed to burden me with.

But the borderline seed had been planted again, nonetheless. So, I spent a solid few weeks ruminating on the matter. I took apart all the so-called symptoms and, just like ten years earlier, found I could almost make everything fit, but not without some squeezing and distortion. I certainly struggled with self-image, but also not really. I only ever struggled in relation to other people. On my own I always felt as if I had an incredibly strong sense of self, almost rigid. In many ways the feeling of me has evolved very little since I was five years old. I just had trouble knowing how to be that person when I was around other people. The "fear of abandonment" thing was also difficult for me to relate to. If anything, it's the whole being tethered to other people that I'm uncomfortable with. I really, really love my own company. It's not that I don't like people, I just find being social really, really exhausting, and it doesn't matter how hard I try, I don't seem to get better at it. But the one point that never made any sense to me at all was the "chronic feelings of emptiness." While I have felt bereft of hope at times, I don't think I've ever felt empty. I have only ever been very full of stuff.

Even as I felt I could dismiss the diagnosis, it kept eating away at me. I brought it up with my psychiatrist and he laughed, much in the same way the therapist had done when I brought up the socio-path thing. "No, no, no," he said gently. "You do not have a disordered personality. You are neurobiologically atypical. Perhaps it may be helpful to find someone who specialises in autism spectrum disorders." This was not the first time someone had given me a nudge toward ASD. My show about my ADHD diagnosis had prompted quite a lot of strangers to suggest that I should get assessed for autism. Despite the frequency of this unsolicited advice, I never entertained the possibility that I was on the autism spectrum, not even a little bit. Every time, I would dismiss it out of hand. I don't know why I was incapable of seeing autism in myself. You would think that my experience with ADHD might have made me more open to dismantling my assumptions about other diagnoses. But it didn't. I wish that it had. Not so that Sam and I could have patched things up. I don't believe we were very well suited to each other. But I do wish I had cottoned on to my autism earlier so that I could have wrought less damage on my way out. Alas, autism apparently did not intrigue my brain as much as sociopathy or borderline personality disorder, so I didn't think to do any research into it. Instead, I began to look into fixing my myriad of reproductive system issues.

Doctor Dog

I made the remark that I would gladly undergo a hysterectomy, assuming my flippancy was inherent in my phrasing: "Why not whip out the whole kit and caboodle." And even if my playful language was not proof enough of my humorous intent, then surely all doubt should have been removed when I added, "I hear de-cluttering is very fashionable at the moment."

We had been discussing the results of a test he had ordered after I had complained to him a week earlier about the gaggle of debilitating side effects attaching themselves to my menstrual cycle. The test had been a distressing ordeal in and of itself, because my doctor had failed to inform me of the specific nature of the ultrasound that he had ordered. I don't know if I necessarily would have fared better had I been told in advance that I was to undergo an internal pelvic examination, but given the fact that the technician was shocked I hadn't been made aware of the ins and outs of the invasive procedure, as it were, I think at the very least I would have felt far less humiliated had I been afforded the dignity of psychological preparation.

With a level of medical professionalism my doctor clearly lacked, the technician gave me the option of rescheduling when she noticed the carnival of distress my human face was expressing. I declined the offer and pulled myself together and submitted to the procedure. The phrase "pulled myself together" is misleading, however. It would be more accurate to say that I detached myself from the situation and just rolled the ball of terror up into a little corner of my brain and held it hostage.

Penetration is an incredibly painful hobby for me. This pain extends beyond the logistics of sexual pursuits; I can't even insert a tampon for fun. Depending on whom you ask, this is due to either a psychological disorder or a physical one. But if you were to ask me, I would tell you, correctly, that it is a very complicated combination of the two. But nobody would ask me, because I'm a woman.

When the technician was unable to access the internal regions of my vaginal holdings, she paused and again offered me the option to reschedule. I declined and just gave her permission to use more force. She nodded, apologised and got the job done.

My powers of detachment are so incredible that although I was being severely triggered, and all I could think about was the time when I had been coerced into having sex with a man who was already raping me, I still managed to remain externally calm throughout the ultrasound procedure. Through the searing pain of the ultrasound I recalled, without emotion, how the man couldn't get himself inside me even after I'd stopped struggling, how he'd told me that he was sorry, but he was going to have to hurt me "in order to get the job done."

And that's what he did. Then he rolled off me and invited his friend to find gainful employment between my legs, but only after announcing proudly that he had popped yet another cherry. Although I was not a virgin, I understood very clearly that my experience bore absolutely no relevance to his reality, so I didn't bother correcting him. Nor did I correct his friend, who had assumed he had a large penis because of the difficulty he was experiencing getting himself inside me.

My powers of detachment, as incredible as they may be, do have a time limit. But fortunately, I managed to make it back home before I crumbled. My skin was still crawling with distress the next day when I returned to my doctor with the results gleaned from my surprise prodding. When I told him that he should have told me the specifics of the tests, I was served a wordless glare and I withered accordingly. I knew at that moment I had very little chance of making it home before I lost my adult responses.

My doctor continued to ignore me for a long time as he looked at the results, all the while taunting me with his aggressively condescending nasal breathing. Eventually, he put the tests down and told me I had fibroids before he turned to type himself a congratulatory note on his computer. He typed like he doctored—aggressively and without the hesitation that his distinct lack of skills demanded. I did not enjoy the unpredictability or the pitch of his tippity-tap, so to drown it out I began to give the side of my head its own tippity-tap. I'd heard of fibroids, but I couldn't recall what the implications were if you were found in possession of some of your own. I pulled out my phone to make sure I had not just been diagnosed with early death, while I waited for my doctor to complete his devastatingly important job of ignoring me. I was only just able to register the benign nature of my affliction before my doctor's angry and raised voice snapped my attention back to the present with such a jolt I burst into tears.

It wasn't that he shouted his request that I put my phone away and give over my undivided attention to his inattentive authority. The thing that really bit into me was that he referred to me as a "little girl." The infuriating thing is that if I'm already distressed when my startle reflex gets a call to action, then I tend to respond eerily like a little girl. Although it was his job as a medical professional to consider the possibility that there may be an underlying medical condition at play if a grown woman starts tapping the side of her head and crying, he chose to ignore his part in our doctor-patient relationship and instead looked away with disgust.

When he eventually spoke, he very calmly corroborated my own Wikipedia-deep research into fibroids, and then handed me a script for a birth control pill.

I had previously told him that I suffered from suicidal ideation and depression when I took the pill, but that fact had been thrown away with other such trivial details like my age and humanity. When

I feebly tried to reintroduce my poor response to the pill, he waved my concern away with his hand. "It's a different one. In any case, we can always change it if you start to feel depressed."

How can a man so drunk on the power of being a doctor have such a devastatingly ignorant understanding of the insidious nature of depression? Even a rude little girl like me knows that when you are depressed you lose access to any memory of ever feeling any other way, you simply accept the depressed state as eternal and immutable. But I didn't think these thoughts at the time, because I was frantically trying to avoid crying like a little girl. I did the only thing I knew how to do, I made a joke, and that is when I flippantly suggested that I should undergo the removal of the whole kit and caboodle of my reproductive real estate.

He turned to face me for the first time so I could fully understand the gravity of my mistake. He spoke low and slow to make absolutely sure I heard him tell me that I had no right to make decisions about my body without first discussing it with my husband. I got up and left. This was going to be another dead end.

A few weeks later I took my scans to another doctor and explained what had happened, but they told me I had to formally request the results from the other clinic, and that was enough for me to stop my proactive search for relief from an affliction that had plagued me since puberty.

I did, however, get my script filled for the pill. I knew they were bad for me, but I was so desperate I was prepared to forget. Fortunately, after about six months I experienced a brief window of clarity where I was able to recognise that I was depressed. I don't think many people would have noticed the red flag that was my decision to spend the evening of my thirty-eighth birthday alone eating congealed porridge out of a pot with a wooden spoon while I thought of ways to kill myself. But fortunately, I am very astute at recognising the more nuanced expressions of depression.

In all honesty, I think it was Douglas who broke through my thick fog of wrong thought, by staring at me with heartbreaking intensity for what may have been hours. People claim that it is the responsibility of keeping another heartbeat in action that is behind the psy-chological benefits of owning a pet. I think this is a rubbish idea that arrogantly diminishes the worth of any existence that is lived outside the realm of human experience. My dog was empathising with me.

I don't believe animals process the world the same as humans do—but I am certain that dogs don't enjoy the vibe of pain in people they share space with. I have no doubt that I was jolted out of my isolated prison of misery because I could feel my distress being reg-istered by my dog. After a while I started pondering how it was that a dog with a taste for his own shit was so much better at producing humanity than my own human doctor. I offered the rest of my por-ridge to Douglas, as a reward, and then opened my laptop and googled the three words that would become the final piece of my puzzle: *women with autism.*

WHIRL,
INTERRUPTED

You don't have to be an expert to know that people with autism don't get to speak about their own experiences. Until very recently, autism has largely only been understood through the prism of the experience of parents and as a list of observations that mostly neurotypical medical professionals have made and assigned meaning to. Most pervasively, autism is known as a side effect of a disease called Andrew Wakefield—the quack who falsely linked autism with vaccinations after he ate an activated walnut and became a Leprechaun.⊗

The myths around ASD and ADHD have wasted enough of my life, so I don't really want to waste any more of my time thinking about them, much less writing them down. These diagnoses have given me a pathway to understanding myself, and for the first time in my life, I am able to like who I am. If that's not enough for you, if you want me to convince you that I am autistic, or prove that ADHD exists, then you can just go fuck yourself.

My neurobiology is at the very core of my thinking and, as such, it sits at the heart of who I am—but it does not define me. I am an

⊗ According to the unverifiable and flawed research I conducted to prove my own biases. A little trick I learnt off Wakefield himself.

incredibly complicated human cocktail just like everybody else, so why should my story be reduced to a quantifying of these ingredients? I want to be able to fold my ASD and ADHD into the rest of the mess that is me, but as the myths are so firmly embedded into popular (mis)understanding, I don't have the luxury to skip over them. It is just a sad reality that I have to waste even more of my time to bring many of you up to speed.❂

So, just for this one step, I will be putting the specifics of my brain function front and centre. But before I do, I want to make sure you understand how potentially catastrophic this process is for me as an individual. When I spoke about my battle with depression on stage, I was drowned by the howling opinionated rage of others, and by drowned, I mean that I was shoved back into the depression I was bragging about not having anymore. I am not an expert. Nor can I speak for everyone on the atypical brain train. Nor am I a static entity. I reserve the right to be able to evolve. On top of that, the field of neurobiology is constantly changing its mind about all things brain-changing. So, just be cool, OK? I am doing my best.

The tolerance level for ADHD was far lower than for depression. That's probably because everybody can at least understand sadness. But, as I discovered, rather brutally, ADHD makes a lot of people very, very angry. Attention deficit hyperactive disorder is not an easy thing to explain. And not just because it is especially complex and has a lot of syllables. The real problem is that too many people have been conditioned to believe that ADHD is a nonsense disease that is not so much overdiagnosed but entirely under-existing. A Western medicine scam made up by pharmaceutical companies who wanted to peddle speed but who were too scared to do business with gangs. A fad. An excuse. A handy label given to energetic young boys with shit parents who give them sugar instead of boundaries. I heard all of these and more.

I don't feel confident that I can change the minds of people who

❂ It's not your fault, Will.

don't want to believe ADHD is a thing.⊛ But I wish I could, because the experience of ADHD has a lot in common with that of PTSD, and as such, it will often present with other debilitating comorbidities, such as depression and anxiety. None of these are fun on their own, but it gets way worse when they gang up. And I should know, I'd collected the whole set.

It is improving, but it is rare for girls and other not-boys, particularly those of my generation, to receive a timely diagnosis. Probably because we were overlooked during the stereotyping process and because girls with ADHD often present as inattentive as opposed to hyperactive. We are the daydreamers. Not the distracters. Sure, ADHD girls fall behind at school but when I was at school, a girl who was not performing to her full potential was not seen as a problem, if she was seen at all. It's always the squeaky wheel that gets the speed.

It's not so much that I have a deficit in attention. I take it all in. I pay attention to everything. If anything, it's attention overload. The deficit is in working out what is important and dealing with it in a timely manner. The bit of the brain that is responsible for prioritising, integrating and sorting out all the incoming—is just a bit shit at its job. My brain is a Ferrari with bicycle brakes, it has no filing system, or what medical professionals might call "executive function." Having a very busy brain without a functioning executive is not an effective tool for this world. It's like having an orchestra without a conductor and it's way, way worse than improvised jazz. And I hate that a lot. Imagine standing in an orchestra pit unable to move your arms or see the music, but still doing your best to conduct, and the oboe is free-forming Acker Bilk over a French horn, the string section has splintered into twenty different tempos, while the timpani section has just taken acid and formed a drumming circle. Imagine that inside your head, then having to make a dentist appointment.

As for the ASD part of my equation, the pathway from hunch to diagnosis was not a difficult process for me, but I don't want to

⊛ Closed minds are a disorder of the highest order.

give you the impression that it is easy for someone to get a formal autism diagnosis, especially later in life. I know for a fact that it can be prohibitively difficult, and I want you to be aware that autism in older women, non-binary, and genderqueer folk remains chronically underdiagnosed. I found accessibility and traction within the system due to my public profile. I didn't go out of my way to access this special treatment for myself, but that doesn't mean I get to erase the fact that I got it anyway.

When I was moving toward the diagnosis, the focus of my research was on all the ways it made sense to me. It had been a thrilling exercise, a mystery to be solved. But as soon as I had my diagnosis, the thrill of it all but disappeared, replaced by a grief that was way too big for any metaphor I can think of. I had always worked under the impression that I would eventually find my way to the starting line of normal, but after I was diagnosed with autism spectrum disorder, I saw that not only was that not true, but I most likely had a very warped sense of what normal actually was. I felt sick for weeks.

For a long time, I worried that I'd been misdiagnosed. It was difficult for me to believe that I wasn't entirely to blame for my life being such a painful struggle, because I was so used to assuming that I was a bad person. It took me a long time to get brave enough to simply share my diagnosis. My experience did not match the popular understanding of autism, and I knew I had to become an expert in neurobiology in order to untangle the myriad of myths surrounding autism—just to beg permission to claim that piece of my identity.

I was right to be cautious, because when I finally did start telling the world of my diagnosis, the dismissals came thick and fast. I was told that I was too fat to be autistic. I was told that I was too social to be autistic. I was told that I was too empathetic to be autistic. I was told I was too female to be autistic. I was told I wasn't autistic enough to be autistic. Nobody who refused me my diagnosis ever considered how painful it might have been for me, and it got real boring real fast.

Ever since I can remember, my thoughts have been plagued with a sense that I was a little out of whack, as if belonging was beyond me. To give this feeling a story, it's as if I am an alien who has been abandoned on earth and left to muddle my way through life, without a reason, a mission, or any memory of home. If you are a conspiracy theorist, this is where you begin to wonder if I might perhaps be a lizard. I am not. Now piss off.

I am a visual thinker. I see my thoughts, but I don't have a photographic memory, nor is my head a static gallery of sensibly collected thoughts that my brain curates into easy sense. It is not linear. It is fluid and flexible, kind of like a private Wikipedia that I am constantly revising and editing, but instead of words, everything is written in my own ever-evolving language of hieroglyphic films filled with hyperlinks to associated and often irrelevant thoughts. I have never managed to develop a reliable system to file and separate my thoughts into individual think-pieces, and so I am utterly incapable of having one thought without at least another hundred coming along for the ride.

Further complicating this issue is the fact that my brain doesn't work in the realm of the abstract. I'm not capable of thinking with imagery that I haven't seen with my own eyes, which means when someone tells me a story, I will see it as something like a film that I must edit together out of all the other films sourced from my own internalised collection. Every single day I have spent on this earth, I have added countless images to my brain library. Needless to say, it is very busy in my head. If it were possible for someone to catch a glimpse of my thoughts being processed, they'd be hard-pressed to make sense out of it. I doubt they'd even believe that the tornado orgy of wingdings and GIFs was anything other than gibberish.

Sadly, the enthusiasm that my brain brings to the collecting of visual records is not then applied to the filing and retrieval process. And because of my inability to quickly and efficiently translate what I see into an externally communicable format, I am wired to have lots of fun and adventure in my head while at the same time failing totally, utterly and miserably at life on the outside, and feeling profoundly alone.

I believe that it is this whirl inside my brain that contributes to my inability to speak at times. To be clear, I don't identify as being nonverbal, but I often lose my verbal ability. Especially if I am overwhelmed by a lot of sensory information at the same time as I am trying to identify, process and regulate emotional distress. This is what is called selective mutism, which is a common comorbidity of ASD, but is not exclusive to it.

Since making my diagnosis public, I have had some parents of nonverbal folk take me to task for identifying as autistic while not being as "disabled" as their child. To those people, I would like to say, I get it. I understand your frustration. It is my bet that you are not supported well enough, and that I seem like a good person to vent at. I don't mind. I can take it. But if it helps, it is not my intention to take anything away from you or your experience. All I want to do is help create something of a window into the inner workings of a manually processing brain. You know as well as I do that no two experiences are the same on the so-called spectrum; but I do know something of how frustrating and painfully lonely it can be from the inside. Ultimately, we are on the same team.

When I told Mum that I was autistic, she said: "Yeah, that makes sense. I always knew that there was a lot going on inside you, but I just couldn't get in. You were like a tin of baked beans and my tin opener wouldn't work on you." It's a tidy metaphor, especially if you know that Mum does not like baked beans.

My childhood was a serendipitously effective buffer for the worst that my ASD threw at me. Small town. Not a lot of change. My family unit was a ready-made social network that I didn't have to navigate cold because I was just a part of it. They looked out for me, but, because we were a big family, no one really noticed if I didn't talk. I was the youngest, so no one expected me to be a leader. No one noticed when I would disappear for hours, and no one thought much of my habit of taking frequent naps in the linen press. I wasn't quirky, I was just Hannah. Nobody thought I was special when I memorised every single question and answer in Trivial Pursuit. Because I wasn't special; everyone cheated one way or another. It was only when I stepped out of the bubble of my family that things went to shit. And, gosh, to shit it went.

For as long as I can remember, I have struggled to grasp even the most basic of life's skills. In my first year of primary school, I forgot to wear underpants so many times that my family started to check me at the door every morning before I left. I assumed I'd get better at stuff as I got older, but it only got worse. And the older I got, the less amused people were by me.

During my adolescence I began to find it more and more difficult to make myself understood, and that is when I developed an instinctual fault-responsibility whenever I didn't understand what was going on around me, which, to be clear, was all the fucking time. This struggle persuaded me to assume that I was unlikable, and eventually I stopped thinking about the world through the lens of my own needs. And anybody who is a human knows that this is not a recipe for good times.

I used to fret about fitting in at school, not because I wanted to, but because I knew I was supposed to. I was at my happiest in my own company, which I took to be an abnormality. It never occurred to me that it could be the epitome of normal behaviour—for me. I was a "girl," and girls were expected to be masters of the mingle, so I tried really hard to be a normal girl but it was a fool's errand, because my neurobiological situation makes it hard for me to "see" all the networks of undercurrent connections that drive the interactions of the more typical thinkers, which in turn makes it incredibly difficult for me to intuitively reflect peer group behaviours. So, the best I could do, and continue to do, is observe, guestimate and imitate, which is often referred to as "masking" in autistic circles. As a coping mechanism for teenage me, masking was an incredibly successful tactic—I was only bullied intermittently during my school years—but as a catalyst for growth, it worked more like castration.

By the time I was middling my thirties, I was no longer living my life. I was merely coping with it, and barely. I felt as if I was a supreme annoyance and a burden to anybody I spent meaningful time with. But nobody seemed to notice that I had major depressive episodes every other year, and debilitating anxiety the rest of the time. Not even me. Nobody noticed that I never made eye contact. Nobody noticed that I often spoke in a patchwork of collected phrases. It took me a long time to even spot those patterns of my own behaviour, because I was too busy trying not to do the wrong thing by guessing, pretending, panicking, then either shutting or melting down.

My meltdowns had always been a mystery to me, so when I was finally diagnosed, I was able to reframe the way I thought about my strange little outbursts. For a start, I became far more compassionate toward myself, which probably halved the distress of the occasions. In the scheme of my life, I have not had very many meltdowns, however. I'm more of a shutdown kind of autistic. From the outside, a shutdown looks very similar to a sulky tantrum, but it is nothing of the sort. I don't have control, for a start. And I am certainly not ruminating on any kind of emotional narrative, because I have gone into fight or flight, but in my body that translates into neither fight nor flight, I just shut down like a maxed-out power grid in the middle of a storm.

Meltdowns are equally distressing, but for different reasons. The worst is knowing that I am out of control, and may accidentally injure myself or, worse, someone else. Meltdowns are often conflated with panic attacks, but they are not the same beast. The biggest difference between them is that a panic attack is agitation and fear, spinning on a kind of mind loop, whereas a meltdown is a maelstrom that begins in the body. Another important difference is that a panic attack will never resolve the anxieties that triggered it. Meltdowns, on the other hand, are a real spring clean. They clear the pipes and can often leave you feeling as if your body has been reset.

I wish more than anything that I had known about my ASD when I was a kid, just so I could've learnt how to look after my own distress, instead of assuming my pain was normal and deserved. There is no one to blame, but I still grieve for the quality of life I lost because I didn't have this key piece to my human puzzle. But until someone unlocks the riddle of time travel, little me will have to flail and fail their way through the world for thirty-odd years.

Once I understood that I was always going to have difficulty with self-regulation, I stopped worrying about it. Once I am distressed, my moods are not mine to control, but my environment is. I am always working to remove myself from all the cycles and patterns of hostile environments, like cafés that have polished concrete floors. And I no longer search my behaviours exclusively for revelations about my character, I use my occasions of distress as ways to map the circumstances and environments I move through, and look for ways I can reduce my exposure to distressing situations. I have learnt how to advocate for my own experiences instead of being ashamed of my pain and confusion. I stopped worrying about what I was expected to do, and worked on building an understanding of what I could do to make myself feel safe and calm.

I am not afraid of pressing pause during a television show when I feel distressed. I seek out spoiler alerts to avoid getting panicked by unexpected plot twists. I leave crowded spaces. I switch off discordant music. I wear headphones at restaurants. I openly express my hatred of the saxophone and electric guitar solos. I don't allow important emotional conversations to take place in cafés with polished concrete floors.

I spend hours alone at home rearranging my little piles of bric-a-brac, because it's really fun. I only wear blue clothes because blue makes me feel calm. I listen to the same music, watch the same shows, and eat the same foods over and over again without any qualms. I find joy in my life where I once couldn't because I was too busy trying to do the "right" thing instead of checking in with my own needs first. I do my best not to bruise other people's feelings with my bluntness, but now I make sure that my boundaries are clear: if you don't want me to be blunt with you, don't engage me in difficult conversations in public spaces with polished concrete floors.

I am lucky. I have the privilege to be able to protect myself . . . now. But it's not because I can do it on my own. I need help. There is not much about my life that is not looked after by another human, sometimes teams of them. That is the beauty of success in show business—other people become quite keen to do all the things for you. I am basically a middle-class white man from the 1950s. But even if I hadn't stumbled into success, I would still need a lot of help just to navigate life. It is absolute bullshit that the only way I could access the help I needed was by accidentally activating some kind of exceptional potential I didn't even know I had until I was nearly thirty years old. Please, stop expecting people with autism to be exceptional. It is a basic human right to have average abilities.

Many people who struggle to find stable employment also contend with things like intergenerational poverty and/or trauma, cycles of abuse, mental illness, systemic discrimination, disability or neurological disorders. Not only are these all chronically stressful and traumatic circumstances, they have all been linked to a high incidence of impaired executive function. Welfare systems are not built to be easy for people who are anxious about using the phone, or people who mix up dates. They are not designed for people who are bad at keeping time, filling out forms, or people who can't easily access all the relevant bank, residential and employment details from the past five years, if they thought to keep that information at all. Welfare systems don't accommodate for transience because welfare systems are not built to be accessible, they are built to be temples of administrative doom, because, apparently, welfare is a treasure that must be protected. Can somebody please do something about that? I am not good enough at organising to be an actual activist. But searching for the connections between the big picture and the little picture, however, is a very ASD thing to do. I am never not cross-referencing the trees with the forests, and it can be a very exhausting way to engage, but I wouldn't change it for the world, because I believe communities need thinkers like me.

I see a fault in the idea, put forward by neurotypical "experts," that autistic people have mind blindness, which essentially suggests that we are unable to understand the inner workings of other people. I believe we all have mind blindness; why else would we invent language? The problem is that communication skills are developed atypically in autistic people, and, most often, very slowly. I have always had difficulty articulating my needs, but as I have gotten older, my language and social skills have improved a great deal. My ability to regulate, however, has not, nor have my sensory sensitivities. My eternal struggle with these distressors often gives the impression to others that I am moody, reactive and inconsistent. I say I want one thing, then moments later I will say that I need the opposite. This is not a reflection of my character but rather it is a reflection of my neurobiological functioning. I am unable to intuitively understand what I am feeling, and I can often take a much longer time to process the effects of external circumstances than neurotypical thinkers. But it is they who get impatient with me, and under that pressure I feel forced to guess my needs before I have had time to process stuff in my own way, and so mistakes are made. I can be cold and not know it. I can be hungry and not know it. I can need to go to the bathroom and not know it. I can be sad and not know it. I can feel distressed and not know it. I can be unsafe and not know it. You know how, when you put your hand under running water and for a brief moment you don't know if it is hot or cold? That is every minute of my life. I am not Bauhaus design.

Being perpetually potentially unsafe is a great recipe for anxiety. And, spoiler alert, anxiety is bad. But if anxiety in a child is left untreated—or worse, unacknowledged—anxiety will not only be magnified, it will inevitably compound into trauma. But it is very difficult to explain to a world that has decided Disneyland is the happiest place on earth that a child's birthday party can trigger a fight-or-flight response in someone with ASD. All you see is a good time that must be had, but inside me it feels like a war zone. Two scoops of PTSD for everybody! Happy fucking birthday.

ALL
PART
OF THE
SOUP

PREPARE THE INGREDIENTS

Anybody unfamiliar with the way that the thinking happens in my head might have thought that my writing a show about Taylor Swift was a sure sign that my mind was losing itself. But in my mind, which probably *was* losing itself, Taylor Swift was the perfect muse for someone who wanted to think a lot about nothing at all.

All my life I have found myself diving into special interest subjects that no one else ever seems to care about, and it can get very lonely. So given that everybody in the world was talking about Taylor, I thought I might finally be able to join in. There was something comforting about doing a deep dive into a subject I wasn't curious about. Why didn't I care about Taylor Swift when so many people loved her to the point of obsession? Why was I so impervious? I wanted to see if it were possible for me to train my mind to learn to like something that I wasn't naturally curious about. The short answer is no. And while I wasn't surprised that I didn't find my inner Swiftie, I did manage to tap into my latent fury for dodgy metaphors.

I called the show *Dogmatic* because being more assertive was one of my "squad goals." That is a little joke. I actually can't remember the reason I called the show that, although it did have a lot of material about Douglas in it, so, maybe that had something to do with it. Look, it wasn't my best show. And I am not alone in that opinion.

My first encounter with a legit Swiftie happened shortly after my show opened in Adelaide. She took to Twitter to let me know that I was not a feminist, because a feminist would not dare take down another woman ... or some kind of tepid logic to that effect. I replied bluntly that perhaps she shouldn't be criticising me ... on account that I was another woman, to which she called into question my right to call myself that, because I look so much like a man. I didn't write back, figuring that she must have been an older fan who had fallen into the Tay Tay cult back in the days when her rain metaphors sometimes came with a subtle garnish of latent homophobia. And to be absolutely clear, I was not and I am still not trying to take Taylor Swift down. I'm not a fool. I did my research. She would absolutely destroy me.⊗

I honestly don't believe that Tay Tay is driven by a nefarious agenda, aside from that whole global domination thing. Ultimately, she is a young woman trying to grow up under immense public scrutiny and that can't be easy, particularly if your persona is built on the idea of being "relatable." Nor can it be easy to find your feminist feet if your whole world is being managed and shaped by a great swarm of music industry men motivated by profit. (Kan)Ye was still right, though. I want to put that on record. Beyoncé was not recognised for the most iconic music video ever made, and it's embarrassing that Taylor Swift tried to position herself as a victim. To be clear, Beyoncé was not recognised for her singular and incredible piece of art *Homecoming* either, and I am so sorry for the small role I played in that. I don't know what to do about this pickle other than quietly position myself behind the fact that James Corden singing with Sir Paul McCartney in a car also won an Emmy over Beyoncé in 2019

I didn't really know what an Emmy was back in 2016, which is a gentle reminder that I am not an American. In Australia we have the Logies. Which is just a fact; I don't have much to say about them, either. But don't think that I am impervious to the allure of external

⊗ Hi, Tay Tay!

validation; it's kind of impossible to avoid getting dragged into awards fever on the festival circuit, because the Best Show controversy is an integral part of any festival ecosystem.

On the one hand, having artists compete for a prestigious award is a great way to draw attention to an artform and even elevate it in the minds of people beyond the bubble of the industry. On the other hand, naming a "winner" of an artform takes subjective decisions steeped in bias and repositions them as objective, measurable facts. Which is a very big part of why people who don't like my work can reach the conclusion that I must not be funny. But all it actually means is that they don't like my work, and I don't like them. Hooray for opinions.

My biggest issue with festival awards is that they always seem to drag you in, whether you want to be or not. In the first ten or so years that I had a show at the Melbourne Comedy Festival, I ended up being part of the Best Show conversation in some capacity. And in the years that I was short-listed, the week between being nominated and, as was the case for me, not winning the award always felt like a completely unnecessary gauntlet of scrutiny, false hope, professional jealousy and imposter syndrome, none of which I would have signed up for, but that is the stuff buzz is built out of.

I knew my work was equal to that of any of the award winners of my world, but I also knew that Anne Edmonds was, and is, the funniest and most exciting stand-up comic working in Australia and she never wins anything. I also knew that Judith Lucy's work has been peerless for decades and she's never been recognised, with either awards or the open access to lucrative media opportunities that so many mediocre men seem to have. All this is to say that the world I was trying to be a part of had made it abundantly clear to me that my voice was not interesting, relevant or important enough to warrant acclaim. And after a decade in comedy, I finally read the room and bowed out. And by "bowed out," I mean that I didn't try to do my absolute best work and just decided to write a show about Taylor Swift instead.

THROW IT ALL IN A POT

"I am very disappointed in your show this year, Hannah, I just don't think there was enough lesbian content."

I ended up immortalising this little nugget of lesbian feedback in *Nanette*. If you've seen the show, you will know that I followed it up with a bit of sass, but in the real world I replied to my naysayer with something closer to blunt petulance. I can't remember what I said, exactly, but it can't have been charming, given her response.

"You have just lost a fan. A real one," she said, not moving. I don't know if she expected me to say something or plead forgiveness. But all I said was "OK." I was keen for her to leave. She was having a lot of feelings that she wanted me to reciprocate, and I just wasn't in the mood to pretend I had feelings about it. Facts are facts.

At first I felt relieved that I no longer had her as a fan, she was annoying; but then the remorse kicked in, because I knew deep down that I had failed my core audience at precisely the wrong moment. The marriage equality debate in Australia had been gurgling away for longer than I had been a comedian, but the year I decided to write a show about something I didn't care about, the debate had kicked into toxic gear.

After Ireland became the first country to legalise gay marriage by popular vote the year before, in 2015, Australia's conservative government had thought, "Gosh, that's a nifty tactic." But, never keen for nuance over controversy, they decided not to dwell on the fact that, unlike Ireland, Australia didn't require a constitutional amendment to change the law. It was political amnesia at its most potent, given that in 2004 the conservative government under John Howard, without any community engagement at all, just casually amended the Marriage Act to change the definition of marriage from being between "two people" to being between "a man and a woman."

There was a great deal of measured caution, from parliamentarians and constituents alike, forecasting the potential damage of putting the legitimacy of queer relationships into the public forum, but ultimately it was decreed that the right to same-sex marriage would be put to a plebiscite—an arcane, expensive, non-compulsory, non-binding nationwide vote.

STOP! FLASHBACK TIME!

It was the Ghost of Homophobic Debates Past. But the reverberations of the Tasmanian gay law reform debate weren't haunting echoes, so much as they were many of the exact same people shouting the exact same hateful rhetoric into the ether. And by "ether," I mean the radios, televisions, post-boxes, eyes, ears, hearts, minds, and social media feeds of the entire Australian public. Eric Abetz, who became a Tasmanian senator the same year that Nick Toonen won his right to privacy, had cautioned that by allowing said privacy, you may as well legalise incest and condone at-home drug abuse while you're at it. Two decades later, Abetz sent his constituents a pamphlet that counseled, "It's ok to vote NO" to the plebiscite, citing that the "real consequences" of marriage equality would include the rejection of "parental rights" and restriction of "freedom of speech."

Meanwhile, Chris Miles of Ulverstone's 1994 "Say No to Sodomy" rally also prepared a pamphlet during the gay marriage debate. After admitting to having no "valid empirical data," it suggested that children raised by same-sex parents would be disproportionately prone to "unemployment," "sexual victimization," "sexual transmitted disease," "drug use/abuse," and "suicidal thoughts." Miles's pamphlet also warned that allowing same-sex marriage would mean "boys will be taught they could marry boys" and "girls will be taught they could marry girls." As this was pretty much the whole idea behind marriage equality to begin with, I'm fairly certain that marking it as a tick in the "against" column is just a blatant display of homophobia at its most basic. And that brings us back to 2016.

My brain had been trained from an early age to be alert to homophobic subtext in public discourse. As such, it was also primed to shift into panic mode if ever homophobic subtext bubbled up and spilled out into open rhetoric. I wanted to ignore the huge, painful, destructive and all-consuming storm brewing inside of me around the debate. I wanted to do my best to block it out like a good snow-flake, which is the other reason I decided to do an extended medita-tion on Taylor Swift. I was clearly having a creative shutdown, I was distressed and my brain wanted to block out all thoughts of the de-bate, but as 2016rolled on, my mind failed to keep the hurt at bay and my creative stasis morphed into a full-blown professional meltdown.

BRING TO THE BOIL

I could tell by her matter-of-fact tone that this was one of five very similar phone calls Mum was having with each of her children, one after the other. I wasn't surprised by the news, as Grandma's health had been declining for quite some time by then.

"I just hope she is better at dying than she was at saying goodbye on the phone."

Grandma was famous for two things: always having at least three desserts on offer at any given mealtime, and being completely inca-pable of hanging the phone up in good time.

"OK. Bye-bye. All right, then, goodbye. Bye, bye, dear. Yes, well, goodbye then. See you later, OK, tutty-byes, bye, bye, ta-ta for now. OK then, All right, bye bye . . ."

Every phone conversation with Grandma always ended with you hanging up on her somewhere in the middle of a goodbye. It was impossible not to. From time to time, I would attempt to stay the course, to see if I could get her to hang up first, but I never managed it, and I stopped trying after she told me off for keeping her on the phone for too long.

There has never been a stereotype that my mum hasn't wanted to smash, so, naturally, she became very good friends with her mother-in-law. They were so close that it was sometimes easy to forget that Grandma was on Dad's side of the family branch. But to be fair, Dad can be so placid that it is sometimes easy to forget he exists at all.

Mum was incredibly sad about Grandma, but I only understood that on an intellectual level, because she refused to offer any obvious grief markers during our conversation, which she ran with her trademark brutal pragmatism.

"Come back now to say goodbye if you want. No point coming home after she's dead."

It was the first time I had ever cancelled a season. Maybe it was partly my own disillusionment with my show that made it an easy decision, but it is my hope that it was mostly to do with my love for Grandma. Some part of the decision to cut my Brisbane run short was definitely due to my lingering guilt that I hadn't gone to the funeral of my childhood anchor, Nan. I'd been at university in Canberra when she had died, and I couldn't afford to get back for it, which was doubly saddening, because Ronnie Barker was being put down around the same time. There was not much I could've done about it, I was very poor and recovering from surgery at the time, but even so, I still regret not going. When I'd first found out that Nan was dying, I'd asked my friend Ada, another one of my old lady friends who lived down the road from me, if she would help me knit Nan a beanie. Nan had always worn woollen hats or cotton wool in her ears, because the wind made her brain whistle. And now as I write that I realise I'd always taken it quite literally. Maybe she had cold ears?

Ada proved not to be a very patient knitting teacher, unlike Nan, who I think must have taught me to knit at least a half dozen times, and was never frustrated by my total lack of clickety-clack ability. But it only took twenty minutes for me to push Ada out of her patience zone, after which she snatched my needles and the two rows of mostly dropped stitches out of my hands and told me to go home and just let her knit it. As promised, she had completed it by morning tea time the following day, but as she handed it over to me Ada told me, with not enough humour, that I hadn't given her enough wool. I thanked her anyway and sent the baby beanie off with my goodbye card to Nan. Nan wrote back and told me that she loved my beanie and that it had made a lovely eye patch for the teddy bear Pop had given her. She finished her note by imploring me not to be sad about not being able to come home, reminding me that she had regrets too. "But it's all part of the soup. Too late to take the onions out now."

I was lucky enough to be able to say goodbye to my grandma on the day she died, but since she was cocooned within herself by then, it was something of a one-sided affair. I sat by Grandma's side for an hour that day. I barely recognised her, she looked so tiny, her face had collapsed in on itself. My grandmother was the devoted matriarch of a large and loving family, which meant that during the last days of her life, she was surrounded by people. *A lot* of people.

I thought about a good many things that day. Things that I hadn't thought about in a long time. In particular, I thought about the letters I used to write to Grandma when I'd first started university. I remembered how I had filled them with funny little stories and small moments, embellished for her amusement. I also remembered how I wasn't able to articulate my feelings to Grandma in those letters, not the profound isolation I felt, not the cascading anxieties, and nothing of all the fears that had crowded the tiny life I was trying to carve out for myself in a world that felt far too big for me. I also recalled how I had found comfort in the act of writing those letters, simply because I had my grandma in my mind as I wrote them. I remembered that, as the world had grown increasingly overwhelming and my ability to negotiate life became worse instead of better, I eventually stopped writing to Grandma. And I remembered that I had stopped because I had just assumed that I wasn't living the kind of life my grandma would've wanted to read about. It was just too full of so much pain, and I didn't know how to share any of it.

I wasn't in the closet with Grandma in the strictest of senses. It had just never come up. At least, not until the year before she died. We'd been sitting in her living room, recovering from a cup of tea, when she'd suddenly asked me if I had a boyfriend. In the few seconds of silence that followed, I made a very conscious decision not to come out. I knew her life was drawing to a close and my time with her was finite, and I just didn't want to talk about how we were different, I wanted to talk about how we were the same. And so, I responded glibly.

"I don't have time for boyfriends," I told her.

"Oh well," she said, seemingly unfazed. "You never know, one day you'll just turn the corner, and there he'll be: Mr. Right!" The subject moved on as quickly as I had hoped, and our chat then turned to all the great dogs we had ever known, and once we ran out of dogs to remember, we plopped our respective recliners back a few notches and took a very lengthy nap together.

At the time, it had felt like the right thing to do. But as I sat in the hospital, bearing witness to my grandmother's life as it tapered to its inevitable end, I wondered if it had been a mistake not to share such a significant part of my life? As I watched her chest rise and fall, I knew that, mistake or not, I had missed my chance. *Oh well,* I thought, *it's all part of the soup. Too late to take the onions out now.*

Out of everyone in my family, the person I felt most akin to was Grandma. I shared much of her manner, the incongruous mix of vague and whip-smart. My sense of humour was a lot like hers as well, ranging, as it were, from silly and ridiculous to dark and very dry, often in the same breath. Both of us had a knack for getting our levity taken seriously and not caring enough to correct course. But for all our similarities, we were worlds apart. Grandma was a mother, a grandmother, a great-grandmother, and a great-great-grandmother. Me? I am not, nor will I ever be, a matriarch. I represent the very end of my branch of the family tree. Which, in and of itself, wasn't a painful thought; it was just that I had never been entirely sure that I was attached to the trunk at all. I supposed that, unlike Grandma, I would die alone.

Grandma died a few hours after I'd left her side. Classic Grandma, making me hang up on her. That evening my parents hosted an informal gathering of extended family, and being that it was Dad's side, it was a very quiet affair, but it did get a bit looser once a bottle of whiskey was introduced after dinner. Dad is the eldest of the six siblings, but he is almost fifteen years older than his youngest brother, David, so, a lot of the stories were interrupted by someone or another saying, "I had already left home by then" or "I wasn't even born yet." "No, I think you were thinking of Peter!"

Most of the memories being shared had been formed long before my time, so I just sat back and enjoyed the show. At first all the stories were familiar to me, but after a while long-forgotten memories began to surface, and it felt a little as if I was intruding upon a conversation between strangers. Maybe it was the grief, maybe it was the whiskey, but that night I was introduced to some skeletons that had never made it out of the closet in my company before.

I'd never met the family member they were talking about. I'd heard his name, but the only thing I really knew about him was that he'd been an alcoholic, and his life had been tinged with tragedy and sadness. What I had not known, until that night, was that he had been gay, and that he and Grandma had been incredibly close. The conversation moved on as quickly as it had begun, and I was too stunned to ask any questions. Why hadn't anyone thought to tell me about this? But that question got swept aside in my mind when I heard someone else mention another relative who they believed had committed suicide. Apparently, he'd also been gay.

There was kindness and regret being expressed about the men I never knew. But I was still stunned that no one seemed to be making a meaningful connection between the sexuality of these men and the tragedy of their broken lives. It was true that there had clearly been an evolution in my family. I was out of the closet; and I was still a part of the family and hiding nothing now that Grandma had taken the last of my secret to her grave. But even as they clearly no longer regarded the subject as taboo, my family's conversation made it abundantly clear that they had no real insight into the pain inherent in a closeted life. And that's when I realised, rather suddenly, that I had never, ever given myself a chance to have that insight either.

I didn't come out to my grandma because I was still ashamed of who I was. Had I known about the affection she'd had for a gay man, perhaps I would not have denied her the chance to love me for exactly who I was. I put my drink down and began to think about how I'd been forced to deal with far too many onions growing up, and how many of those onions had not become part of my soup as Nan had promised. They were still very raw and stung like an absolute bitch. With that thought, my traumas began to sweep through me. The violence, the abuse, the rape . . . and then, in this mixed-up cluster of dark memories, I could suddenly see how tightly I was wrapped in the tendrils of my internalised shame.

REDUCE TO A SIMMER

Mum had dropped me off at the airport hours before my departure, because she wanted to pick up my sister on the same trip. I didn't mind, as it gave me less of an opportunity to miss my flight. As I came down the steps into the terminal, I saw that there was a large group of school kids clogging up the thoroughfare. I knew I'd have more of a chance parting a body of water than a group of teenagers, so I diverted my path and skirted the wall. Besides, I am terrified of teenagers. Which I don't find problematic. I like to think that any-body who was even a little bit bullied at school will always carry a healthy fear of school-aged children. If any of those kids saw me, they made no attempt to make room for my passage. This didn't bother me, because I have a tendency to worry about the well-being of adolescents before I judge them. It's a frightening time of life, why shouldn't they take up a lot of space?

But as I went in search of a seat as far away from them as possi-ble, I began to wonder whose job it was to teach kids that public spaces are shared spaces. The answer to my question came when two fat-bellied businessmen charged straight through the middle of the group, barely breaking either their stride or their self-important conversation. They seemed impervious to the openly hostile recep-tion they received from about three-quarters of the group they'd scattered. *Well, they obviously never got bullied at school,* I thought to myself.

"Kids today!" I heard one of them scoff as they plonked them-selves down opposite me, piling their newspapers and bags on the three empty seats between them. Leaning back in their seats, legs spread comically wide, they resumed their conversing at a half shout and I began to wonder whose job it was to teach these guys that public spaces are shared spaces.

As the two men talked about hitting their targets, getting their bonuses, and finishing their quarterly reports, I began to make a list of all the things that made these two men far less impressive than they wanted everybody in earshot to believe. Firstly, they were talking loudly. Which I decided meant they either had nothing valuable to say or they were very unreliable holders of valuable information. Either way, I marked them down. Then there was the fact that they were both wearing the same green gingham shirt, which I took to mean that they worked for the same company and that this was their uniform. Wearing a uniform means the same thing as an adult as it does when you are at school: you are not in charge. I marked them down a few more notches for that. Then I noticed that both men were wearing socks embellished with cartoon characters—which I decided meant that they had children who hated them. Novelty socks are the gift you get adult men who have everything except a personality. It was at that point that I began to feel pity for them. Which is a weird thing to feel for two men who were taking up so much space in the world.

I was trying to regain my disdain for the two men when I heard someone say my name. It was not that I'd been recognised that caught me by surprise; ever since I'd been a picture crossword clue in the Hobart *Mercury*, I had been regularly recognised in Tasmania. It was the way he said my name that struck me. There was something about the way he linked my first and last name together that told me this was somebody who knew me from school.

His face was very familiar, he was definitely someone I went to school with, but I still had no idea who he was. I stood up to greet him as warmly as I could, but he must have registered my confusion because he offered his name as a prompt. Unfortunately, his was a very ubiquitous Smithton name, so I still couldn't place him as an individual. He was sporting a non-ironic mullet, his clothes had clearly not visited a washing machine in recent history, and his breath smelt like stale cigarettes and what I reckoned was premixed bourbon from a can. That I even know what that smells like means I'm in no position to judge him.

"I went to school with your brother," he added, obviously registering all the confusion I was failing to hide. I had no idea which of my brothers he was talking about, but, as I was keen to keep our interaction brief, I smiled in false recognition and braced myself for the awkward conversation I felt sure I was about to have.

"I just wanted to say congratulations," he began. I nodded and mumbled a few thanks as he lurched his way through what was clearly a speech he'd prepared just moments earlier. I've never been particularly good at hearing good things about myself, but over the years, as my public profile has grown, I've learnt how to give the appearance of listening. I tuned back in when I sensed that he was nearing the end of what he had to say.

"We are just all so proud. Seeing you doing so well, on TV and all? No one can believe it, eh? Someone from Smithton, eh? Famous, eh!?" As soon as he stopped talking, he turned abruptly and walked away, leaving me standing a bit stupidly and saying my thanks at his back. Something of this exchange had caught the attention of one of the men sitting across from me and he gave me a conspiring look of condescension. I sat down quickly, ignoring both him and his look.

I was relieved when the businessmen picked themselves and most of their debris up and made their way to the gate. Theirs was the flight before mine, so I stayed where I was and watched the rush of people around me. Toward the end of the line, I saw the familiar stranger from my past. He was standing with another man and a woman; all of them were what my mum calls "a bit rough around the edges." Even if he'd gone to school with my eldest brother, that still would've only made him less than ten years older than me, but he looked as old as my parents. His eyes were downcast and his shoulders were slumped, as if he was trying to take up the least space humanly possible. I began to wonder whose job it was to teach people like him that public spaces were shared spaces, and that he was allowed to take up space.

STICK A FORK IN IT

Smithton had always been a pretty tough place to live, but in the twenty-odd years since I'd left, it had been ripped even further apart by industries that stripped resources and then skipped town with the profits and no Plan B. It was not a place I returned to often, and as such it remained in a kind of time capsule. Occasionally people from school would contact me on Facebook, but for the most part the town of my childhood lives in my mind as if suspended in childish amber.

The last time I'd gone back to Smithton was for my fifteen-year high school reunion, which had been in 2009 That was a sobering thought to me, as I sat watching the line pass through the gate one at a time. Seven years does not seem like a considerable passage of time but, thinking about it, I felt like I had been a very, very different person seven years ago. For a start, I didn't remember having such strong opinions about novelty socks.

Around the time I'd gotten my invitation to the reunion, Smithton had been in the news because of a murder investigation. Two men had been slain in their home, and those responsible were at large for quite some time before being brought in and charged. As brutal as it all was, I followed the story with half a mind of amusement simply because it all took place in a town called Penguin. Once I'd read the headline penguin police on lookout for murder weapon, it stopped being a terrible crime in my head and just became a fantastic episode of *CSI Antarctica*.

But my amusement dried up once I found out that the murderer was from Smithton, and that he'd used a tomahawk to butcher the two men, rumoured to be his ex–gay lover and his father. I'd felt so uneasy about the whole thing, I began to have second thoughts about going to the reunion. It also didn't help that around this time the North West Coast of Tasmania had officially been mapped as the most homophobic part of Australia. I did end up going, how-

ever, because I was a comedian and mining life for material is what
we do.

The reunion wasn't a terrible affair, but I still built a wonderful
narrative about it which went on to become the centrepiece of my
2011 stand-up show, *Mrs. Chuckles*. I won't share all the gory details
here; my profile has grown significantly since then, and I feel like I
would be bullying if I turned it into material now. But I do want to
share something I heard during a conversation a group of us were
having about Smithton's very own axe murderer. We'd all been workshopping our disbelief and shock about the whole thing, agreeing
that it felt a bit too close for comfort. Not many of us had had any
direct dealings with the guy, but that hardly matters in a town where
kids inherit their grandfathers' nicknames. At first, the conversation
seemed to be going in the way you'd expect, but I had mistakenly assumed we were shocked that we knew someone capable of hacking
people to death with a tomahawk. But a couple of people in that
conversation, it turns out, were more horrified to find out that they
knew an "actual fucking faggot."

In that instant, I can remember how the protective barrier I'd
been painstakingly building for years completely fell apart. Although
it was only a mere moment in a much larger evening, it turned into
the only moment I really was able to have, because of the way it cata-
pulted me back into another moment I'd had at a bus stop. There is
no more to that reunion story. I was triggered, I went into panic, I
drank some more beer very quickly, the evening rolled on and I just
kept drinking until I could safely vomit myself into oblivion. No
doubt I must have looked pretty cool.

The familiar stranger from Smithton had unsettled me, and I
couldn't quite work out why. He was someone who would've terrified me when I was growing up, and he represented so many of the
things that had pushed me into the margins and held me there. And
yet, after a decade of performing and building confidence, I'd finally
grown comfortable taking up my fair share of space in the world.
This is not to say I always feel visible to, respected by, or even safe

around the people I sometimes share a room with, but I no longer live under the assumption that I should have to shrink myself because I am less than anyone else. And this, I guess, is because I am no longer governed by shame alone.

The way my familiar stranger from Smithton had looked down at the ground as if willing it to swallow him up, reminded me of the way I used to be. I recognised the way he held himself, twisting his body away, shoulders rolled forward and down. That was how I used to be. He had spoken flatly and struggled to finish each word, often swallowing the end of his sentence completely. I used to do that. I could see so clearly that this young man was living in a state of deep shame.

Making that connection, I found myself comprehending a new facet of the cruelty of putting same sex marriage to a public vote. Here I was again being thrown up as a debatable citizen and almost forced to be an oppositional slice of humanity to the likes of my familiar stranger from Smithton. It was clear that neither of us really mattered to the world, we were both just caught in the crossfire of a process neither of us understood. The difference between us was that he'd been promised the world, and I had not, which made him the underdog, whereas I was just a dog.

STIR. STIR. STIR

A couple of friends of mine, Zoë Coombs Marr and Rhys Nicholson, were planning to get married on stage during the Melbourne Comedy Festival that year, and they asked me to give a speech. I agreed without hesitation and then immediately regretted doing so. It was a protest event; they were both in long-term committed same-sex relationships with other people, and they wanted to show just how ludicrous marriage inequality was. They could marry each other for laughs, but not their own partners for love. It was an incredible idea from two incredible performers. Both of them had solo shows at the festival that year which were dominating the festival buzz. Zoë's show *Trigger Warning* went on to take the Best Show award that year, in what was something of a watershed moment for the long overdue recognition of women at the festival (more on that later). Personally, I would categorise Zoë's show as one of the most significant pieces of work I have ever seen live. I can't tell you how cathartic it was for me to see a queer woman so joyously demolish the worst of toxic masculinity in comedy, in a mega-meta performance that was as juvenile as it was dizzyingly complex.

The marriage "event" that Zoë and Rhys were planning was going to be a feast of raucous comic disruption that involved some of my favourite peers—Geraldine Hickey, Adrienne Truscott, Judith Lucy and Denise Scott, amongst others. But, as the performance approached, I began to seriously doubt my place on the stage, because I had all but lost access to any impulse to be even remotely funny.

I'd become increasingly annoyed that Tasmania had been the mascot of homophobia when I was growing up. Although it was not an undeserved label, it was the embedded certainty with which we were characterised as being an isolated pocket of homophobia, outliers amongst the broader Australian population. This has never been corrected on the public historical record; nobody seems to want to acknowledge the fact that so many of the politicians who facilitated the toxic debate were mainlanders, and many of them also relentlessly perpetuated the worst side of the marriage equality debate.

I didn't need a pamphlet to understand that the "conservative" side were already engaging in the same kind of hate-mustering that they did when I was a kid, taking advantage of the desperation of struggling communities, and distracting them with an invitation to channel their frustrations toward the gay community, who all seemed to be living a very lovely life in the cities. We know that there is a strong correlation between low literacy levels and homophobia. But instead of investing in education, leaders were investing in hate, again. I knew that the complexity of this kind of social change was never going to get the care it needed under the kind of combative leadership style that drives the Australian political landscape. And it was breaking me.

Fortunately, when I pitched the possibility of doing a straight-up serious speech to help get some things off my chest, Zoë and Rhys very generously and graciously gave me the all-clear to do whatever I wanted.

Their show was an absolute triumph. It was fun, political and an utterly joyous spectacle, despite my very serious interruption. Looking back on it, it was the only time during the whole marriage equality clusterfuck debate that I was able to engage with the subject without being weighed down by my own pain. It was also the first time in my entire comedy career that the greenroom was not defined by the tension of competitiveness. All of us who were performing that night were linked by a comradery, a common sense of purpose; we all understood that the audience and the stage were something we were sharing. It gave me a glimpse into a world that comedy might have been had it not been defined by so many brittle egos with loud voices.

THE SPEECH

We are gathered here today to witness the union of Rhys Nicholson and Zoë Coombs Marr. The concept behind this wedding between Rhys and Zoë will be familiar to anybody who is familiar with the closet. Why be happy when you can be normal? (Thanks, Jeanette Winterson.)

Is this a real marriage? Am I a real woman? Many have said no. But they would not dare to today. And certainly not in this room. Because what you are witnessing this evening is not a protest. It is a celebration.

As we all know, Marriage is between a man and a woman to the exclusion of all others. Although we are ALL excluded from this union between Rhys and Zoë, I would like to make a special mention to Keiren and Kate. As the LONG-TERM partners of Zoë and Rhys, I am sure this exclusion is all the more special for them.

But when one is queer, one is familiar with exclusion.

Zoë and Rhys first met when they were flaunting their lifestyles at the Sydney Gay and Lesbian Mardi Gras. Because, before they met, Zoë and Rhys were gay. And they will continue to be gay whether or not they, or anybody else, acknowledges that. Because that is kind of how it works. It is not a choice.

But don't think that just because being gay is not a choice that gay people don't like choice. People who are blind like to be seen. People born without legs still like to move through space. Neutered dogs still like to hump beanbags.

Us gayers know that we technically have access to the same rights as de factos; heterosexual couples that choose not to marry. But it is the choose bit I would like you to consider. Giving someone an air-conditioner unit is not the same as leaving someone out in the cold.

Exclusion is not a simple act. When you say to a person: "No. You cannot join in. You do not belong in this community." The end of that sentence is not the end of the story. The ramifications are traumatic to the individual. To actively isolate a fellow human being is nothing short of structural violence.

You are here this evening because you are the friends, the family and the community of Rhys and Zoë and it is incredibly important to them that you are here. It is also incredibly important that you paid for your ticket to this event. Because they really do want to uphold the sanctity of marriage this evening, and the institution of marriage is fundamentally, if you strip away all the namby-pamby love shit, is and always has been a glorified financial transaction.

The most common argument put forward against same sex marriage is "Think of the children."

And OF COURSE, people will listen to the church on this. Many people believe they are the guardians of marriage. They are not. And they never should have been the guardians of children, either.

I want you to know that I do not want the legalisation of gay marriage for myself. It is too late for me. Thanks to my old friend exclusion, I'm dead inside. Rhys and Zoë are on the cusp. There is still hope for these beautiful and talented bright sparks. EVEN so, this is not even really for them.

Rhys and Zoë are doing this because they are thinking of the children. And not just all those vulnerable baby queers. Although at this point I would like to say that all profits from this evening go to charities supporting the well-being of LGBTQI youth.

BUT, Rhys and Zoë are doing this for ALL of the children. Because at the moment, what we are doing in this country right now is saying to ALL of the children that it is OK to exclude a minority. It is OK to be a BULLY.

Through their union, filled with love and respect, from both within and without, what Rhys and Zoë would like to say to all children is that being inclusive is JUST as important as being included.

Now, I know that by ensuring this room is filled with friends and family we are only really preaching to the choir.

But who said the choir isn't supposed to have a fucking brilliant time?

SHAME BOILETH OVER

I made the mistake of scrolling through my social media while I was jet-lagged. I don't know why I thought that going to London would be enough to stop all the opinions about the worth of my existence reaching me, but I was still shocked by the stream of debate dominating my feeds. I snapped. Why was this happening again? Perhaps it was because the jet lag had been so brutal, but I completely lost my will to try and rise above it, and so I decided to transcribe a little piece of my mind. As soon as I pressed publish on Facebook, I finally got the sleep that jet lag had been withholding.

When I woke up, I was full of regret. I knew better than to try and communicate with the world when I'm on my way to shutdown. The worst thing was, I had not made any attempt to hide my earnestness. And if there's one thing that will get a comedian cancelled, it is earnestness. What had I done? As I logged in, still blurry from my midnight nap, I braced myself for the inevitable ridicule, but much to my surprise, I discovered that my post had gone viral. It had had the shit clicked out of it. More people read that post than had ever seen me perform. The problem was that my post contained exactly zero jokes. Was I losing my ability to do the only thing I was able to do? What was I becoming? And why was I not being slammed and hate-bombed? Why was everyone being so nice? I couldn't process it, so I went back to sleep.

THE POST

Oh! hey guys . . . this plebiscite thing is a very bad idea. The very idea of an ongoing debate around marriage equality makes my stomach turn. It's not a pleasant turn either.

Let me be clear. I don't care about marriage equality for myself because I do not have an aptitude for relationships.

The reason I care about this is because I don't want young kids to hear the kind of horrific bile I was forced to listen to in the 1990s when Tasmania debated on whether to legalise homosexuality. For many, the debate was theatre.

For me, it made me hate myself so deeply I have never been able to develop an aptitude for relationships.

In the mid-nineties I was the age when I should have been learning how to be vulnerable, how to handle a broken heart, how to deal with rejection and how to deal with all the other great silly things about young love which help pave the way to the more substantial adult version.

But instead, I learnt how to close myself off and rot quietly in self-hatred. I learnt this because I learnt that I was subhuman during a debate where only the most horrible voices and ideas were amplified by the media.

These voices also gave permission to others to tell me that I was less than them, with looks, words and on one occasion, violence. Every day of my life I deal with the effects of anxiety and low self-

esteem. It is not nearly as debilitating as it used to be but I don't imagine I will ever be truly free of it.

Just imagine how brilliant I could have been if I hadn't been given such a shit show at such a vulnerable time in my life.

I am very concerned that the plebiscite debate is going to be another open season for hate. I fear for those, particularly in regional Australia, who are isolated from positive voices. If this plebiscite has to happen then let's try and drown out the hate-filled commentators. They might not have the numbers but they will no doubt be handed a megaphone in the name of entertainment.

But this kind of entertainment will not only ruin young lives . . . it will end some of them. Speech is not free when it comes at such a cost.

This plebiscite is FUCKED.

ADD A PINCH OF SALTY

I thought I had been sent to heaven when my documentary about "the nude in art" was greenlit. I just couldn't believe the luck of it; my first love was going to be my actual job. I had been interrogating the history of the nude in Western art since I was a tortured teenager searching for a clue to my own existence, and I had not stopped thinking about it ever since. Sadly, the project ended up being the absolute worst experience of my professional life. I'd gone into it hoping to break open the generally constricted and whitewashed narrative of the history of the nude in art that persists to this day, even though the canon has apparently been destroyed. But I was brick-walled again and again. The biggest issue, I suppose, is that I failed to communicate just how important the subject was to me, as an artist.

In one interview, an artist took me for an idiot and refused to change his mind. That was fun. "Every culture on earth celebrates the human body through their art," he declared, rather incorrectly. One of the central motifs of his work was the nude form as an unambiguous echo of the Ancient Greek ideal, so I guess I shouldn't have been surprised by the staggering certainty behind his reverence of the "canon." But I was, so I asked him why he didn't think Islamic art qualified as "culture." I didn't get my question out with a great deal of eloquence, which is probably why he didn't feel obliged to address the glaring inaccuracies in his gross generalisation, and just continued on with his "point." When I asked why he only used the one body type in his work, he told me it was because "the ideal human form best communicates the human condition." When I asked him how he knew what the ideal human form looked like, he scoffed and then used the enduring popularity of Ancient Greek art as proof that the ideal human form is universally understood. So I asked why it might be that some cultures only found out about this so-called ideal human form after they'd been colonised by the West? I knew I'd breached his logic, but he didn't feel I was worth engaging with, and waved me away again.

Another of my interview subjects, a life-drawing instructor, thought I needed a lesson on the concept of beauty, so he got up and pulled out a replica of the Venus of Willendorf and passed it to me. The tiny cellulite-ridden body very closely resembled my own, and as it pre-dated the Ancient Greek ideal I was trying to destabilise, it was the perfect object for the conversation I had been trying and failing to initiate. But instead of having a conversation, the instructor went on to mansplain it to me. I tried to participate, but I couldn't get any purchase because he was obviously delivering something he'd pre-pared earlier. I tried to be patient, but when he told me that it was a symbol of beauty, with his eyes closed as if in revery, I couldn't be polite any longer and I called bullshit.

I explained that our understanding of beauty has been inherited from the Ancient Greeks and so he is incorrect, and, as somebody who has existed in such a body all her life, I knew life would be so much easier if he was right. But he wasn't right, I told him, because "beauty" is a construct. And to which I should have added that the construct of beauty that dominates my lived experience has nothing to do with my lived experience. The construct of beauty that I have to negotiate is an invention born out of the colonising eye of the Western patriarchy. And by "negotiate" I mean it is demanded that I be willing to literally break my back bending myself in order to achieve it, or else be shamed and shunned into some kind of projected moral ugliness. But, of course, I stupidly left my response to just the tip of that idea-berg. And that's when his real lecture began: "Beauty, m'dear, is in the eye of the beholder!" Looking back at the footage, you can see the precise moment my blood began to boil.

By far the most aggravating interview, however, was one I'd had with a curator. I'd wanted to engage critically with an exhibition he'd curated, but at every turn I was stymied, because he was too busy patting himself on the back for ensuring that there was at least one female artist represented in every room of his exhibition. *Does he not understand,* I thought to myself, *that that's a pretty fucking dangerous circumstance for a woman to be put in? "Metaphorically" or otherwise?*

At one point I got in a thorny question about a painting by Picasso, in which his penis dominates one side of his famous "muse" Marie-Thérèse Walter's sleeping face. I think I used the term "tea bagging," but the curator was not impressed with my worldly reference, and went on to try to sell it to me as an expression of tenderness and desire, and not just garden-variety sexual assault. Once he was done gaslighting me, he went on to explain what a metaphor was. As someone who was raped as a young woman while I was asleep, I was not particularly interested in metaphor.

I then asked him why we must keep romanticising Pablo Picasso's relationship with the seventeen-year-old Marie-Thérèse Walter, despite all the very clear evidence it was an often-abusive relationship that she'd been coerced into by a much older and powerful man. I thought it was a reasonable question but the curator dismissed it, chiding me that I should not apply current-day worldviews onto the past. Then why bother with history at all, I asked? Why not burn all the galleries and museums down, if the past has nothing in common with the present? Rather than answer me, he laughed as if I had made a joke and just moved on to the next room. What did he think? That a comedian should give the same shits as an historian?

I am an artist, and as such I am engaging in the themes of the artist, not the context of the world the art was created in, but in the context of the world that is consuming it now.

I had wanted to keep in the film all the tense exchanges I'd had with all the white men. I thought it was interesting that they chose to speak over the top of me so they could make dumb and sexist statements, but I was told that it would make me look bad, because I came across as angry. It didn't matter to me that I might appear angry. I had no problem coming across as angry. But apparently I don't get to choose how I look, which I guess, in a documentary about Western art, is pretty on-brand.

I'd wanted to end the documentary with the glass artist Yhonnie Scarce, a descendant of the Kokatha and Nukunu peoples of what is now known as South Australia. I did manage to interview her, and we had a really rich conversation about the effects of colonisation on Indigenous Australians, but, sadly, it never made the cut. I was disappointed but unsurprised, as her art did not overtly represent the human body and I am shit at convincing people that I might know what I am talking about. So, I will just share it here, because I truly believe that the only universal "body" is our breath, because breath is the only thing that all human bodies experience and as such, it is something we all must share, not just with each other, but, in one way or another, with all living things on earth. To this day, I still can't think of a better way of truly breaking us free from the visual rut that the canon of Western art has left us languishing in, than the breath of an Indigenous Australian woman.

Perhaps I couldn't make myself understood clearly enough. Perhaps it was because the documentary was funded by people who had an interest in not destroying the more comfortable version of events. Perhaps I was being too esoteric. Perhaps it was because I was a comedian and had no right to be serious. Whichever way you cut it, I didn't get to make the documentary I wanted to make. And why should I get to do what I want? Picasso got to do whatever he wanted, whenever he wanted. And by the time Picasso died, he didn't have a scrap of humanity to call his own.

THAT IS BAD SOUP

While I was suffering through the documentary making, I was also trying to write a play about my relationship with one of my favourite artists, Claude Cahun. This was proving to be a far better experience, but even so, it became clear that my creative process was at odds with yet another avenue of expression. Theatre has lots of rules, you see, and not all of them made sense to me, so I tried to work around them, which seemed to prevent other people being able to make sense of me. It was a familiar cycle, but painful nonetheless.

Another alternative avenue of expression was simultaneously being damned by my own shortcomings. *The New York Times* had approached me shortly after my Facebook post had gone viral, to see if I might write an opinion piece about Australia's marriage equality debate. I was honoured but, two drafts in, I had all the evidence I needed that I couldn't form appropriate opinions. I wasn't sad, I actually felt that I'd said everything I had to say on the matter in my post, and I wasn't particularly interested in wrestling with the question further in an even more public forum. At one point I set up a meeting with Rodney Croome, one of the key activists in Tasmanian gay law reform in the 1990s. He was more than happy for me to pick his brain for my *New York Times* piece. We had a great conversation, but I still couldn't seem to find the exact opinion the *Times* editor had in mind.

My mounting frustration over the documentary had led me into something of a writing spiral, which had begun to take precedent over any other work. I was beginning to see all kinds of interesting connections between art history and the current socio-political events, and this line of thinking led me to pitch a different piece to *The New York Times*. One that was not devoted to the marriage debate, but instead drew a direct line from Picasso to Trump. Apart from the pithy line "Let's not make art that great again," it was a mess of an idea and I was not surprised that the editor basically ghosted me.

I was in a very bad state of mind. My conversation with Rodney Croome had driven that home. He'd lived through the same 1990s Tasmania that I had but he was in a much, much better place than me. He was very actively engaged in the marriage equality debate and in being a proper constructive leader, whereas I was just upset and scared. Even so, I really felt as if I had something profound to express, but there didn't seem to be a format that would allow me to channel all my creative urgency. I was bad at making documentaries. I couldn't make theatre bend to my voice. Social media felt too much like a toxic nonstop conversation, and I just don't have the correct neurobiological setup to participate in that. I couldn't even form an opinion correctly, and, apparently, I'd become too serious for comedy. But I was desperate to funnel my ideas somewhere. I wanted to make something angry and urgent, but there were too many ideas swirling in my head to know what to make out of it all.

And then I met Nanette.

GATHERING STRANDS

YOUR BARISTA FOR THE DAY

I often feel quite tense in small towns, because I tend to stick out like dog's balls, only worse, because intact dogs are welcome in small towns, unlike suit-wearing butch lesbians with statement glasses and fancy shoes. I'd done a show in Wagga Wagga the night before and was racing back to Melbourne for a gig that evening. I was feeling pretty smug about my time-saving tactic of wearing my stage clothes en route until I climbed out of my car and onto the main street curb of a very small town where my well-dressed presence was met with a lot of side-eye glances, double takes and straight-up stares.

I relaxed as soon as I entered the café, because I know nanna décor when I see it and this place was chockablock with it: lace doilies on the tables, cross-stitch samplers home-sweet-homing the walls, and a great stack of homemade cakes on the counter, wrapped so tightly in plastic wrap it looked as if Madame Tussauds had taken up baking. Everything looked as though it had just been wiped down, even the fly strips I had to fight through at the door had that just-been-cleaned sheen; the air was thick with a heady mix of bleach and lavender, and I couldn't help but to relax, because nannas are my favourite people.

The café was empty, but I knew better than to be a stranger in a hurry, so I just stood and waited. I noticed a little blackboard propped up on the counter; it was graced with some very fancy chalk work, lightly traced with the telltale wobble of a hand losing its strength to age. It wasn't easy to make out the message as it was written in old school cursive, with every letter holding hands, so I ventured a closer look:

"Your barista for the day is Nanette"

If nans are cute, then, in my feeble thinking, "Nanette" signalled a doubling-down on the adorability, and so I quite convinced myself that I was about to meet cute squared to the power of puppy.

Nanette appeared very suddenly. One moment I'd been alone in the café and then BAM!, there she was. I don't know how she travelled, she didn't walk, she certainly didn't glide, she just kind of landed. And there she was, glowering at me from behind the counter. She was a square human; she went straight down from her ears to her feet in pretty much a straight line, a four-by-four, as my grandma used to say. She had the look of someone who'd had a tough life combined with too much sun, her face was a wrinkle farm. I'd bet she was a smoker too; the middle and index fingers of her right hand were stained with the yellow ghosts of cigarettes past. My barista for the day was not a kindly nan at all, however; she was a furious thumb in an apron, mean squared to the power of guppy.

Nanette fixed me with a radioactive scowl I was familiar with. She was looking at me as if I represented everything that was wrong with the world: a left-wing, bleeding-heart, arty-farty, fancy gay from the big city. I was one of those "coastal elites" who "thinks they know it all" and who is not in touch with "real Australia." I hated that people always just assumed I lived in the big smoke. I hated it because it was true—I was living in Melbourne at the time—but the thing is, I don't belong in a city. I don't walk or talk fast enough to flourish in a city. I belong in a small town, but I didn't live in a small town, because people like Nanette had the habit of making me feel very unwelcome.

I guess I panicked. I stuttered an apology and left her territory, as if I'd never meant to be there in the first place, and I got straight back into my car and got out of town fast, as if I had been chased. I hadn't been chased. I was just a little brokenhearted. I knew that if both Nanette and I had had the chance to clear the slate of our starting assumptions, we might have been able to have a really nice chat. She looked as tired of life as I felt; it was clear to me that she worked hard, and I wanted to let her know that I appreciated her chalkboard flourish. But I didn't give her a chance.

PUNCH A SHARK IN THE FACE

When it came to registering for all the festivals for my 2017 season, I had a hard time choosing between two names and, ostensibly, the two competing ideas that I had attached to them. As you might have already worked out, I ended up going with the title *Nanette*. But the other title in hot contention was *Punch a Shark in the Face*. Which, in terms of the content of the show, might have been a much more apt title than *Nanette*. But I am glad I didn't go with it, because I love sharks.

The title had been gifted to me by an awful young man who'd told me an awful story about the time he'd been free-diving and a shark had kept stealing fish from his catch stash up the line. So, he decided to ambush the shark the next time it tried to steal from him and teach it a lesson. How do you teach a shark a lesson? You don't punch it in the face. Because that's what this guy did and the shark paid him back by taking two of his fingers clean off his hand. I like that he lost his fingers, and it would have been a great story had the jerk not told everyone at the time that it was a completely unprovoked attack, and so the shark was caught and killed. I still hate that guy.⊗

Most of the ideas that I had attached to my shark title, however, were worlds away from the aggression it seemed to suggest. I was actually thinking about writing a show entirely about the colour

⊗ I should have punched his dick in the face.

blue. Blue had long held a fascination for me, and even though it was a deeply personal topic, I didn't think it was possible to write anything about blue that Maggie Nelson hadn't already written better in her magnificent book *Bluets*. So, I went with *Nanette*.

I had visited Giotto's Scrovegni Chapel in Padua after the Edinburgh Fringe in 2010, and I have been obsessed by the power of blue ever since. I'd found the depth of the lapis blue that dominates those frescoes so overwhelming, I was unable to think. To this day it remains one of the very few pieces of art that has affected me viscerally, without any intervention from my thinking. It simply enveloped me with wonder. But it was the road trip I took from Perth up the West Coast of Australia to Exmouth that really introduced me to the healing quality of blue. I have never taken a better breath than the ones I took as I stared for hours at the horizon where the turquoise of the Ningaloo Reef crossed with the deep blue of the Indian Ocean, meeting a cloudless blue sky.

I had taken the trip to meet up with Hamish, who'd flown over to swim with the whale sharks for his fortieth birthday. Had I not been breathing through snorkel gear as I swam beside this magnificent creature, that breath would have been even better. Even so, swimming through nothing but blue with that gentleman mega-fauna, with his fairy-light markings and ethereal, unceasing side-to-side glide, was the most exquisite thing I have ever experienced.

At the time, I was only just beginning to understand the complexity of my sensorial experience of the world. So many things were painful to me, and I'd never really understood it. Things I had previously thought of as being simply "unpleasant"—the feeling of mushrooms in my mouth, the beeping of a truck in reverse, the squeal of a happy child—actually caused me something akin to pain. I don't simply dislike the colour yellow; the colour yellow makes me angry. But as I swam beside my whale shark friend—and not at all punching it—I was suddenly aware of a profound sense of beauty living inside me as a sensation.

It was not long afterward that I began to take actions to protect myself against the hostilities of my environments, things like taking my noise-cancelling headphones with me absolutely everywhere, and wearing sunglasses in supermarkets. That's also when I began my habit of wearing exclusively blue clothing. But this one was not a preventative measure; it was a proactive engagement in positive self-stimulation. Which makes it the first significant step that I made toward embracing my autistic identity.

STICKING BUTTERFLIES WITH PINS

I'd heard Mum talking and I assumed she was chatting to Douglas, but as I got closer, I saw that Doug was still in the car. A little scared to know the answer, I asked the question anyway: "Who were you talking to, Mum?"

"Oh . . . just a butterfly," she said, stubbing out her cigarette before climbing into the passenger seat beside me. "It's so strange to think that people collect butterflies," she mused as I pulled back out onto the highway. "Isn't it?"

"Yes. I suppose it is," I said, meaning it.

I was driving with Mum from Melbourne to Adelaide to spend Christmas with my sister and her family. The plan was to give Mum and Dad some time apart, because they'd been fighting quite a bit in the months before. Mum had been annoyed with Dad because he was sulking.

"It doesn't matter what I say," she'd complain. "He just sits there and huffs and puffs."

Dad, who'd been put on a plane to Adelaide, didn't mention what it was that annoyed him about Mum—probably because he was really ill. None of us knew it yet, but Dad was about to be diagnosed with melanoma.

The drive to Adelaide from Melbourne can be dull at times, long stretches of straight with not much to pass but fields and fields of monotonous crops. I was happy driving, though, I liked being lost in my thoughts, but Mum was getting bored and had begun to read every single road sign as we passed them. Eventually I had to tell her to stop, as it was disrupting the train of my thoughts about my new show, *Nanette*. She obliged but then began sighing to let me know she had something to say, and wanted me to ask her what it was, but I didn't. And after a while the sighing stopped and the silence between us resumed. For about a minute.

"Look at that beautiful little church!" Mum jolted me out of my thinking.

"I would love to look, Mum, but I am driving quite fast."

"It was so beautiful!" she exclaimed, then added with thinly veiled venom, "It's just a shame about the owners." I don't know exactly what the story is with Mum's Catholic school days—she has never felt ready to talk about it—I just know it must be a doozy, because of the way she spits with fury whenever she's on the topic of nuns.

"I'm really proud I raised you kids without religion," Mum declared, as if reading my thoughts.

"Good for you," I said a bit dismissively.

"I am!" she said louder, demanding I get off my own train of thought and climb aboard hers. "I'm really proud of it," she continued. "I've brought up five children with minds of their own."

It couldn't have been easy to raise five children with less money than was useful in a town far too small for her personality, and I'm sure her choice to keep her kids out of Church culture isolated her even further. But I wasn't really in the mood to match my thinking to hers.

"Are there any parenting decisions you aren't proud of?" I teased.

Mum didn't answer and instead just looked out the window. I felt bad; I'd only asked in jest, and I assumed she'd reply in kind. Sometimes I like to tell her that she used to terrify the life out of me, and she usually responds by telling me that she didn't like me very much. It's fun. It's our love language. But this was not how this interaction was going.

"I think the thing I regret most," she said eventually, "was that I raised you as if you were straight."

I was stunned. I had not been expecting that at all. I was thinking about all the homemade clothes she'd forced me to wear.

"I guess I wanted you to change, because I knew the world wouldn't. I should have been your friend, you know, but I wasn't. I'll never forgive myself for that."

They say that time heals all wounds, and while I'm certain that time is better at wound care than Vicks VapoRub, time alone is not enough. Effort is required. And until Mum said that, I don't think I appreciated just how much effort she had to put in over the years. As we drove on, I began to think back to the moment I'd come out to Mum all those years ago, and much to my surprise, it was still painful to recall.

"What if I told you I was a murderer!?"

I had repeated Mum's response to my coming out so many times on stage that it had separated itself from my actual memory. It worried me that I had become unable to think about my coming out story as it had actually happened, without all the silly jokes I wrote into the story crashing into my memory. There was nothing funny about it, and yet by telling my story for laughs, I'd trimmed away the darkness, my trauma, for the comfort of my audiences, and by doing so, I had shoved all my pain into a closet of its own. It's not that I strayed very far from truth in my comedy version of events, but I still got it wrong, simply because I made it funny.

It wasn't funny. I don't remember being pithy and cavalier. I was in too much pain. I remember crying snot and shouting at her, "I'm not a criminal!" but only after the phone had been cut off, and me with it. I remember sliding down the wall and sitting on the kitchen floor, absolutely shattered. Devastated. I had just got the confirmation that all the dread that had been building inside of me for years was entirely justified, and I was completely alone in the world. It was as brutal a moment as I'd ever experienced. And even then, after mining it for laughs for years, it was still an open wound.

I find it too easy to forget that I was the one who hung the phone up on Mum when I came out. I'd hung up because I couldn't bear the thought of her rejecting me. I also find it easy to forget that it was

Mum who phoned me back immediately; the cruel anger had left her as she softly pleaded for me to forgive her. "I just need time," she cried.

This moment of vulnerability was easy for me to forget, because Mum needed quite a bit of time. Years, in fact. And as completely accepted as I felt fifteen years later, I couldn't so easily forgive the time it took Mum to come around to my queerness.

One of the biggest faults I built into my coming out narrative was that I blamed my mum for my pain. I thought she was responsible for what I had to endure. But I'd been so self-absorbed that I'd never been able to believe anyone else got hurt. I took the lion's share of the brunt, sure, but my family were not the architects of my position in life. I'm only now beginning to appreciate the complicated nature of this kind of fracture: it doesn't matter which side you're on, you still get hurt. But I was too naive at the time to understand that my mum had not rejected me. She had been afraid. She was afraid because she couldn't control the world for me, and it frightened her. And it frightened me.

Our family unit had been collateral damage, nothing more than pawn porn for the juvenile and toxic political games being played out well above our heads. That is the shit that ruined my life. I couldn't see that until then, but once I did, I became furious and filled with an unrelenting urge to update the way I told my story. It's not that I wanted to forget the jokes, I loved them, I really did. I needed them for a long time, and I know that if it hadn't been for all the armour they provided me over the years, I probably wouldn't have been able to find the self-acceptance that I now possess. But the story was wrong and it was incomplete. The metamorphosis was not mine alone to claim, my entire family weathered the storm as much as I had. I needed to update my story. Not for me, but for all of us.

We had been sitting in very comfortable silence for what felt like hours after that, when Mum pulled me out of my thinking again with a sudden and urgent declaration.

"What a stupid bloody thing to do."

"What is?" I asked.

"Sticking pins into butterflies," she said, indignantly, without even looking at me. I agreed wholeheartedly, and without saying a word, I decided it was time that I took out the pin that I had kept sticking into my own story.

And that is when I can say, for sure, that I truly met *Nanette* for the first time.

WOMEN'S WORK

ONE-BLOCK WONDER . . .

The first thing I do when putting together a new show is to settle on the shape and the feeling that best reflects what I want to communicate. And look, I know that all sounds a bit esoteric, but that is how the processing gets done in my head. I find it annoying too, but I think it's a bit late to try and make believe that I have a normal brain. In a way, this process has something in common with Michelangelo's approach to sculpture. When he carved his figures out of marble, he didn't try and make the marble fit his intention, but rather worked to fit his intentions around what he found inside the stone. In other words, he did not try and master the medium; he had a conversation with it.

My slabs of marble are all the thoughts that my brain most wants to wrangle with, my preoccupations if you will, my tools are all the rules of comedy and my shows were simply what I discovered while chipping away at my thoughts with the chisel of setups and the hammer of punch lines. To be clear, I am not suggesting my finished pieces are comparable to Michelangelo's giants of Renaissance greatness. What do you think I am? Some kind of man with some kind of man ego? I am way better than that. That's a little joke. Chip. Chip.

Michelangelo's most recognisable sculpture, *David,* is housed in the Galleria dell'Accademia in Florence, and if you ever have the chance to visit make sure you give yourself some time to spend with the four "prisoners" that are flanking his entrance, so to speak. The jury is still out as to why Michelangelo left these figures only partially freed from their marble cocoons, but whenever I look at them, I don't see a decision or a failure, I just feel as if I've interrupted a very difficult conversation. And in my humble opinion, in comparison, *David* is not much more than small talk.

This opinion is very personal. You don't have to take your research much further than Tripadvisor to know that *David* is very popular. My taste is driven by my own fascination with process, and I only offer it as a light, subjective amuse-bouche of an idea, because experience has taught me that most people prefer to believe that art is just a magic trick. Hell, even Michelangelo thought he was God's hand on earth. Who am I to argue?

Three weeks out from my first trial show of *Nanette,* all I had was a name and a million very unruly ideas. And yet, even with the immovable deadline of my tour hurtling toward me, I couldn't seem to make an official stab at wrangling the nonsense in my head into something I could say out loud. I'd not been procrastinating, exactly. *Nanette* had been all I could think about for months. It was just that whenever I came close to making a start, the tangle in my head would expand and totally overwhelm me like a backseat airbag. Even if I only gave it a sideways glance, I could become distressed. And if I ignored that red flag and tried to push beyond it, it wouldn't take long before I'd begin to feel physical pain. At which point I would wonder if I was experiencing some form of insanity. How else can you explain a brain eating itself with its own thoughts?

Despite my lifelong passion for the mechanics of process, in my own work I have always been careful to cover my tracks. For most of my career, my number one rule when writing material was: Don't make comedy about comedy. Would you carve a slab of marble out of a slab of marble?

What I didn't know in the weeks leading into my first *Nanette,* however, was that I was about to break this, my biggest rule, and that once I did, I was opening the floodgates of a murderous rule-breaking spree. But it was never my intention to break the rules of comedy. Truly. I love rules too much for that. What drove me was my failure to solve the riddle that was *Nanette*.

Very early on, I knew exactly the feeling I wanted to impart with my new show; I wanted to punch my audience in their metaphorical guts. But despite the clarity of that intention, the shape of the show remained frustratingly elusive. It didn't matter which way I carved my thinking; I just couldn't find a way to grip onto the shape of *Nanette*, and the intellectual struggle of it only further exacerbated my sadness and pain. Writing has always been a challenging process for me, but no other show had ever felt as discombobulating and potentially injurious to create as *Nanette*. But conversely, none had felt so important, so pressing, or necessary.

NANETTE

THE PROBLEM WITH
COMEDY

I FEAR THAT IF I
PRIORITISE PUNCHLINES
I WON'T BE ABLE
TO CONTINUE MATURING
ENOUGH TO KEEP
AHEAD OF SUICIDE.

Full disclosure: It is very difficult for me to find a coherent way to peel back all the many layers of process that went into creating *Nanette*. This is in part because, for me, a creative process is beyond words, even when the process is in the service of words themselves. The biggest issue for me is that the process itself was traumatic, because I was not chipping away at a mere tangle of competing ideas, I was digging into a hotbed of my own trauma. And if I have said it once, I have said it a thousand times: there is no straight line to be found through trauma. There is part of me that wants to leave this alone, and let you believe that what I did was magic. But there is a bigger part of me that wants the world to know what I did, because I don't think many of the people with strong opinions about *Nanette* have managed to scratch very far below her surface. So, if you don't mind, I will manufacture some artificial lines through my process, just to give you an appreciation for the metaphorical iceberg that is *Nanette*. But to be sure, none of this was linear.

I'd always thought homophobia was behind my bus stop beating. In many ways this was a completely reasonable assumption given that Tasmania was rife with it at the time. But as I began to re-examine what happened, I could no longer believe that I was assaulted because of my sexuality alone, it was my gender expression that had invited the brunt of the violence. If I had looked like what he expected a woman to look like, it would never have happened as it did. I think he hit me because he saw me as being incorrectly female. I think he hit me because he saw me as a threat to his masculinity. But most of all, I think he hit me because he saw it as his job, as a man, to enforce the rules as he understood them. And at the time, I could only agree with him because I had been raised in the same school of toxic masculinity.

It had taken me a long time to free myself from the worst of that memory. Thinking about it used to be so raw, so painful and debilitating. But as time passed, the intensity dropped and it became just a slight churn of my stomach, a tightening of my chest, and eventually, it shrank to be nothing but a vague crawling of my skin, everywhere and nowhere at once. For years I had been able to think about it without devastation following, but as the marriage equality debate kicked off, I felt the tide turn on my recovery.

As I was wrestling with *Nanette*, I thought a lot about how I'd turned this trauma into material for my first ever stand-up comedy show. How heavily I had to edit the reality, namely the violence, so I could make it work within a comedy context. It had been very difficult turning something that dark into laughs, and I'd once been proud that I was able to do so. But laughter had not been the medicine it promised, and I began to wonder if I needed to try again, to use *Nanette* to try and tell the full version. Surely, I had the experience and skills to make it funny without shaving off the violence and trauma.

As I was wrangling this idea, I was plagued with imaginary questions: *Do you need to tell your story in public again? Have you heard of a therapist, babe? Why do we have to hear about all this misery? None of this is relevant! Times have changed! We need to keep the economy spinning and you interrupt to talk about something that happened last century?* But to my mind, the "last century" was bleeding painfully into the right now. I was not coping with all the public debating of marriage equality. It was hurting me. Physically hurting me. I had been drowning in that fucking shit my whole life and I just couldn't bear hearing any more people having their first ever thoughts on the matter, out loud and unfiltered. I had lived this shit. But I felt too overwhelmed to do anything about it. I felt too small and too weak, which is to say, I felt too traumatised.

And still, I knew beyond any doubt that there was genuine value to be found in my story. I felt as if I had something constructive to offer that went beyond the flash point of political divisions. I had the story of my family and how it was not destroyed by my queerness. Despite the trauma thrust upon us by external forces, the love of my family not only survived, it evolved into something even stronger. I had a story of healing, but I didn't know how to safely participate in the debate because I was too angry. And I was angry because I had not been able to heal myself.

Common wisdom has it that the pathway out of trauma is a coherent narrative; but I had a coherent narrative and I was still stuck in the painful maze of my Trauma. I'd tried everything in my power to heal and I was left to wonder whether it was entirely my responsibility. What good is a coherent narrative if people don't want to hear it? Because trauma won't leave you alone until you feel safe, and safety is not something that an individual can summon on their own. Safety is not a gun. Safety is being able to trust that those around you WANT to protect you from harm. But if those around you don't believe you are "like them," then they will focus on the discomfort you make them feel, and that discomfort is not a safe space.

Nanette was too much of a beast to be tackled in one fell swoop. There were too many ideas demanding my attention, and it became clear that my usual process was not up to the challenge. I had to try something new. The first thing I did was rid myself of the self-imposed pressure to do it all at once and decided to take baby steps. I spent a good couple of weeks siphoning everything out of my head and onto the page. It was a frenzied effort, and if anybody had intruded upon me during that time, I may very well have been committed to some kind of interventionist treatment.

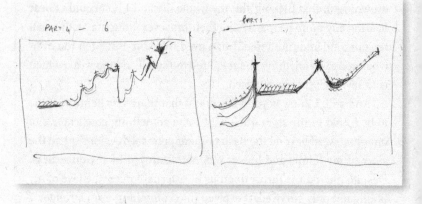

It was very much a two-steps forward, one-step back situation. As each idea was loosened and freed from my head cocoon, the pressure inside me would begin to ease off, but then I would see a multitude of possible idea-prisoners and I didn't know how to choose which one to give shape to. Every time I felt myself panicking about the impossibility of making all the pieces fit, I reminded myself: *one idea at a time.* And I would set the unfinished idea aside and strike up a conversation with a different one, like a regular Michelangelo.

The history of Western art is how I think about the world. Even as I am trying to explain my creative process here, I can only think of examples pertaining to this, my biggest branch of special interest. But to be clear, I don't point back into the history of art to prove a point about art; I don't use it to prove that I am right about one thing or another. I use it to remind myself that paradox has always been the animating life force at the heart of the human condition. And therein lies my problem.

Western culture is built around the fucked-up and demonstrably false premise that "white men" are the natural peak of the human pyramid. By that measure, history becomes nothing more than a glorified mood diary for white men. But this history of art is not only sexist and racist, it has also totally rewritten the narrative of queer bodies, and by rewritten, I mean erased. We see ourselves all the time, but time and time again we have been gaslit out of ever existing, and, yet, paradoxically, thinking about the history of art has only ever reminded me that I do exist. Because isn't it possible that hidden amongst all the things that history has forgotten is what holds the key to what we are missing now?

In my mind I could see *Nanette* taking shape; the problem was, she was three different, contradictory shapes, and it didn't matter which way I twisted them, I couldn't find a way to make one cohesive form. If I had three hours to kill on stage, maybe I could have forced those shapes to work for my purpose, but it would have become a show that undermined the intensity of the "punch" I was aiming for. But on their own, each piece seemed too weak, or too thin to hold the weight of all that I was trying to communicate.

I decided to remove two very big ideas from the palette of thought I was painting *Nanette* with: autism and my body. My ASD was an easy drop; I knew that by bringing it into the conversation, everything I had to say about anything else would be measured against the mountains of misinformation that is built into most people's understanding of it. That is not to say that *Nanette* has nothing to say on the topic; I would argue she is hardwired with my autistic thinking, and as such, she is a flaunting of my atypical brain, but it's a quiet celebration that lives only in the underside of the iceberg.

It was easy to disappear the prejudice of neurobiology from *Nanette*, but I knew I couldn't disappear my physical existence. I knew that everything I said could only ever find meaning in the minds of others once it had been filtered through the lens of my body and all the distortions it seems to engender. But I made a decision not to diminish my ambiguity by explaining it; people would just have to sort me out on their own. It was, after all, their problem.

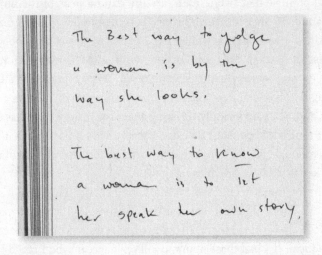

The Best way to judge
a woman is by the
way she looks.

The best way to know
a woman is to let
her speak her own story.

Not so long before I began working on *Nanette*, I stumbled upon a photograph of myself when I was about twelve years old. I am standing knee-deep in a river with two of my brothers, and, despite the mullet and the big teeth, I look utterly adorable. I am clearly unaware that the two white fleshy drumsticks emerging from the leg holes of my bathers were going to attract so much brutal and unwanted attention into my life. And it is precisely because I am so clearly unbothered by my body that makes me look so adorable. One of the saddest things I know is that just about everyone who chances upon an image of their younger self will experience the same grief I felt looking at myself in that photo. We don't grieve for what we've lost but for what we never knew. We grieve because none of us can reconcile the beauty we can see in our past with the ugliness we were told to remember.

I decided that I did not want to waste any more of my precious energy trying to police what others have to say about my body or even try and change what it is they believe my body says about my worth as a human. I have not changed my mind since then. I know that so long as my body is understood as female, then my body will always be a target for the hostility and cruel judgment of others. I have every confidence that I will continue to hear all the same horrific things about how I look, and I am sure I will continue to find it painful, but for me this is the last time I will speak about it. I have never identified with how people see me. I have a great big universe of stuff inside of me. None of it is gendered. None of it. I love who I am. It's only on the other side of my skin where the pain begins. But I will not negotiate anymore. I am proud to be Queer.

~~Just for a brief~~
Just for one breathe: I was the pinnacle of NORMAL.

Once the load of my ideas was relieved of the significant burden of explaining my brain and body, I discovered that it was possible to layer my three shapes on top of each other. And that pretty much cracked the code. It felt very good, I won't lie. It was as if I had popped a thought pimple the size of my whole brain, and in almost an instant, the pressure of my thinking fell away and the game was back on.

One shape became the "material," the surface of the show, things like topics, delivery and attitude. My plan was to perform as a mirror of "masculine" action, by mimicking a specific type of male comedian, the kind who likes to throw around all their opinions with arrogance and anger. Not in an attempt at caricature, mind you, but simply to "appear" as someone "acceptable." I was already a master of the art of masking, so I had no problem stepping up to the funny-man plate.

The second layer would be purpose-built to hold all the meaning I wanted to convey. In other words, the function. This function, however, was not just a subtext; it was at war with the form. My intent was for the means and method to be in direct opposition to one another. I was really beginning to lean into my limited understanding of Taoism at this stage (apologies to proper Taoists), and so, I began to think of the form and function as representing the yin and yang, or ebb and flow, or "masculine" and "feminine." Which is how I ended up shouting about the merits of whispering.

The third shape was to live in the space that would necessarily open up between these two opposing ideas, and my guess was that this third shape would represent me, but I called it *Nanette*.

This layering idea very quickly evolved to become a process better described as weaving. This allowed me to sometimes bring the implicit to the surface, such as when I spoke about the colour blue being the epitome of feminine strength. Weaving was the perfect process to draw *Nanette* out of my mind, given that the show was in part a tribute to all the women in my life who've helped hold me together. My mum, Nan, Grandma and Sister along with my fierce friends Cheryl, Suz, Caz and Annie and all their knitting, quilting, stitching, solving, caring and healing. Woven throughout *Nanette* is my best effort at my own atypical appreciation for all the emotional labour so many people have invested in me, but that which I am often too slow to process until much, much later.

With my freshly baked layer cake weaving its way into existence, I finally had to accept that the form of comedy, as I understood it, was never going to be sophisticated enough to carry the complexity of what I was attempting to do. If I wanted to tell the truth, and create a cohesive narrative for myself, one that was not dysphoric, if I wanted to share the literal, visceral pain of my trauma, I knew I had to invent something new.

And, so, I began to write a comedy show that was not funny. A comedy show in which I refused to seek the laugh, refused to pull my punches and turn them into tickles as a comedian is supposed to. I began to write a show that would drive my punches deeper into the metaphorical guts of my audience. I was going to repurpose comedy into something that could allow me to express the heat of my anger and the pain of my trauma, but without transferring it. It was a bold idea, but bold ideas will often happen when desperation pushes a creative brain to find a solution.

LET THE TRIALS BEGIN

I stared down at my handwritten note in panic, desperately searching my chaotic brain for why it was I was so angry about reputations. I knew I had a reason somewhere in the thicket of my thinking, but apparently I'd lost my grasp on it. Unsure of what to say, I looked up and saw that the first two rows of my audience were sitting bolt-upright, silent and stricken; behind them in the darkness there were another sixty people and although I couldn't see them, I'm fairly certain I'd traumatised them, too. When I'd woken up that morning, I knew I didn't have a hope of getting my show together in time. I had barely slept. My brain, determined to keep the fingers of my thinking running at full speed, had refused to let me shut it down. Even so, I still couldn't solve it. I understood everything with unnerving clarity, on some level, but I couldn't seem to even begin to turn it into something I could externalise.

I had spent the week leading up to this moment furiously distilling all of my expanded thoughts back into smaller bite-sized ideas. This had always been my favourite part of the offstage process— culling extraneous language, finding the most economical way to express ideas, searching for the perfect words and sequences to best convey meaning and shaping them into rhythms and sounds that my brain can reliably release for my mouth to speak.

I don't want to brag but I did some very excellent polishing in that week. But I will brag, because I think it is incredible that when I took to the stage at the end of January 2017 to perform my first ever iteration of *Nanette,* I held in my hands note cards filled with some of the exact same phrases that I would go on to deliver the very last time *Nanette* lived on stage eighteen months later, in Montreal.

I should hasten to add that not everything was in its finished form, I had a great stack of cards filled with twisted threads that looked nothing like what they needed to be, and many more that would never make it beyond that first *Nanette.* I knew I had too much material for a one-hour show, but I knew, beyond any doubt, that everything I needed was in that great stack somewhere.

My friend Annie had offered to give me a lift to the venue. I don't remember accepting her offer, but thankfully she understood that I wasn't living in the actual world, so she turned up anyway. Annie and I had known each other for years, but our friendship really cemented itself during the time we worked together on *Please Like Me.* She'd been the first assistant director, and we discovered our mutual love for staring at dogs. I think Annie must have recognised what was happening when I'd first begun to plummet into the depths of *Nanette*, and she had positioned herself as my spiritual lifeguard and I, apparently, positioned myself as another dog she could stare at with love.⊗ Which is another way of saying: I don't think I could have done it without her.

When we got to the venue, Annie herded me and my bundle of fifty or so cue cards to the nearest table and made me a cup of tea as I continued with my frenzy of shuffling. I cut it very fine, with just two minutes to spare, but I finally cracked the code. It wasn't a very close match to the best beast I had in my mind, but I knew it was significantly closer than any of the other attempts I'd made that day. As I stacked all my cards into their new order, I felt the blinding pressure of my thinking release, as if I were literally transferring the responsibility of holding weeks and weeks of work from my head over to the cards in my hands. And then I dropped them all.

I told the audience exactly what had happened, and they laughed. Of course they did. They had no idea how much work I had put into that stack. They didn't know that when I dropped my cards, I had dropped everything. They didn't know how scrambled and frazzled my brain was, they didn't know that all my thoughts had scattered out of my grasp with those cards. All they knew is that they'd scored free tickets to watch Hannah Gadsby try out some new jokes. I plucked one of my cards out of the great pile Annie and I had dumped into a basket and scanned the angry scribble:

Fuck you Mr. Art History. I was raped in my sleep and it was not what I would call "ideal."

It was not the kind of icebreaker I was looking for, so I tossed it back into the basket.

⊗ Midway through the *Nanette* process, Annie accompanied me to adopt another dog, an adorable and anxiety-ridden little fluff, Jasper. Jasper and Annie became firm friends, to the point that he usually lives with her these days. Delightfully affirming the slippery-slope argument, we are the strangest little family now.

"Too soon!" I quipped, and the audience laughed. Of course they did. They still thought this was a comedy show. Shit.

It was not the first time I'd stood in front of an audience like this—without a show, a desperate work in progress. But this was a different kind of uncooked because *Nanette* was a very different kind of monster. Even in this, her most raw state, *Nanette* did not feel like a comedy show . . . she felt more like someone, me, had kicked off at a family reunion and no one had seen it coming. As I plunged my hand back into the basket to fish for a better starter card, I noticed I was shaking, and then I noticed that I was holding my breath, and then, when I tried to exhale I found my lungs were already empty. That is when I realised that I was about to experience the most terrifying thing that could happen to me while performing.

It is not unusual for me to have a shutdown on stage; the lights are shockingly bright up there and audiences can make a lot of noise; and so, if I've been having a rough day, or even just an intense one, my brain sometimes disconnects my sensory input from my memory bank to save on processing power. I once received a standing ovation at the Royal Albert Hall in London and as I walked off stage I thought, *Gee, they were a bit quiet.* To be clear, that is close to five thousand people on their feet clapping on top of whatever mouth sounds they were making, and I don't remember hearing a thing. This is definitely a function of my autism; if my brain were more typical then the extreme public speaking aspect of comedy would trigger my fight or flight well before sound and light were even relevant. But my brain is not typical, and so the idea of thousands of people witnessing me fail in real time has never really bothered me.

Shutdowns, however, only ever happen at good gigs, because bad gigs are never loud enough, and nor are trial shows. But this was not a shutdown, this was a meltdown. I'd never had a meltdown on stage before, and I didn't want to start now, because when I have a meltdown, my brain cuts the power to my ability to regulate, which means some kind of emotional outburst would most likely follow; the other thing that gets short-circuited in a meltdown is my ability to speak. Like I said, just about the worst thing that could happen.

I can't remember how I figured it out, but as soon as I knew that it wasn't a meltdown after all, I found I could breathe again. Gathering my wits, I looked up and flashed a smile at the crowd. They laughed and I laughed back. I wouldn't say that we shared a laugh, however, because they were laughing at the awkwardness of the moment whereas I was laughing at something far, far darker: I had just triggered myself on stage with my own rape joke that was not a joke. It must have been the absurdity of it that pulled me back from the brink, but not wanting to lose my brittle hold on myself, I yanked out another card and I just read it out: "Picasso is not my hero."

The audience didn't quite know how to respond and so they sat patiently, waiting to see what I did with it. I did nothing and it felt good. The card had a printed Picasso quote stapled to the back of it, so, I flipped it over and I read it out:

> "Every time I change wives I should burn the last one. That way I'd be rid of them. They wouldn't be around to complicate my existence. Maybe, that would bring back my youth, too. You kill the woman and you wipe out the past she represents."
> — Pablo Picasso

Silence. But I didn't care, I just tossed it to the ground and put my hand back into the basket. The audience found that funny, and so I waited for them to finish laughing before I read them the next card. I'm glad I did. It was the last laugh they had that night.

I eventually got myself on some kind of rough track and then, when my mouth finally found a way on board my train of thoughts, I began picking up speed and almost spitting my ideas out. Each card got its own little rant before I tossed it aside and grabbed a new one. I did not pause at all, and my intensity and delivery built and built, but I still didn't get anywhere. It was a train wreck of a show, a staccato of seemingly unrelated ideas butting against each other as I feebly tried to keep my own distress in check. It was clear my audience was in shock. Their silence had been unbroken for almost an hour, but it wasn't the unsettled silence you get when jokes fail, it was thick with tension. I felt terrible about what I had just done. I knew it was my job to put them at ease, I knew I should make a joke, to lighten the mood, but instead I just glanced back down at the last card in the basket:

When I got home after that first trial, the only thing I remembered was being triggered. I am ashamed to admit that this was when I first truly understood that what I was attempting to do was quite dangerous, not just for my audience but also for me. I already knew *Nanette* had to serve a purpose above and beyond my own story, that I had a responsibility to create some kind of narrative catharsis for anybody who might be triggered by my material, but at the same time I did not want to offer that same catharsis to anybody whose discomfort was just inconvenience. But after that first trial, I understood that before I could even attempt to walk that line, I had to make it safe for me.

Usually, when I find myself with a big new problem like that to solve, I need a lot of time to process and workshop. But for this one, I had barely articulated my question to myself before the answer made itself known, and it came in the form of a sound: my teacup hitting its saucer. Somewhere in the basket of cards I had that sound written down.

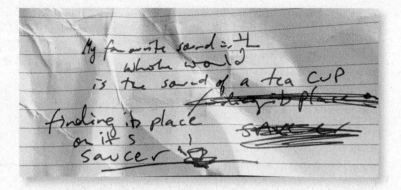

My favourite sound in the
whole world
is the sound of a tea cup
finding its place
on its
saucer

I had long known that sounds had the potential to trigger physical pain in my body, but I had only just begun to actively search for sounds that triggered pleasant responses. The list of good-feeling sounds, however, is nowhere near as long as that of the painful ones; but of them, there are a handful that feel exquisite; and of those, the most important to me is the sound of a teacup hitting its saucer. The sound does not simply feel beautiful, but it comes attached with memories of being loved and feeling safe.

I had been funnelling every bit of my thinking into the creative process, so it is quite possible that I wasn't working with my best decision-making mind at the time. But I did what I did. And this is what I did, in the order I did it: First, I went through all of my cards and picked out ten that I felt really good about. Then I cleared the next four days of absolutely everything. Stocked my kitchen up with nourishing food, locked the front door and turned my phone off, and spent the next few days repeating each of those ten phrases over and over and over again under the influence of my best guess at micro-doses of MDMA.

I feel obliged to tell you not to try this at home. But that feels cheap after I just told you that I did exactly that. But I would also tell you to never write a show out of your own trauma and then perform it two hundred times all over the world. That is more likely to shorten your life than experimenting with a bit of molly.

What I was attempting to do was shortcut some neuroplasticity for myself, so I could create and disguise some very specific stimming into the text. Stimming—self-stimulation or self-soothing—is an all too often denied expression for autistic people, and we know it. I have always tried to disguise or delay stimming, preferring to wait until I am alone to make myself feel better by tapping my temple and rocking; this is part of the masking process, and it only ever compounds my distress.

But I knew that if I let my tics out into the open during a performance of *Nanette,* I would lose my authority on stage. At the same time, I knew that if I tried to repress or delay my self-protective behaviour, then I would get to a point where I would be unable to regulate my emotions, which would give my trauma free rein to overwhelm me. My theory was that if I could force the coupling of my chosen phrases with the very good feelings unleashed by the MDMA, then I could create my own *Nanette*-specific stimming sequence.

Not all of my safety phrases stayed with *Nanette* for the term of her natural life. But many of them did. The teacup was predictably effective as one of my self-soothing touchstones, but the two that ended up feeling like actual lifesavers had additional performative qualities that must have contributed to their getting all the way into my body memory. I had always enjoyed impersonating Mum on stage, because it had always felt like a holiday away from me; I guess that's why they call it acting. But after I spent the weekend repeating her apology over and over and over again under the influence of good feelings, I discovered a new layer of protection. I felt the pain she was trying to communicate disappear inside of me. Every time I performed *Nanette* thereafter, I felt something of that profound catharsis each time I used her voice, and my distress would reset to nothing, just like that. I am no expert, but I do reckon an expert should really study this.

The other lifesaver was the phrase "I am in my prime." When I was repeating it over that weekend, I was giving it a subdued but resolute firmness. At the time, I did not believe it was true to me personally, I was thinking more about older women in general, but I gave myself a little tap on the chest in any case. During the next few months, as I worked *Nanette* into shape, that safety phrase became a real chest-pounder. Probably because I found that I was in my prime after all.

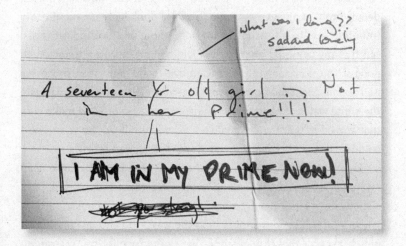

I only came up with the idea when a friend who was leaving for the U.K. left me a small measure of MDMA as a parting gift. I was delighted, as I like feeling good but hate going out of my way to break the law. I had been educating myself on all things trauma for a few years by then, and had become quite intrigued by the research being done into the microdosing of various mind-altering substances. To be clear, I am under no illusions that I am an expert. I know exactly what I was: I was desperate. I had been swamped with the effects of trauma for as long as I could remember, and it was clear that the cutting edge of medical science was not going to cut through my trauma in my lifetime, because the cutting edge never seems terribly concerned with the biological specifics of autistic women, or any women for that matter. What did I have to lose?

I had intended to try and see if microdosing could help me develop a buffer between me and the uncontrollable panic that thinking directly about my trauma inevitably invited. But after I was triggered in the first minute of my first show, I thought better of it and decided to pursue my experimental lily-pad sequence of positive stimming instead.

I felt a responsibility to my audience, you see. I knew that the material I was covering in *Nanette* had the potential to be very triggering for many people, and, as I was not giving them fair warning, this felt deeply problematic to me, and to this day I don't feel easy about it. My intention was to ultimately create something of a healing catharsis, but it is my personal philosophy that good intentions are not much good if you don't do your best to imbed "good" into your processes and actions. So, I did not attempt to build myself a life raft to navigate the white water of my trauma rapids, because I wanted to make sure that my body was the most alive and vulnerable in the room, so I could go down safely with my own ship like a good captain.

Upon reflection, it is quite outrageous that I did all these deep layers of performance preparation at a time when I didn't even have a show. But I knew exactly what I was doing even if I couldn't articulate it. And I did end up doing it, by the way. I did end up creating an epic beast of a show and a somewhat safer space for trauma-ridden audience members, who are all too often disregarded in the context of comedy. I also managed to take the worst of the sting out of my own trauma through performing *Nanette* over and over again. Maybe it's just a coincidence. Maybe the required time had just passed and my wounds were always going to heal slowly over the same two-year period that *Nanette* happened. Impossible to say.

Just in case you might think that it all came together quite easily after that, let me tell you how awful the first few months were. Really awful. I don't know how else to describe it. It was just awful. I got heckled, I got abused, I had people demanding refunds, I threw up, and I cried myself to sleep. And that was just opening night. And it didn't get any easier for quite some time. I headed into my tour knowing I was going to have a rough time of it in the beginning. *Nanette* had thrown me into a bit of a catch-22 because she was never going to be safe to perform until she was finished, but there was only one place that I would be able to finish my weaving proper, and that was on stage.

NANETTE

I don't think I could think of a less appropriate city to debut *Nanette* than Perth, Western Australia. No offence to my Perth friends, but you really do bring little-dick energy to just about everything you do. That being said, Perth was the most defining season of *Nanette*'s early life.

The Heath Ledger Theatre made it feel like a posher "occasion" than the comedy usual, and I think that helped the crowd settle into a slightly more respectful demeanour, but at the same time, looking out and seeing people sink into the soft velvety seating, I knew *Nanette* was going to struggle to live up to the "I PAID FOR THIS FUCKING TICKET" standard.

The "script" was approaching an acceptable structure by then, the only thing missing was the beginning and the end, which is not as bad as it sounds, although it isn't great. The real issue, however, was me. Not only was I a hot mess, I also didn't know my material well enough to have control over my delivery. Under normal circumstances, this was something I could bluff my way through during the first run of a new show. But *Nanette* was not normal circumstances. What I was most afraid of happening was that all of the stress inherent in remembering a brand-new show on opening night would weaken my ability to keep my distress responses in check. In other words, I could self-trigger my trauma and have a meltdown on stage. And that is precisely what happened.

I think I kept it together for about ten minutes before I lost all access to self-regulation. After that, I spent the rest of the time shouting all my raw unfiltered distress at that poor audience. The only thing that kept me from totally losing my grip was my decision to keep the microphone in its stand. Had I not physically rooted myself firmly onto that stage and tethered myself, I might very well have blown too far off course before *Nanette* had the chance to gather into the fierce storm she eventually became.

Two things happened during that fateful show in Perth that made *Nanette, Nanette*. The first was the silence. Despite my over-heated delivery and the chaotic structure of that show, I still managed to strike the audience twice in their guts, and while it was exactly what I had wanted, I had no idea what that would translate to inside of me. The first silence happened shortly after I had shared my laundry list of traumas. At first I didn't notice it because I was in such a heightened state, but when I couldn't think of what I was supposed to say next I paused, and that's when I felt it, the entire crowd of five hundred or so people gripped rigid with tension, and I went blank inside my body. It was the weirdest feeling and I don't know how else to describe it other than time stood still.

The second silence happened about five minutes later, when, halfway through my rant about Picasso, a man in the second row decided that what I needed was a heckle from him. I stopped mid-sentence and looked down at him and I could tell he had absolutely no idea of the fury I was about to unleash on him. He was sitting slouched in his seat, his arms folded sulkily over his chest, and his legs were spread so wide I could see yesterday's skid mark. Usually when a hostile heckle interrupts a show the audience becomes restless until your response gives them direction for how they should respond. But not this time. The tension returned, and with it so did my calm. I had heard what he had said, but I got him to repeat it. Which he did with exaggerated impatience, "I said: What. Year. Are. You. Talking. About?"

He was being cocky. I knew he was trying to trip me up, but what he had chosen not to assume was that I knew what I was talking about and had enough material at my fingertips to publicly humiliate him for at least ten relentless minutes.

"What year am I talking about? Why do you ask?"

The silence was getting thicker and thicker, and I tried to use it to gather my calm, but I was losing my grip, fast.

"Just curious?" he said, with such a lathering of smugness that I nearly lost it there and then, but I managed to keep myself almost steady.

"Curious? No shit," I spat back coolly. "Of course, you are curious. That's what a question means, you dumb cunt. Now *why* did you ask *that* question?"

"Nah, well, it's just that shit you are talking about happened a long time ago. Times have changed. It's irrelevant. Just get on with the jokes already."

And with that the floodgates of my rage opened with a snap.

"Times have changed, have they? Well, I beg to differ and I would say at least one in three women in this room have firsthand experience that will back me up. Now let me tell you why you really asked your stupid little question, you stupid little man. You weren't curious. You just think you have a right to speak. You don't. Not in my house. I have the loud stick, little man, and now I am going to tear you a new arsehole. But before I do, let me answer your stupid little question. It was 1932. Now just shut the fuck up, put your legs together and listen to me." I then shouted at him for another five minutes or so. I don't think I made a lot of sense after that, but it didn't matter, the point was that I was wiping the floor with him and the crowd did not make a single sound the entire time. *Fuck it,* I thought, *I knew this show was going to alienate a lot of people.* This was the bed I had made and I was ready to lie in it.

It was only once I turned away from my heckler and repositioned my gaze back to the broader audience that the room erupted. I was more than a little thrown. I didn't know what to say. This had not been part of the plan. I still hadn't gathered my thoughts by the time the applause had died down, and it was all I could do to to pick up where I had left off.

"I quit!!" I shouted. It had been written as a sly little joke, but I couldn't deliver it that way that night. I sounded as if I meant it, and my audience obviously did not know what to do with that, and so they kept their silence, waiting, and I reiterated, "I quit. It's not a joke. I'm quitting comedy. I have to. I can't do this anymore."

I didn't know what I was trying to say when I spat that out but as soon as I did, I knew exactly what I was doing: I was committing to a one-way journey. I was going to tell the truth as I knew it. I was prepared to lose my audience, my livelihood and my own reputation in order to do so. My stunned audience remained so still and quiet, I had them in the palm of my hand, and that's when I first really understood that despite having little power in the world, I did have incredible power over a room when I was on stage. The time had come to wield it. As this realisation dawned on me, it brought with it an urgent and profoundly unfamiliar feeling. To this day I don't have a satisfactory name for what I felt in that moment, but it stayed with me as I left the stage. In fact, it stayed with me for the best part of two years.

I didn't have time to reflect on that idea for very long, because I had a much more pressing problem: I had to make the show bulletproof. And fast. I couldn't leave room for heckling; it would have been too dangerous for me, which, in turn, would make it unsafe for my audience. So, over the course of the next week, I worked feverishly to stack the front half of the show with as many jokes as I could. I scaled back the intensity of my delivery, as best I could, and disguised my antagonism by swaddling it in a bit of gentle cheek.

THAT JOKE IS NOT MY JOKE. I DIDN'T WRITE IT. IT'S A CLASSIC. OLDIE BUT A GOLDIE. THAT JOKE HAS BEEN AROUND SINCE BEFORE WOMEN WERE FUNNY. BUT BACK THEN, BACK THEN IN THE GOOD OLD DAYS, "LESBIAN" HAD A DIFFERENT MEANING TO WHAT IT DOES TODAY—BACK THEN A LESBIAN WAS JUST ANY WOMAN NOT LAUGHING AT A MAN. (NANETTE: PERTH EDIT)

Some of the criticism that has been levelled at *Nanette* has been directed at this first half, describing it as weak, or not as strong, comparative to the second half of the show. This is neither here nor there for me. It was designed to be comfortable, that was its purpose. If I had loaded the front half with "belly laughs," then I don't think the "gut punch" that came after it would have been nearly as impactful. It would be like going from freezing cold water to boiling hot. Both are extremes and so, on a certain level, the body will not register the second sensation as a shock distinct from the first. But if you were relaxing in a nice warm bath and I came over and tipped a bucket of volcanic lava all over you, that would be a crime. See what I did there? I led you to believe that I was going to make a serious point but instead I did a little dad joke. Shocking.

By stacking the front of my show with gentle cerebral comedy, I was doing many different things at once. Firstly, I was giving my audience a false sense of security. Secondly, I was creating a buffer for myself, to make sure I could deliver my difficult material responsibly. And finally, I was employing my absolute favourite autistic style of communication: wordplay and dad jokes. *Nanette* is absolutely brimming with duelling ideas like this one. I won't share all of them with you, I'll keep the best secrets to myself, because I am not done quitting comedy just yet. But I would like to make it clear to anybody still with me on this ride that *Nanette* was a real high-wire balancing act. The feelings I launched at my audience might have been very blunt, but the structure is a precise, delicate, subtle and complex piece of work.

I suspect many of the people who hate the show—and there are enough of them to justify this small measure of response—are most likely only responding to the feelings I gave them, and not engaging with my work with much in the way of critical thinking. And that's OK, I pulled the triggers on their reactivity myself. I wanted to distract that very large segment of the world which is prone to devolving into reactive anger when it comes to women speaking unapologetically in public. I wanted to make sure their cognitive skills had been shut down before I allowed myself to be truly vulnerable on stage. I knew that by rubbishing straight white cis men I would be culling the worst of those who identified as such. I knew by rubbishing "comedy" I would be cutting loose the most toxic of my peers. I wanted to make them experience intensely negative feelings but not allow them any capacity to connect meaningfully with me at my most vulnerable.

For everybody else, I tried to provide as many different safety threads as I could think of for them to grab onto. And the biggest safety rail of all was making it absolutely clear that I was not in the business of prioritising the comfort of powerful people. And now I feel obliged to thank that little man in Perth who wrongly believed that his voice was welcome in my house, because without him, I may not have found this important key to my own safety in time.

Perth set *Nanette* on the right course, but there was a lot of wrangling-into-shape to come. All the guardrails I had put in place for myself were an enormous help to me over those gruelling first few months, but they weren't enough. The only reason I was able to hang in there was because of the people around me who saw what I was doing and closed ranks, and closed ranks hard. Every time I walked off stage I was always met by someone from my production team, either Kath, Rowan, Erin, Helen or Kev. I am also indebted to the other comedians who were being produced by the team that year; I probably took up way more than my fair share of their time. Soz about that.

Kevin had recognised the potential impact of *Nanette* well before I ever did. After that first, disastrous trial show, he'd bounded over as

I was gathering all my scattered cards from off of the floor and told me in no uncertain terms that this was going to be a hit, before he added with the kind of glee only a manager can muster: "Get ready to sell out your Wednesdays!"

I had built my audiences steadily throughout the years, and I would always technically sell out my shows, but the Wednesdays would always drag their selling feet. I didn't really believe Kevin when he told me this show was going to be popular, but once *Nanette* landed in Melbourne, I finally understood just how right he was. Once the word-of-mouth kicked in during the first week, the Wednesdays didn't just sell out, my whole season did. And then came the extra shows in massive venues. And that's when I got the shock of my life.

The show at the Forum was the first time *Nanette* got a run in a really big venue. Unlike all the other rooms up until then, the Forum is a grand venue, the kind of cavernous space that can turn a show into an event and, apparently, turn a *Nanette* into a monster. I think part of it had to do with the fact that I had finally found a true and consistent balance between all the many moving parts of the show. I was familiar with everything I had to say and, more importantly, I was better practiced in how to deliver it all. It was the most precise version of the show I had ever delivered and after it was over, I vowed never to let myself get that comfortable again.

When I took control over that room, I found I could play the tension in the audience like a conductor of an orchestra, and I felt like I had an insight into what Hitler must have felt giving one of his famous "orations." I don't say that glibly. I honestly felt as if I could have convinced that crowd to undertake any manner of mob job. The tension was pricked through with an expectation, an anticipation of leadership. I understood that I was not just in control of a moment, but in control of people, real people, and I did not care for that feeling at all. That kind of power feels too big to comprehend, too dangerous for anybody to wield, but especially someone who was running the gauntlet of their own triggers and traumas. I had wanted to create a show that served as my tool, not my weapon.

WHY WAS IT OK TO PICK ME OFF THE PACK AND DO THAT TO
ME? IT WOULD HAVE BEEN MORE HUMANE TO TAKE ME OUT
TO THE BACK PADDOCK AND PUT A BULLET IN MY HEAD IF IT
WAS SUCH A CRIME TO BE DIFFERENT. DO YOU KNOW WHY
I NEVER REPORTED ANY OF THESE MEN WHO ABUSED, RAPED,
AND BEAT ME UP? BECAUSE I AM NOT AN IDIOT. I KNEW I WAS
WORTH NOTHING COMPARED TO A MAN. I KNEW THE STORY
OFF BY HEART: I DO NOT MATTER. (NANETTE: MELBOURNE
EDIT)

I came up with a number of possible solutions, but I settled on the rather crass but effective strategy that I described in my head as "flipping the board." I took all of the material that I had whittled the last ten minutes of the show down from, which was roughly about twenty-five minutes' worth, and I flooded it back into the tail of the show, and then I jumbled it around in my head, loosened the connections and tossed the order like a salad. My theory was that by keeping the end of my show in flux, making it a veritable panic grab, then I would force myself to stay in the room, as a way of reverse engineering my own vulnerability, as genuinely as possible. And that is how *Nanette* lived every single performance thereafter, save for the ones that were filmed for posterity and Netflix. Those I locked in tighter than a fish's asshole. But more on that later.

Mum and Dad saw the show in Hobart. It was not the same show anybody else saw. Knowing they were going to be there, I edited out the more traumatic sentiments of the show and I completely curbed the bus-stop story of my assault. I changed the show because I didn't think it was fair on my parents to witness my pain while sitting in a room full of strangers. But even so, the heat of my anger was still very much present and the air ran thick with tension several times during the show. As had become the norm by then, nobody was game to break the silence—except my mum. Naturally.

"Hah!"

There was no mistaking her laugh, so I told the crowd that it had been my mum. The crowd, mildly scandalised, stayed silent, and this time so did my mum. But I knew my mum had not laughed at my expense, it was not the kind of laugh that indicated amusement, mockery, resistance or derision. It was a sound that seemed to want to let me know that she was there, that she knew what I was doing, and that she was afraid for me.

Usually, after performing *Nanette*, I would have to go directly to a quiet, dark and safe place and decompress. But as there was no trauma in the Hobart show, I was able to head out to find my parents. Dad had already left but I found Mum in high spirits and holding court over a table full of family and friends.

"It's the best show you've ever done!" she declared as I sat down. I didn't know what I had been expecting her to say but that wasn't it.

"Really?"

"Yes," she said. "Because you didn't put yourself down!"

"Or you," I countered.

"Same thing." She shrugged as she took a swig of wine and turned back to the rest of the table, all of whom seemed a bit subdued. After a while a woman approached the table, having apparently overheard my mum making no secret about her relationship to me.

"Are you really Hannah's mum?" she asked excitedly, apparently totally unaware that I was sitting right beside her.

"Well"—Mum looked up at her, trying to find the measure of the woman—"I can't say for sure, but she is what grew out of the baby they handed me at the hospital." The woman forced a small laugh, then just stood for an agonising moment. "Well, you must be very proud of Hannah," she finally declared, before turning and scurrying away.

"Who is this Hannah?" Mum asked, loud enough for the retreating woman to hear. Mum had been right all along. She is funnier than me.

IF HOLDING MY HEAD HIGH MEANS THAT MY COMEDY CAREER IS OVER, THEN SO BE IT. I CAN LIVE WITH THAT. (NANETTE: HOBART EDIT).

When I saw Dad the next day, he didn't have much to say about the show. He mumbled a vague compliment that was no different to any other he had given anybody about anything.

"He didn't like it because he's a man!" Mum explained.

Dad didn't argue but he didn't have to, I knew that had nothing to do with it. He was undergoing treatment for melanoma, and he was sick, tired and scared. I was just happy he was able to see the show at all.

As the show toured, all of my immediate family saw *Nanette* and as such, I forced them to process the parts of my life and trauma that they'd not known before. We've had some conversations but really, I said everything on stage, and my family have all made it clear, in their own way, that they are on Team Me, so much so that despite the lack of chat between us—I now feel closer to my family than I ever have in my adult life.

My favourite response was probably Justin's because it was so Justin, and so supremely awkward, and so funny.

"Yeah, nah, yeah. I mean, nah, but yeah. Look, I don't have a problem with anything you said up there, eh." And then he gave me one of his big sweet bus driver hugs.

Justin had seen *Nanette* in her second iteration at the Adelaide Fringe, which meant that the greenroom this conversation took place in was a length of rubber mat that ran between a shipping container and a portaloo. The Garden of Unearthly Delights, which turns Adelaide's fairly nondescript Rundle Park into a heavily tented carnival dreamscape for the duration of the festival, had always been the primo venue for Fringe performers. One of the defining features of putting on a show at any festival is the inevitable chaos that happens in the turning of shows around in impossibly narrow time frames. I think this is another incredible benefit that comes with being a festival comic, because unlike the usually invisible and underappreciated tech component of most comedy clubs, a festival venue forces performers to witness the artistry of the crew. It is truly humbling.

The year that *Nanette* was in Adelaide might have been one of the most interesting changeovers I've ever witnessed, because in less than ten minutes my stunned and emotionally wrought audience were pushed through the exit and replaced by the very pumped-up and white-wine-drunk audience of *Puppetry of the Penis,* which is a show that is exactly literally what it sounds like. The two performers making puppetry of their respective peni, Rich Binning and Barry Brisco, had been nothing short of delightful to me throughout the run, so respectful and so kind, but they still needed to warm up, and so as Justin tried to put his feelings into words, all I could see out of the corner of my eye was two strapping young men, dressed in nothing but a cape and boots, standing next to a portaloo and going through some rather spectacular motions. Isn't it funny how humour can help ease tension? Who knew?

YOU KNOW WHY I MAKE FUN OF STRAIGHT WHITE MEN? BECAUSE THEY ARE SUCH GOOD SPORTS, THEY GET IT! GOOD JOKE ABOUT ME. REFRESHING PERSPECTIVE! (NANETTE: *ADELAIDE EDIT*)

I had deliberately written a great deal of flexibility into *Nanette*'s central premise, as I'd been thinking of how to adapt the show to the different audiences I'd be sharing her with, from my hometown crowd in Melbourne, to the always potentially hostile cynics in London, to the misogynist broth that tends to flavour an audience in more regional stops. But interestingly, I had not anticipated that performing *Nanette* would destabilise the landscape inside me quite so erratically. Thankfully, the flexibility I designed for my audience also accommodated me and I was able to reconfigure *Nanette* so that she could be whatever I felt she needed to be. In that way, *Nanette* became many different things to me throughout the many different phases of her life. Sometimes she was an utter pain in my arse and I wanted to screech the whole thing to an immediate stop. At other times she was giving me a powerful boost of spiritual steroids. There were times when she made me mostly sad and only a little mad, while other times I was a vibrating skin sack full of unadulterated rage. Then there were the occasions I was just good old-fashioned dead inside. One thing was for sure, neither *Nanette* nor I was ever static. We were a living, breathing double act, both responding to the ebb and flow that I suppose must come with navigating an immensely high-stress circumstance over a prolonged period of time.

WE NEED TO STOP ROMANTICISING MENTAL ILLNESS AS A PATH-WAY TO ARTISTIC GREATNESS. MENTAL ILLNESS IS NOT A ROMANCE—A TICKET TO GENIUS—IT IS EXCRUCIATINGLY ISOLATING. IT IS A TICKET TO FUCKING NOWHERE. (NANETTE: BRISBANE EDIT)

For all the brutally direct specificity that I employed to get many of my points across, I also deployed quite a lot of purposefully non-sensical phrasing. I did this to make sure I provided enough space for a broad audience to potentially connect to my considerably idio-syncratic life.

"To be rendered powerless does not destroy your humanity. Your resilience is your humanity."

This does not make any sense whatsoever. Surely resilience is more a tool for survival than an accurate indicator of this so-called humanity. But I figured it might be helpful to reframe resilience as an active power-pose instead of a passive state of just getting by, because I knew better than most that "coping" takes a fuck-tonne more effort and energy than "thriving" ever will. But even as I wanted to champion it, I must admit that I don't really know what resilience is, exactly. I am sure it is a complicated mix of a lot of things. But again.

Not the point. The point was to almost say something profound, and in the space between the words said and the meaning I didn't make, other people might be able to turn it into something that they were searching for. It is a little trick I learnt from Tony Robbins, except I left out his messiah complex and victim-blaming rhetoric and replaced it with the faith that people are capable of finding their own meanings. There are quite a few of these non-wisdoms scattered throughout *Nanette;* most of them obviously did their job, as I see that many a meme has been created in their honour. *Nanette* is basically *Eat Pray Love* for autistic queer folk.

To be clear, people are not wrong to find meaning in a meaningless phrase. When it comes to trauma, no two experiences are the same, so who am I to say it is impossible to find any meaning in places I can't? If you are someone who found meaning in those two sentences, then I want you to know that you did the real work. And just between you, me and the fencepost, there were times when I was performing *Nanette* when I absolutely believed that I had a grasp on the meaning of my own pseudo-wisdoms, because I was in a distressed state and was desperately searching for some kind of solace to grip onto. Logic be damned when you are in fight-or-flight. Am I right? Probably. But it depends on how you feel, I suppose.

Every run I did with *Nanette* forced me to adjust and adapt things to suit the conditions, but none of them challenged me as much or as painfully as my season at the Edinburgh Fringe. I had decided to take *Nanette* to Edinburgh because I knew she was exactly the kind of show that would blow up that festival. She was already the show that I had hoped all my others could be, and I figured I had nothing to lose—the fact that I was even considering doing the Edinburgh Fringe again meant my sanity was already well and truly lost.

I had stopped taking shows to Edinburgh after *The Exhibitionist* in 2015 because I couldn't justify it anymore. What I had once placed at the pinnacle of my year had become a gigantic waste of my time and resources. In the beginning it seemed to hold the key to breaking through into the U.K. scene, which in turn felt like a necessary step in terms of career growth, given Australia's comparatively tiny population. The great Australian creative pilgrimage to the mother-land has a long and illustrious history. I won't list the many alumni of reverse colonisation here, as many of them have become more than a tad transphobic, openly misogynistic and intellectually calcified in recent years. But suffice it to say, I had taken a well-worn path for Australian creatives and all I found was a well-worn path, and eventually I just got tired.

NOW, SMARTER MEN THAN I HAVE GONE TO GREAT LENGTHS TO PROVE THAT ALTHOUGH THEY MET WHEN SHE WAS UNDERAGE— THEY DID NOT SLEEP TOGETHER UNTIL HER EIGHTEENTH BIRTHDAY. GET FUCKED. YOU DON'T GET TO SELL PABLO PICASSO AS A PASSIONATE, VIRILE, TORMENTED, AND PATIENT MAN. NO! HE FUCKED AN UNDERAGE GIRL. (NANETTE: EDINBURGH EDIT)

Nanette was not built to thrive in a small room in the middle of the afternoon. That much had been made abundantly clear to me by that first clusterfuck of a trial show. It might seem strange for me then to choose a tiny sixty-seat lecture theatre as a venue for what was already going to be a pretty miserable month, but anybody who has failed at the Fringe as many times as I had would know that when it comes to that festival there are no good choices, only fifty shades of shitty ones. So, I weighed my big room ego against my most favourite of safety nets—thoroughly underestimating myself— and I just couldn't get past the logic of setting myself up for small-scale failure.

Of course, that is not what happened. *Nanette* totally scorched the Edinburgh Fringe. Every show sold out within the first week. I put on extra shows in some much larger venues and they sold out too. I got a massive swag of glowing reviews; I became the talk of the Fringe and *Nanette* was the hottest ticket in town. Celebrities filed through the door, I got standing ovations every night, and I won the Edinburgh Fringe comedy award—the holy fucking grail of my small world if ever there was one. And still, it was one of the worst months of my entire life.

The small room was an utterly horrific place for *Nanette*. The tension was gutting, I was barely able to avoid onstage meltdowns. Not even the supremely absurd sight of all the hands of my terrified audiences folded neatly on the little desks in front of them was enough to cut through the pain of it. Then, ten days into the festival one of my wisdom teeth impacted and the gum infection that followed forced me to get it removed by a Scottish Dentist. And if you don't find that a frightening enough concept, you should just google "Scottish teeth" and get back to me.

To make things worse, Dad had to have a chunk of his own face removed because his melanoma was proving to be quite the coloniser. I'd never really felt much in the way of homesickness if I was busy working, but I'd become so worried by the idea that Dad's face being altered would change the way I understood him, I'd become totally resentful about having to be on the other side of the world with no one else to blame but myself. When I called Mum to find out how the procedure went, she responded by telling me that she didn't think I would be able to love Dad anymore and I felt so sad in my heart, I felt pain.

"Why not?" I asked feebly, and I heard Mum take a drag on a cigarette. "Well," she eventually began. "He looks a lot like one of those Picasso paintings now." Dad thought he looked more like a Van Gogh. "It's the bandages," he added. Unnecessarily.

Even though the 2017 Edinburgh Fringe was by far the worst I had ever endured, I did not implode in the September that followed. I was tired, sure, but I did not once want to stab myself in the eye. I put this minor miracle down to three things. One was that *Nanette* was actually working to strip me of the worst of the debilitating effects of my residual trauma. Wow. The second was that I had learnt to manage my environment better, and had avoided all the usual ASD pitfalls that had drained my reserves in previous years, things like talking to people, and also socialising with people who talk, and not to mention other things like talking to people who talk. But it is the third thing that I believe really gave Edinburgh the safety net that allowed me to recover from the extreme duress, and that thing, ironically, involved people talking to me.

I had worked with my producers, Rebecca Austin and Hannah Norris, in previous years, but in the year of *Nanette* they didn't just produce, they kept me alive. There were also a handful of other performers who had made it their business to make sure I was always surrounded and supported, but they all did it with such kindness and deep consideration for my need for quiet and solitude, it makes me want to cry. I won't actually cry though, it's only an intellectual idea. They get it. What made this so much more enriching was that these quiet little champions were all people whose work I admired and who had all had an influence on *Nanette*. Sarah Kendall is the best storyteller who has ever graced the Fringe. Adrienne Truscott was responsible for one of the most powerful shows critiquing rape culture in comedy—and I include *Nanette* when I say that. I have already mentioned Zoë Coombs Marr but I will do it again. Zoë Coombs Marr. And finally, Ursula Martinez, who could just build a brick wall on stage and I would be riveted.

I had pulled most of my material about Australia's marriage equality plebiscite out of the Edinburgh and London versions of *Nanette* for the purpose of being relevant to a non-Australian audience, but the plebiscite was reaching its toxic peak in August, so I still couldn't escape it. Then, from September through November 2017, it reached fever pitch as the votes rolled in.

It was to my immense relief that the result came in a resounding "yes," as in "yes, let's not be homophobic and let the gays get married already." Of the nearly 80 percent of eligible voters who participated, over 60 percent were in favour of same-sex marriage, including a majority in every state and territory. The Marriage Act amendment was passed formally in Parliament shortly thereafter, though not without several representatives who indignantly voted "no," against the voice of their districts. Ultimately it was a win, but personally, I felt like the damage had already been done.

The debate had forced me into a dark corner, and I know it forced a lot of others into similarly dark places. I knew several people for whom the debate was the final nudge they needed to make an attempt on their lives. One of them didn't make it. I didn't know them very well, so their story is not mine to tell. But to this day I can't think about that debate without thinking about them. It was so incredibly avoidable. So many of us sounded the alarm, but we were ignored. And we continue to be ignored as the win is being painted into history as a "victory" pure and simple. It was not. The lives of a vulnerable minority should never have been put into the hands of the majority in a media landscape that is all too happy to be powered by the fumes of a toxic debate. So, while everybody else was doing victory laps, I could only seem to grieve.

Not long after the Edinburgh Fringe, another seismic event put the wobble on things. Just like in 2006, when Tarana Burke first used the phrase as a solidarity tool for sexual assault survivors, I completely missed the #metoo movement. I did not follow Alyssa Jayne Milano on Twitter; in fact, by October 2017 I wasn't on Twitter at all. I had withdrawn from social media because *Nanette* had inspired a bit of unnecessary hate and a lot of sharing of trauma. Neither of which I felt robust enough to process without doing damage to myself. Of course, I followed the story very closely in the news, which pretty much puts my experience of #metoo on par with most blokes', the main difference being that it didn't provoke shock, sorrow or reactive anger. It was more of a quiet and relieved: "Finally!"

AND WE CAN'T EVEN BEGIN THE CONVERSATION THAT MEN GET RAPED AND WOMEN RAPE . . . OR THAT A MAN IS MORE LIKELY TO BE RAPED THAN HE IS TO BE FALSELY ACCUSED OF RAPE. AND WE CAN'T HAVE THESE CONVERSATIONS BECAUSE THESE THINGS ALL THREATEN TO RUIN THE "REPUTATION" OF MASCULINITY. FUCK REPUTATION . . . I JUST WANT BETTER HUMANS IN MY WORLD! (NANETTE: LONDON EDIT)

The interesting thing for me is that #metoo didn't change *Nanette* as a piece of work. Other than adding a few names to my already quite substantial list of famous predators, *Nanette* didn't need to do anything to absorb the moment; she was, after all, created out of the same zeitgeist. This is not to say that the #metoo moment didn't impact *Nanette* at all, quite the opposite. For a start, I can pinpoint October as the month that the hateful and violent reactions to me and my work really began to flood my DMs. Fortunately, I was already detached from online engagement.

The other big difference was one I could only detect within the rooms I performed. I first noticed the change during my run at the Sydney Opera House and my return season at Hamer Hall in Melbourne, in the latter half of the year. During the parts of the show where I had once only prompted anguished silence, I had begun to detect an air of excitement. Of course, part of that was due to the traumatic heart of *Nanette* no longer being a surprise, there'd been enough press and buzz about the show to make sure most people would have been, at least in part, prepared to get the wind knocked out of them. But the frisson, as it were, was too cohesive for the change to be about the spoiler alert factor alone. I believe it was mostly down to the fact that victims of sexual assault were no longer separated and silenced within their own bubbles of suffering.

The relief and excitement were palpable to me on stage, as was the fury of some men, who apparently felt so victimised by the moment that they thought I should have to help them process their feelings in the middle of my show. Fortunately, by that time I had absolutely no problem smacking heckles right back in the face of anyone foolhardy enough to try. But sometimes I didn't have to say anything, and on one occasion all I had to do was pause and wait as a woman frog-marched her heckling husband out of the auditorium to the tune of two thousand people applauding.

Another very significant impact that the #metoo movement has had on *Nanette* is that she has now been recontextualised as merely my response to it, and not as something I created under a completely separate set of very personal compulsions. Which is a real shame, I reckon, because I feel it diminishes the risks I took, casts a shadow over my originality and intentions, and it all but erases the profound isolation I'd experienced throughout the process. I had in no way felt as if *Nanette* and I were part of any kind of sisterhood prior to that October. But, on the other hand, it was nice to have that eventually and, at the end of the day, I don't think I would have gotten a Netflix special at all without the #metoo movement giving the streaming platform something to capitalise on.

By committing *Nanette* to the screen, I felt as if I were taking a living, breathing, ever-evolving entity and suspending it in amber. I was collecting a butterfly, so to speak, and we all know what a bloody stupid thing that is to do. There was quite a lot that I knew would be lost from *Nanette* once the live performance aspect had been removed. But I am not a purist, clearly, and I believed that there were enough people out there who would appreciate the opportunity to experience something of it rather than nothing at all.

Nanette was filmed on January 27, 2018, in the Sydney Opera House Concert Hall. We'd felt that a prestige venue might help trick an international audience into believing I was worth listening to.[⊛] I guess it worked. What we didn't know until much later was that it was also an acoustically perfect room. One of the most defining qualities of the live experience of *Nanette* was the strangely audible quality of the silences that haunted every room she graced, but we never believed that this could possibly be captured by a recording. But the Opera House proved us wrong, and we were able to capture one of the most profound silences of *Nanette*'s life. It was so thick with tension it was loud enough to drown the sound of a thousand pins dropping.

The only thing I'd ever had on stage with me during the live tour

⊛ To balance out the grandeur of the iconic Sydney Opera House, it was important to me that we film the opening sequence of the special at my home, my beloved Bloomfield, to demonstrate that, as magnificent as the Concert Hall was, it was not my natural habitat. So, the first image that viewers would see was me in my very humble abode, enjoying a cuppa on my chesterfield, surrounded by my books— including the ones I stole from the Smithton school library—and joined by my best friend, Douglas, and his new pal, Jasper.

was a stool and mic stand, because nothing screams *I am a man doing comedy like a man* better than a stool and mic stand. But as the Opera House stage is quite large, we decided to create a set, a bit of razzle-dazzle for the camera. Now, nothing screams *I am a man filming a comedy special like a man* better than having your name spelt out in lights behind you. But I decided it might be a nice idea to contradict all the man comedy context clues and commission a piece of art.

I asked Sydney-based artist Caroline Rothwell because I was intrigued by the way her work combines the traditionally masculine medium of sculpture with the traditionally relegated feminine medium of textile. I didn't give her much in the way of direction as I wanted something that was a response to my work, as opposed to an extension of my own ideas. Although, I am sure if I hadn't liked her idea, I would have changed my mind. But I loved it.

It is my humble belief that Rothwell completely nailed the alchemy at the heart of *Nanette*. She used an overlay of images, one being a scratched-up negative of a colonial landscape photograph she'd found in a museum archive, the other being a giant reproduction of my eye. (Which is hilarious, given how I hate making eye contact.) The composite image was split over five huge textile banners that had been stiffened so as to have the appearance of being both hard and soft. And best of all, it could completely dominate the stage and disappear at the same time. Much like the laughter in *Nanette*.

Recording at the Sydney Opera House also meant that we were able to involve many of the people who had kept *Nanette* on the road for the preceding year, as the touring team worked with the TV folks to transpose the stage for the filming. It was all hands on deck. While Rowan unfurled Caroline's banners with the production team and then hoisted them up over the stage, the TV crew set the cameras, and Kath was ruling every other aspect of the world. The sparkling accents of the Concert Hall meant that the stage had to be carpeted and drapes piled in front of hard surfaces, both for the microphones and my senses.

It was great to have the old team in place for the special, but we also wanted to bring in some fresh blood and were particularly keen to share this opportunity with an emerging female director. Madeleine Parry was a documentary producer and new to both directing and live events, but we wanted her eye, so we paired her with a more experienced event director to give her the confidence while upholding her perspective.

You may have noticed that most comedy specials use multiple camera angles. There are close-ups, mid-range shots and wide views—intercut with a jib, budget depending—and maybe a roaming camera or two. This is not an effort to re-create the live experience, clearly, because when you go to a comedy show you don't tend to change your seats every few seconds to change up your perspective. The point is to replace the naturally occurring dynamism that a large crowd generates, with an artificial one. *Look here, now here, what about here, now look here, back here now, look at these people laughing at this joke, you should laugh too, now look here, now here!* And so on and so forth. It's not as cynical an exercise as all that, it's more due to the fact that if there are no edit points, people will eventually fall asleep watching a screen. It doesn't matter how funny or exciting the content is, we all need a reminder to blink.

We did not mess with this idea entirely when we filmed *Nanette*, but we did tweak a few mainstays. Save for the backs of heads you see in the wide shot, there are no audience response shots at all. One of the core premises I had built into *Nanette* was that I wanted to prevent my audiences from feeding off of each other. I wanted to force people to think for themselves and not fall into the excuse of mob mentality. So, it made sense not to show a viewer at home how other people were responding in the room. The other bold decision we made was to pretty much lock off the last ten or so minutes into a mid- to close-range shot of my face. Providing you don't fall asleep, that shit is fucking intense. Or so I have been told. I've never seen *Nanette*. I've heard it's not very funny. A little joke there. You're welcome. But seriously, I have not seen *Nanette* and I don't think I will anytime soon. I have my own relationship with her.

As the filming date began to loom larger and larger, I experienced a mounting of extreme pressure that was threatening to break me completely. And just when I didn't think I could withstand any more pressure, Mum informed me that she wanted to be there for the filming. Now look, Mum wanting to support me is ultimately a very wonderful thing. I think it is what you call love. My issue was that the version of *Nanette* she had seen was not anything like the version I was hoping to immortalise. She hadn't heard the list of my worst traumas, and she certainly didn't get to see me tell a room full of strangers that I had been beaten and kicked, raped and molested. I knew there was a chance that she might have read about it somewhere, but we had never spoken about it. Which meant that on top of all the other shit I was trying to keep on top of, I had to now have a frank and open conversation with my mum, and that was something I had been really hoping I could continue to avoid.

Thankfully, Hamish and Jessica had also decided to come for the filming, and we had a few conversations about the best way to tell Mum the truth of what she was about to witness. We agreed it was best if we didn't give her too much time to stew over the harsh reality, and that I should tell her just before the show. There was never a doubt in my mind that this was the right course of action, even as I knew it was going to be all Dread City for me until it was over. Which was not ideal, given that I was also trying to film a show all about my trauma.

Mum had not been to Sydney since she was a teenager, and I didn't like the idea of her travelling alone as she is a bit like me when it comes to new experiences and I didn't want her to land in Sydney full of pent-up anxiety. I wanted her to feel safe. I needed her to feel safe. So, I flew down to Tasmania with Annie to pick her up.

Dad and Ben came to the airport to see us, and we all had lunch together at the airport café. Dad was too unwell to travel, but he was adorably excited at lunch, telling Annie, for no apparent reason, that he was a morning person and Mum was better in the evenings. "We are like the owl and the fowl," he said. Ben and I looked at each other. Who was this chatty man? Next, he spoke about all the trouble he'd had keeping up with all the articles and reviews that I'd gotten over the last year. Annie said later that he'd told her he'd had to start in on the third volume of *My Comedy Career*, pushing me to explain what the hell that was.

I told her about his passion for archiving everything that had ever been written about me, and how that's the most painful thing about all the hate I was getting online. I didn't have a Google Alert for my name, but Dad did. I was used to reading my own rape threats, I didn't think Dad was really in the right place for all of that, what with his melanoma spreading and being my father and all. Annie burst into tears, and for a brief moment I began to panic that I wasn't upset, but then I remembered that I was autistic and I finished my snack.

A few months later I would be in New York doing an extended off-Broadway run of *Nanette*, and I had a very rare conversation with Dad. He and Mum had just gotten back from Alice Springs and he was full of chat. Not long after I had filmed *Nanette*, Dad got the news that his melanoma had begun to spread and Jessica had asked him if there was anything he really wanted to do. He told her that there wasn't. "I have had a very good life. Couldn't be happier with it." Jessica told him to think about it. And then all of us kids pitched in to send Dad away to tick off the one and only item on his hastily thrown together bucket list: to see Uluru. I am not sure what Dad made of Australia's great red rock monolith; he only told me about every single meal they ate, including all the plane snacks.

After he finished telling me about all the hot chips he'd had in Alice Springs, I told him about how I'd woken up so sad that morning, and that I didn't realise until well after lunch that I had only dreamt that he'd died. "Ha," he said, pausing for a moment before adding "What did you have for lunch?"

I gave him a brief rundown of my most recent sandwich, and then I asked if he had seen my review in *The New York Times*. He told me that he had, before launching into a very long complaint about how ridiculous some of my reviews had become. "I can't even fit some of them onto one page, double-sided! I think I might have to stop. I'm not made of toner, you know." Dad has never had to tell me that he was proud of me, he just showed me through the medium of scrapbooking. And I never told Dad how scared I was about him dying, or how much I loved him. I just showed him through the medium of committing our conversations to my memory as if they were going to be our last,[*] and also by not hanging up on him whenever he took to telling me all about his scrapbooking. Again. Ours is a very uncomplicated relationship. It is perfect.

DON'T TELL ME TO SEPARATE THE MAN FROM THE ART . . . WHY DON'T YOU SEPARATE THE MAN FROM THE ART. TAKE PICASSO'S NAME OFF HIS ART AND SEE HOW MUCH HIS LITTLE DOODLES WOULD SELL FOR AT AUCTION. FUCK. ALL. NOBODY OWNS A CIRCULAR LEGO NUDE, THEY OWN A PICASSO. AND PICASSO WAS A VIOLENT, ABUSIVE MISOGYNIST AND WE ROMANTICISE THAT FOR PROFIT. (NANETTE: NEW YORK EDIT)

Mum had been so adorably excited throughout the flight to Sydney. Everything was a thrill—the shitty coffee, the man breathing heavily across the aisle, even the seat-back pocket became a source of fascination. She was like a little kid save for her desire for a cigarette. She'd been asking me for weeks if there was going to be anywhere for her to smoke at the pub we were staying at in Sydney. We'd all been booked into a posh hotel on the harbour, and when she asked again on the flight, I reminded her that we were fancy now and she could just smash the penthouse window with a TV and smoke out of that. "You're a dickhead," she told me and the small audience of fellow passengers who were very much enjoying our little double act.

I was trying very hard to enjoy Mum's enjoyment, or at least take in all the details of it so I might be able to enjoy it later, but I was finding it very difficult to focus. When my parents had made the trip

---

[*] They weren't. Sometimes medical trials are medical miracles.

to Melbourne to see my second show at the Comedy Festival ten or so years earlier, I had taken them out for dinner afterward at a nice restaurant in the city and can still remember the feeling of pride spilling out from all of us. There we were, eating fish-and-chips on white tablecloths on the mainland. And I was paying. I knew, intellectually, this was a far bigger moment, but my brain didn't have room to process any feelings.

"Are we really staying in a penthouse?" Mum whispered a few moments later. I told her that I didn't think we were, and that I wasn't even sure what a penthouse was. "I think it's a magazine, darling."

The seatbelt sign had barely been switched off before Mum was off the plane and racing up the exit ramp. Annie and I only managed to catch up to her because her suitcase had gotten stuck when she tried to cut a corner. I could tell she was really agitated, so I sent Annie off ahead with Mum's suitcase, and asked Mum to walk with me. "But you walk so slowly!" she complained as she scampered off. I do walk slowly, I always have. I've been told by quite a few people that I fall as if I am in slow motion too. It is as if I exist in my own bubble of molasses. Unlike Mum, who walks very quickly and falls even quicker.

The sound of Mum's knee cracking on the floor is not something I am likely ever to forget. Annie had made the mistake of stopping to make sure Mum was following, but Mum was not just following, she was tailgating, and gawking at absolutely everything except the ground in front of her, so she didn't notice the stoppage until after she'd run full-pelt into her own suitcase. It was quite spectacular really.

In the few extra moments that it had taken me to catch up to the scene, I had already made peace with the fact that I was going to be spending the rest of the day navigating a hospital emergency department. I'd even started drafting the conversation I was going to have to have with Jessica, so she could project manage the debacle. Where had all this brain space come from? When I reached Annie, I could see she was upset before she even grabbed my arm. "I broke the fowl!" she cried. "She's the owl," I corrected her, and patted her on the shoulder and smiled. What was wrong with me?

Mum was wincing painfully and trying to get up when I put my hand on her back. "I'm fine!" she said, answering the question I had not asked. She looked so small; she'd shrunk dramatically over the past few years, and she looked nothing like the strapping woman who had wrangled me into adulthood. And with that thought my brain lost its mojo again, cotton wool replaced my thinking, and it was all I could do to just pat her like a dog I was about to put down. That very weird little moment was thankfully broken by an officious-sounding voice: "Don't get up, madam! Don't move." A young man from the airline tried to push past me to take charge, and while I was very happy for that to happen, I did caution him as I stood up.

"Careful, I wouldn't tell her what to do, if I were you." He stopped in his tracks and stared at me. "Trust me. That's my mum." He didn't know what to think, and I silently welcomed him to the club, as I watched him squat down beside Mum as cautiously as you would a wild animal. "Are you OK, madam?" he asked gently. Mum looked up at him. "Well," she said, studying him with contempt. "What do you think? Do I look good on the ground?"

Fortunately, my mum had not needed to get put down. She didn't even have to go to hospital, and even with her new and dramatic limp, she still walked faster than me.

As soon as we arrived at the hotel, Hamish and Jessica swooped in to take over Mum duties, leaving me to work on the end of *Nanette* and let the dread build about the conversation I didn't know how to have with Mum. I was beginning to panic. I knew I couldn't just let Mum go into this blind, it was unfair, and she was the last person who needed to be gut-punched by me, by a show I had written partly as tribute to her. My issue was that I just didn't know how to carve out the right kind of time. Mum's like quicksilver, especially when she wants to avoid a difficult conversation. She won't be cornered, and I regretted not taking the opportunity to talk to her while she'd been spread-eagled on the airport concourse. In the end, I asked

Kevin and Erin for their advice, and they helped me hatch a very good plan.

Mum was coming to the first show, and the plan was for Erin and Annie to bring her backstage to see me about half an hour before we were set to start. They would leave us alone for ten minutes, during which time I was to have the dreaded chat. Kevin would then knock, and walk Mum to her seat. The logic was that Kevin would be able to follow up our difficult chat with his trademark matter-of-fact, not-so-emotional chitchat, so as to avoid giving Mum a chance to circle the difficult stuff too much and flee the scene completely. At the end of which he would have delivered Mum to Hamish and Jessica, who would be waiting to flank her during the show. It might've been perfect had it worked. But it didn't, because Mum managed to quicksilver herself out of it somehow.

Kevin was with me backstage when Erin and Annie arrived with Mum. He'd been helping me consolidate the last ten minutes of *Nanette*, workshopping the best sequence and exact wording. It was a great distraction to all the mounting stress, and I was able to focus on the task with unusual tenacity. I finished a few minutes before Mum was to be delivered into our trap, and I did not know what to do. My hair and makeup had been done, now all I had to do was keep a safe hold over the show in my head, put my jacket on and tell Mum I had been molested, beaten and raped, and then film a Netflix special about all that in front of her. At the Sydney Opera House. Pretty average day.

"Trevor!" Mum exclaimed as she barrelled into the room. Mum really liked Kevin but she hated his name, deciding to call him Trevor. Kevin didn't mind, he was just confused as to how Trevor was any better: "It's just a sidestep. It's still a bland man's name with a V in the middle." But Mum has never been one to be deterred by logic. After everybody had left us alone, Mum began circling the room like a caged tiger while I stood rooted to the spot in the middle of the room, which was a fairly standard holding pattern for us. I waited for her to run out of chat: "Look at this piano! Do you eat all this cheese? Look you can see the bridge! I touched a woman's boob today, I wanted to grab the handrail but she tried to push past. So, I grabbed her boob. She looked pissed-off, but I said, lady, if you don't want your boob grabbed don't get between an old lady and her handrail, and get off your phone and look where you're going, stupid little turd. I don't think they were real. Her boobs. Do you want to see my bruise? I took three Panadol last night and I was fine."

She was running the clock down. Did she know I had an agenda?

"Mum?"

"What?"

"You need to know something about the show . . ."

"No!"

"Look, I think you do."

"Well, I don't. It's OK. What time does the show start? I need a puffer." Mum was clawing at the window now, as if she was looking for a way out.

"If I could just . . ."

"Now where is that Trevor?" And then, as if she had summoned him, TrevKev arrived. I looked at him and threw my hands up in the air. "Don't worry about anything," he reassured me, "I will do it. You just focus on the show." I nodded, not knowing how the fuck I was supposed to do that now. The door closed behind them, leaving me alone with nothing but my not-thoughts.

PICASSO'S MISTAKE WAS HIS ARROGANCE, THAT HE ASSUMED HE HAD THE POWER TO REPRESENT ALL THE PERSPECTIVES. OUR MISTAKE WAS TO INVALIDATE THE PERSPECTIVE OF A SEVENTEEN-YEAR-OLD GIRL BECAUSE WE BELIEVED HER POTENTIAL WOULD NEVER BE EQUAL TO HIS. (NANETTE: NETFLIX EDIT. WRITTEN BACKSTAGE WHILE WAITING FOR MUM.)

Until the moment I walked out onto the stage, I had been in a complete daze of non-thinking. But as soon as I headed into *Nanette* mode, I began to return to myself. The banners looked spectacular, the crowd was electric, I felt my confidence building as I walked across the stage. I felt powerful, I felt like a fucking witch, I felt *Nanette* return to me and I knew we were about to do the best show of our lives. I felt invincible, and then a baby started crying in the front row. What the fuck?

I was about five minutes in when I stopped the show to make sure I wasn't making it up. "I'm sorry, is there . . . is there a baby in here?"

There sure was, and I could tell it was a real freshy, too, because I got a good chance to look when its mother held it aloft like we were in the middle of some kind of fucked-up adaptation of the *Lion King.* How did a baby get past the ushers? You weren't even allowed to take glassware in.

I had to kick the pair out; a baby was a dangerous thing to have when you have microphones hanging over the audience and a very sound-sensitive performer workshopping their trauma on stage. Despite feeling confident that it was the right thing to do, I had to be careful, because it was critical that before shit got real in *Nanette,* I be as charming and delightful as possible, and I didn't think kicking a mother and her newborn out of the room would fall under that umbrella. So, I pretty much told the audience all of that, and fortunately they found that charming and delightful. And so I kicked them out.

With the newborn booted, I picked up the show where I'd left off and found that the crowd was even more on my side than before, and I can remember thinking: *I am not going to fuck this up after all!* That fresh confidence lasted a good twenty minutes before it all came crashing down as I scanned the crowd during a potent silence, and in that sea of heads, made more visible by the lighting needed to film, I found Mum, smack-bang in the middle of the auditorium. I didn't need to double-check; her silhouette, crowned by her distinctive mop of silver hair, was unmistakable. This wasn't meant to happen.

The show had never been easy for me. Every single time I'd laid out my trauma, I'd felt something of the pain of it. It had lessened over time but, by design, I had never become completely conditioned and so I was affected every single time. After my eye had accidentally found Mum in the audience, I did my best to avoid putting her back in my sight line. But the damage had already been done, and as the show built to its worst moment, I began to buckle under my distress. But there was nothing to do but suffer through it and do my best to keep the *Nanette* train on track.

I didn't mean to pick Mum out with my eyes when I reached the traumatic peak of the show, but I did, and as I delivered the worst of it, I saw her shoulders slump and her head drop. I felt my heart do something and it was very unpleasant. I never wanted to trigger her guilt, her pain, and here I was doing exactly that in the most public of ways. I forced myself to look away for a time, and when my eyes found Mum again a few minutes later I could see the heads of Hamish and Jessica had joined with hers, as they were all huddling and holding onto each other.

I don't remember anything else really. I finished the show. I got a massive standing ovation. Then I got another one, because we had to trick it for the cameras. It was a triumph, as they say. But I didn't feel as if it was any such thing. I was too overwhelmed by everything to feel or think anything. I just sat alone in my dressing room and let myself melt down.

"How did Mum take it?" I asked KevTrev when he popped in to check on me. I didn't have a chance to check in on Mum myself, because the turnaround between shows was too tight.

"I couldn't tell her either!" Kevin reported, incredulous. He told me that he had never met anyone more slippery to an emotional conversation.

"Like quicksilver," I said.

"Like quicksilver," he agreed. "Ready to do that all again?"

I was and I did. Like only slow gold could.

As I stood on stage and did it all again, Hamish and Jessica went to a bar and had a stiff drink together. Hamish told me later that it had been really beautiful, I said thank you, and he said, "No! Not the show, our conversation. I mean, the show was great too. Well done, Gods." Jessica had a much better crack at conveying her feelings. Of course, I couldn't reciprocate, but I keep her words close to my heart to this very day.

Annie had been left in charge of Mum while I did the second show, and on Mum's insistence, she'd taken her out for some fresh air. It was a beautiful summer evening, and there were quite a few people out, so they picked their way over to an out-of-the-way spot. And while I was somewhere inside the building delivering *Nanette* for the second time that evening, my mum sat on the steps of the Sydney Opera House, and sobbed like a baby. When she eventually gathered herself, she lit a cigarette, took a big old drag and then asked Annie if she could call my dad for her, so she could tell him all about the wonderful news of me.

Prologue

HOW SIFFIN SOFFON BECAME FRIENDLY WITH A DRAGON

Part One

One day Mrs. Soffon had an egg. "Not again!" Said Mr. Soffon.

The next day the egg hatched and out popped their baby. They couldn't decide what to name their new baby. "What about Kinnowin?" Said Mr. Soffon. "NO! That's a stupid name." Said Mrs. Soffon. Finally, they agreed that Siffin was a good name.

That night while everyone was sleeping Siffin woke up and drank all the lemonade and ate all the jelly. In the morning Mr. Soffon woke up and saw that all the jelly and lemonade had gone missing.

"Oh well. We'll just have to have pizza and cake for breakfast."

The Soffons decided to move to a bigger house. They looked all over the land and there was only one pretty garden and house.

It was a cave.

They went and explored the back of the cave. It was full of snakes. They caught the Soffons and took them outside and stopped at a guillotine. They tied Mr. Soffon up and cut off his head.

All the years past until Siffin was big and strong. One Day the snakes were going to hang mother. Siffin broke through the bars to stop the snakes that were going to hang her. But it was too late. Siffin ran away as fast as he could.

Siffin found a ship on the shore, and he got on. But the ship was cut in half by sharks. Siffin held onto the side of the one half and kicked and kicked and kicked until all the sharks were dead and the water was mostly blood. He was near China so he swam to shore. The China people pulled him out and they invited Siffin to eat with them.

"You will fight the champion tomorrow." They said. Siffin was very scared but the food was delicious.

The next day Siffin had to fight the great champion of China. The Big Barnshed.

The bell rang. "START!!!" Shouted the Starter. Big Barnshed ran toward Siffin who kicked him in the mouth. Blood came out and he fell down dead.

Siffin was very tired after his fight and fell into a deep sleep after a meal of honey chicken and prawn crackers. He dreamt about being a dog again.

There was a CRASH BANG SPLAT! And there was a monster sitting on a brick of the China Wall. He took Siffin to a strange land. It was full of creatures just like Siffin. And there were uncle Joe, cousin Andrew and Grandma!

Grandma said: "We are going on holiday to Hooky Pooky."

"Andrew . . . Get some clothes for Siffin."

Andrew got Siffin some clothes. But they were too small. The only thing that fitted Siffin was a dress!! Siffin felt very uncomfortable in the dress.

The next day, on their way to Hooky Pooky, Siffin was run over by a bus. Uncle Joe called an ambulance. The ambulance man said: "Can you hop on both legs?" Siffin tried but it really hurt. "You have definitely broken your leg" said the ambulance man. He rubbed on Vicks VapoRub and put plaster on Siffin's leg. "There, you can go on your holiday now!"

When they got to Hooky Pooky they found a dragon. The Dragon ate Grandma, Joe and Andrew. He looked at Siffin.

"Hi" said Siffin.

"Hi" said the Dragon.

They shook hands.

The Dragon got a magic kettle and said: "Take Siffin and I to where nobody lives."

Siffin and the Dragon landed on an island called Holiday Island. There was lots and lots of food.

the en d

"When I was growing up, all the women in my house were using needles. I've always had a fascination with the needle. The magic power of needle. The needle is used to repair damage. It's a claim to forgiveness. It is never aggressive, it's not a pin."

—LOUISE BOURGEOIS

ACKNOWLEDGMENTS

I have been failing to finishing this book for a very long time. I am very pleased with the end product, sure, but I feel compelled to let you know that the writing of this has been a monumental pain in the spiritual arse of my life. It might surprise many of you to discover that the first time I missed the deadline for this manuscript, the last five metaphorical steps of this book had not yet even happened. And I have a sneaking certainty of a suspicion that without my continued failure to carve a book out of the impossible tangle of my lived life, *Nanette* would never have been. How about that? So, it is with a great deal of gratitude that I will dedicate this first tier of acknowledgments to those people who extended to me superhuman levels of patience, support, and professional kindness during this woeful process.

Laurie Liss and the team at Sterling Lord Literistic.

Kelly Fagan and Claire Kingston and the entire team at Allen and Unwin Australia.

Sara Weiss and all the good folk at Ballantine.

Clare Drysdale and the team at Atlantic (UK).

A big and humble thanks to Erin Zamagni and Helen Townshend at Token for being so patient with me during the extended period of overwhelm that went into this book. You made me feel very safe and I can't thank you enough. Janette Linden at PBJ, I thank you for your care and hair. And of course, Kevin Whyte. Let me keep those feelings where they belong and just say "potato."

My inability to shape this book into a whole and sensible procession of story would often reduce me to a frustrated puddle of "I can't do this." Usually when this happened, I would do the only thing I knew how to: quit. But on a few occasions, I did reach out to some writers and gifted readers for some help. And help they did. So now I would like to thank these wonderful folks for their time, care, and the confidence they taught me to have in my own writing.

Lori Lober, Sadie Hasler, Stella Nall, Carolyn Whyte, and Sinsa Mansell (for making sure my ignorance didn't shine too brightly).

If I can call myself a writer, it has only been the process of writing this book that has dragged me kicking and screaming into that particular professional arena. But really, what I am, and probably always will be, is a comedian first. And even if you do not want to allow me the honour of calling myself a comedian, I am, at the very least, a speaker of sorts. And as a professional speaker of sorts, it was that skill set that very heavily informed my approach to this task. Apparently, I am unable to commit to the page anything that I have not first trialled out loud and in the presence of another. For years and years, I have been cornering many of my nearest and dearest, and the odd stranger, so I could read and reread passages of my stumbling attempts at written prose at them. So, it is to those most generous ears I will be dedicating this next round of heartfelt appreciation, because without them, this book would have been forever shelved as unfinished.

Annie Maver, Ben Bennett, Suzanne Dayton, Cheryl Crilly, Caroline Davies, Amelia Jane Hunter, Jen Brister and robot Chloe, Deborah Frances-White, Geraldine Hickey, DeAnne Smith, Nicole J Georges, Phyllida Law, Emma Thompson, and Kate Woodroofe.

My skills are limited to the stage and to the stage only. So, I would like to extend my thanks to all the people who made sure that *Nanette* could exist at all.

Australia: Kathleen McCarthy, Rowan Smith, and the Token Events team.

Susan Provan, Brigit Bantick, Claire Hammond, Sean Ford, and the team at MICF.

Edinburgh and London: Rebecca Austin and Hannah Norris! Steve Lock, Kelly Fogarty, and the Soho Theatre team in London. Heather Ruck, William Burdett-Coutts, and the team at Assembly.

New York and LA: Arnold Engelman, Darren Lee Cole, Leigh Lotocki, and the Soho Playhouse team. And, of course, Flanny and the team at Largo.

I would also like to thank the team at the Sydney Opera House, especially for the recording of *Nanette*. On top of that, I would like to thank Caroline Rothwell, Madeleine Parry, Jon Olb, and Frank Bruzzese. And a robust thanks to Netflix, especially to Robbie Praw, Caitlin Hotchkiss, and Cindy Holland.

What? More? Yes. Next in line are my post-*Nanette* champions:

My team at UTA—Blair, Nick, Lucinda, Skikne, Bjorn, Larry, and Josh.

The legends at ID—Kelly Bush-Novak, Molly, Court, Amanda, and Lori.

Lawyers? Why not . . . thanks Karl and Michael!

Next! I would like to offer a big, huge, and humble thanks to my fans! Especially to those of you who have been with me since before I "quit" comedy. You are an integral part of this story. Please keep supporting local live performances of any art form; you keep our world turning.

Thanks also to all the activists who fought for gay law reform in Tasmania: Rodney Croome, Nick Toonen, and the rest of Equality Tasmania (formerly known as the TGLRG) for all your personal sacrifice and leadership. Thanks also to the leaders and activists who rallied to get Australian marriage equality over the line. Also, Penny Wong and Bob Brown. I have always been so thankful to hear your voices rise above the Parliamentary fray on most matters, but especially on those that cut closer to my identity bone. And, finally, a little salute to Panti Bliss. I saw what you did and I took courage from it. But ultimately, just a blanket thanks to everyone who fights for inclusion in the face of any hateful moral panic.

And now for the penultimate thanks, my extraordinary spouse lady, Jenney Shamash. THANK YOU! Not only did you usher this book over the line—handling that big cluster of technical tasks that would have been impossible for me to get through on my own—but you have helped me navigate my very frightening post-*Nanette* world. Thank you for the joy you bring and the low-level lights you shine for my overly sensitive eyes.

And now, last but certainly not least, I would like to draw my acknowledgment attention to my family. Thank you for trusting me with the parts of your story that couldn't be separated from mine.

To my siblings: Justin, Jessica, Ben, and Hamish. Thank you so much for always being there for me, and for all the support you've shown me throughout my career and especially for all the propping up of my existence that you do and have always done.

And, of course, to my parents: Kay and Roger, AKA Mum and Dad. Thank you. I love you.

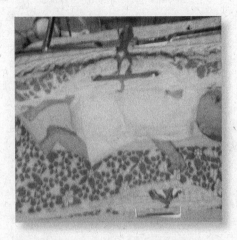

Tasmania's own HANNAH GADSBY stopped stand-up comedy in its tracks with their multi-award-winning show, *Nanette*. Its launch on Netflix in 2018, and subsequent Emmy and Peabody wins, took *Nanette* (and Hannah) to the world. Hannah's second special was named *Douglas*, after their dog. Hannah walked *Douglas* around the globe, selling out the Royal Festival Hall in London, the Opera House in Sydney, and the Kennedy Center in DC. *Douglas* was nominated for an Emmy and is available throughout the world on Netflix.

Hannah Gadsby's "overnight" success was more than ten years in the making, with their award-winning stand-up shows having been a fixture in festivals across Australia and the U.K. since 2009. They played a character called "Hannah" on the TV series *Please Like Me* and have hosted multiple art documentaries, inspired by their comedy art lectures. In 2021, they were awarded a Doctorate of Letters *honoris causa* from the University of Tasmania. This is Dr. Gadsby's first book.

ABOUT THE TYPE

This book was set in Scala, a typeface designed by Martin Majoor in 1991. It was originally designed for a music company in the Netherlands and then was published by the international type house FSI FontShop. Its distinctive extended serifs add to the articulation of the letterforms to make it a very readable typeface.